In Good Time

'Harold's unwavering commitment to peace and reconciliation was instrumental to the success of the Northern Ireland peace process. I have the greatest respect for the role he played – particularly his steadfast dedication to fostering trust and understanding among divided communities and his tireless advocacy for peaceful cooperation. Harold's legacy is now set out in this insightful memoir and will continue to inspire efforts towards enduring peace for future generations.'

Tony Blair, Prime Minister of the UK 1997–2007

'In the long and dark history of the Troubles in Ireland, Harold Good stands tall as an enduring and courageous advocate of peace. From his early work as a young Methodist minister on the Shankill Road at the outbreak of the Troubles, this remarkable man of faith never wavered from the view that the answer to the conflict would never be discovered in the sound of gunfire but rather in quiet places through dialogue. His memoir is an essential and timely contribution to our understanding of the peace process, written by a man who has devoted his life and ministry to the pursuit of peace and reconciliation between the two traditions in Ireland.'

Bertie Ahern, Taoiseach of Ireland 1997–2008

'If you want to know the price of peace and the pathway out of conflict to peace then Harold Good's memoir is as sure and true a guide as there is. In Northern Ireland – where Christ surely wept at the hatreds and histories that kept its Christian citizens at each other's throats – there were the few, epitomised by Harold, who courageously led, who never counted the personal cost but in hope and faith witnessed to a burning love of neighbour that made new friends of old enemies and gave us a future to look forward to.'

Mary McAleese, President of Ireland 1997–2011

'Rev. Harold Good is one of the unsung heroes of the Northern Ireland peace process. His wisdom and decency were respected by all sides as the Northern Ireland peace process entered a new phase after the Good Friday Agreement. That respect was evident when he was trusted by the entire community to oversee the vital weapons decommissioning with his close friend Fr Alec Reid. His story is one of faith, reconciliation, charity, and hope, and the story of his life is inspirational.'

Senator George Mitchell, U.S. Special Envoy for Northern Ireland 1995–2001

'There are those who talk about peace. And then, there are those who make it happen. Harold Good worked on the paths out of conflict – and showed others the way. What is his contribution to this process? That he believed and that he saved lives. His is a book of experience and learning, written from the inside of some of the most important moments in our recent history.'

Brian Rowan, a former BBC correspondent and an author on the peace process

'Over the years I have waited impatiently for a glimpse into the extraordinary life of Harold Good, one of the best-known and much-admired peacemakers of our time. The waiting is now over, hallelujah. This memoir skilfully combines insights into Harold's ministry in the Methodist Church with jaw-dropping revelations about friendships painstakingly built between high-profile politicians, once arch-enemies. It truly is a fascinating read.'

Sylvia Hermon, MP for North Down 2001– 2019

'Little did I think all those years ago that my companion at a school desk in Methodist College would end up as President of the Methodist Church at the same time as I was Archbishop of Armagh. Nor did I imagine in those far-off days that we would find ourselves deeply involved in the cause of peace in Northern Ireland. But in fact I now think of Harold Good as a pioneer and courageous advocate for human understanding and peace. I am pleased that this important memoir sheds some light on Harold's immense contribution to peace-making in our lifetime.'

Robin Eames, life peer, Church of Ireland Archbishop of Armagh and Primate of All-Ireland 1986–2006

'Rev. Harold Good has written a remarkable and fascinating life story inspired by his Christian faith and passionate desire to make and build peace. His outstanding contribution to the peace process, alongside that of my confrère Fr Alec Reid, was made possible by his bona fides and trustworthiness, which was recognised both by republicans and unionists. This book is both an illuminating testament to what we have endured and a helpful guide to how we might become more productive in the work of healing and reconciliation.'

Peter Burns C.Ss.R., Rector, Clonard Monastery, Belfast, 2002–2007 and 2018–2023

'For decades, Harold Good has been applying the prophet Micah's advice to "walk humbly, do justice." His memoir is a testimony of how to do that and his stories are a joy to read.'

Monica McWilliams, founder member and co-leader of the Women's Coalition 1996–2006

'Harold Good's warm, engaging personality beams out of these pages. He was a symbol of hope throughout "The Troubles", but even his friends will be astonished to learn just how many things he did to build peace in Ireland and many other places. Those who are too young to remember those days will be enthralled by the extraordinary person they meet in the book, and without doubt some will be inspired by his faith, devotion, and powerful life story to give themselves to work for better relations in our troubled world too. A wonderful book, and an extraordinary legacy!'

John Alderdice, life peer, Speaker of the Northern Ireland Assembly 1998–2004

'I am so grateful to Harold for taking me under his wing and into some incredible rooms where I was able to witness first-hand his grace, generosity and humility as he brought people together in the pursuit of peace. I'm delighted that he has finally written this book and pray that the stories and lessons he shares profoundly shape and inspire a new generation of peacemakers.'

David Smyth, head of Evangelical Alliance Northern Ireland

In Good Time

A Memoir

Harold Good
with
Martin O'Brien

Published by
Red Stripe Press
Upper Floor, Unit B3
Hume Centre
Hume Avenue
Park West Industrial Estate
Dublin 12
Ireland

email: info@redstripepress.com
www.redstripepress.com

© Harold Good and Martin O'Brien, 2024

Paperback ISBN 978-1-78605-241-4
ePub ISBN 978-1-78605-242-1

A catalogue record for this book is available from the British Library. All rights reserved. No part of this publication may be reproduced, stored in a retrieval system or transmitted in any form or by any means, electronic, mechanical, photocopying, recording or otherwise, without the prior, written permission of the publisher.

This book is sold subject to the condition that it shall not, by way of trade or otherwise, be lent, resold, hired out, or otherwise circulated without the publisher's prior consent in any form of binding or cover other than that in which it is published and without a similar condition including this condition being imposed on the subsequent purchaser.

Every reasonable effort has been made to secure permission for the use of all photographs in this book. If you can identify any omissions or errors please notify the publishers, who will rectify the situation at the earliest opportunity.

Typeset by www.typesetting.ie

Printed in Dublin by SPRINTBOOKS

For

Clodagh

Who for 60 years

has been

my loving,

ever-patient

and loyal companion

and the anchor in our family

And for

Carolyn, Sharon, Jonathan, Richard and Denise

Their 'other halves'

John, Edgar, Jenny, Melissa and Colin

And their collective additions to our family

Sarah now with Gareth

Stephen now with Chloe

Grace now with Matthew

Jamie, Gareth and Andrew

Michael

David and Josie

Christopher, Matthew and Connor

With great-grandchildren

Patrick, Eden, Tom and ? soon to follow

OUR FAMILY TREE

Author's Note on Terminology

For those less familiar with the intricacies of Northern Ireland I would like to give a little background and explain some terminology. Northern Ireland is a region that is politically part of the United Kingdom and geographically part of the island of Ireland.

Numerically there are two dominant communities within the population: unionists and nationalists.

Unionists are mainly from the Protestant tradition, largely identify as being British and support Northern Ireland remaining part of the United Kingdom of Great Britain and Northern Ireland (UK).

Nationalists are largely from the Roman Catholic tradition, generally identify as being Irish and aspire to Northern Ireland leaving the UK and forming part of a united Ireland, which would include what is currently the Republic of Ireland.

There is also a growing sector of the population who regard themselves as 'non-aligned' and politically neutral regarding the Union.

Within nationalism are republicans who are more forceful in promoting the cause of a united Ireland. The Republican Movement comprised the Provisional IRA and its political wing, Sinn Féin. During that period of conflict known as 'The Troubles', the Provisional IRA carried out the majority of violent attacks in pursuit of a united Ireland, resulting in great loss of life.

In the last few years unionists have been increasingly referred to as comprising 'the PUL community', those letters standing for Protestant,

Unionist, Loyalist. Unionists are sometimes divided into small 'u' and large 'U' unionists: small 'u' unionists are those who believe, in principle, that Northern Ireland's best future is to remain in the United Kingdom of Great Britain and Northern Ireland, while large 'U' unionists are those who identify culturally as being British and Protestant and are most likely to support one of the Unionist political parties.

Within the PUL community are large working-class areas from which the loyalist paramilitary organisations recruit and draw their support. There are two main groups, the Ulster Defence Association and Ulster Volunteer Force, who during the conflict also killed many people in defence, as they saw it, of the union with Britain and the Crown.

'The Troubles' refers to the period of violent conflict that ensued for about thirty years, resulting in more than 3,500 lost lives and over 40,000 wounded until the negotiation and ratification of the Good Friday Agreement (aka the Belfast Agreement) in 1998.

Contents

Author's Note on Terminology	viii
Acknowledgements	xiii
Prologue	xv
Introduction	xxi
1. Good Beginnings	1
2. A Sickly but Privileged Child	15
3. Boy Preacher	30
4. An American Journey	45
5. Home Again	61
6. Pastures New and Less Familiar	87
7. Return to Parish	101
8. 'A People Called Methodists': Who and What We Seek To Be	113
9. Decommissioning: A Witness to History	131
10. Ian Paisley: As I Came to Know Him	155
11. Martin McGuinness: As I Knew Him	178
12. When Martin Met Jeffrey	200
13. Father Alec: My Fellow Traveller	219
14. The World as a Parish	238
15. Guns and No Guns! Up Close with ETA and FARC	257
16. Questions for Our Churches	283

Epilogue	295
Endnotes	310
Appendix I: Joint Statement by the Independent Eyewitnesses, Reverend Harold Good and Father Alec Reid, on the Decommissioning of IRA Weapons (26 September 2005)	312
Appendix II: Report of the Independent International Commission on Decommissioning	315
Appendix III: Address at a Graduation Ceremony in Queen's University Belfast, 3 July 2008	317
Appendix IV: *'From Prison to Peace'* – Address in Bayonne, Basque Country, southwest France, 7 April 2018, to mark the first anniversary of the disarmament of ETA	321
Index	330

Acknowledgements

To adequately acknowledge all of the people who have been significant in the story of my life would fill many more pages than this book could contain. But amongst them are those without whose encouragement and professional counsel and skill this book would not have seen the light of day.

It was at the insistence of my good friend and coffee-mate Brian (Barney) Rowan that I began to put pen to paper, and it was he who gave me reason to believe that there actually were people who would be interested to read it. Thank you, Barney, for your friendship and encouragement in this as in other things we have shared. And for introducing me to Mervyn Jess, who cast his critical eye over later drafts and suggested valuable improvements.

Needing a confidant with whom I would share my story and upon whom I would depend for professional guidance and technical skill, I was well guided in my choice of Martin O'Brien. Knowing of his distinguished career in journalism and broadcasting, I was delighted and privileged when he so readily agreed to my request. Thank you, Martin, for your friendship, your generous gift of time and patience, and for the heavy lifting when it came to the 'nuts and bolts' of writing and publication. Not recorded are the countless early and late-night calls, the immeasurable cups of tea, goodwill and constructive criticism, which for me has been an introduction to an otherwise unfamiliar world of book-writing and publishing.

Speaking of the latter, Martin and I were very pleased by the instantly positive response of Michael Brennan of Red Stripe Press. Thank you, Michael, and your very professional editor, Eileen O'Brien, and the many unseen people involved in the production of this memoir. Thank you for your faith in us and for ensuring that it really was published *In Good Time*.

These are the people who have made it possible for me to tell my story. But within and beyond these pages are those who have been my story and without whom there would be no story to share. Fellow pilgrims in my journey of faith, within other traditions as well as my own and within the congregations I have been so privileged to serve. But no less dear to me have been the trusted friendships I have made in so many committees and commitments in the wider community. I wish it were possible to name them all, but they will know who they are. Valued colleagues from whom I have learned so much and who remain the most personal of my many friends, even long after we have completed our shared responsibilities.

And thank you to those who have given endorsement to this book. I have been profoundly humbled as well as honoured by their most generous comments and commendation.

Less visible but central to my story have been Clodagh and our family, to whom I have dedicated this memoir. I trust that in helping them to understand what it was that kept me much too busy they will forgive those times when they did not get their fair share of my time and attention. I will be forever grateful for their unconditional love.

Harold Good
August 2024

Prologue

'What's past is prologue.'
　　　　　　　　　William Shakespeare, *The Tempest*

On numerous occasions, not least since my participation in the secret decommissioning of the IRA's remaining weapons back in 2005, it has been suggested to me by close friends and others that 'it's about time you wrote *that* book.'

Now in the second half of my ninth decade, sixty-two years since my ordination and more than twenty years into retirement, and while there is yet time, I have chosen the title *In Good Time*.

In this sharing of memories I have been anxious lest unintentionally I might betray confidences and dishonour the trust that has been placed in me throughout my ministry and more public life.

The most important code in peacemaking is confidentiality, which means that there are things I cannot share. But as time passes it does become possible to say more about things that in their time may have been considered secret or not for sharing.

And if what I have said in these pages sounds in any way egotistical, forgive me. That is the risk that goes with the telling of any personal story.

As I write, the headlines are of the brutal Israeli-Palestine conflict and the cruel Russian invasion of Ukraine, and I am reminded that however imperfect some may feel our peace to be, we all know that we are now in a dramatically different and much safer place in Northern Ireland. But while recognising the statesmanship, hope and vision of those who brokered the landmark Good Friday Agreement, we are on an unfinished journey, which is why I have written into this book things I believe we need to say to each other at this time.

It is my hope that these messages will speak to our unhealed wounds, unresolved differences, irreconcilable narratives, our uncertain constitutional future and our as yet unanchored peace.

Let me summarise what I believe to be the key lessons which I and others have learned over these turbulent years and which I wish to share in the pages that follow. How paths have been made for politicians and governments by lesser-known people and the need for bold leadership in both church and state.

THE NEED TO *TALK*

Being prepared to put oneself in the shoes of 'the other', whoever that might be, listening and journeying with each other, is a prerequisite for the resolution of any conflict. And as is so wrongly perceived, being prepared to engage in such a way does not mean that one is capitulating or surrendering one's own position.

In this book I refer to many times when people of differing and diametrically opposing views sat at my kitchen table while I poured the tea. As I listened to them, and they to each other, I was profoundly moved by the evolving spirit of trust which broke down barriers and opened doors of understanding and new possibilities.

In much of what I have written, there may be those who feel that I have been overly attentive in both time and attention to those from the republican/nationalist tradition. In response I refer to what is a fundamental first step in the bridging of any chasm. For the architect and builder this will inevitably involve what may appear to be a disproportionate amount of time given to an understanding of the side of the river with which he or she is less familiar.

Having said that, let it not be thought that in *our* outreach to others that I or others with me were tolerant of terror or unmindful of the horror and grief which has been inflicted upon so many on either 'side'. Having known and ministered to many victims of violence, nothing could be further from the truth.

THE NEED FOR *TRUTH*

To emphasise the need for honest conversation is not to be confused with the politics of condemnation, finger-pointing or 'whataboutery'. The endless recital of a litany of blame and denial of responsibility was something in which we became well practiced in public as well as in political life during our weary years of conflict. I have witnessed enough of such exchanges to know that they never will provide an environment in which people will be open to one another. On the contrary, they are more likely to retreat into their respective and defensive corners.

But having said that, uncomfortable though such conversations may be, in every fractured relationship, be it personal or communal, truth does demand mutual acknowledgement of responsibility for what each has inflicted upon the other.

For it is truth that sets us free. Not your 'opinion' nor my 'opinion', but truth, however unpalatable, which is a prerequisite to *trust*.

THE NEED FOR *TRUST*

The level of trust of which I speak only becomes possible when people are prepared to build personal relationships, show leadership, take risks and venture out of their comfort zones.

Later in this book I will I refer to times when at my kitchen table I sat with people of very differing and diametrically opposing views. But as I listened to them, and they to each other, I was profoundly moved by the evolving spirit of trust which broke down barriers and opened doors of understanding and new possibilities. Such engagement is no less needed today than then.

When addressing a variety of audiences in university or community groups, here and elsewhere, I have spoken of the importance of a relaxed setting for serious conversations. Such as our kitchen table with a pot of tea and scones baked by my wife, Clodagh. I go on to speak of these three 'Ts' – *talk*, *truth* and *trust* – which are fundamental in the process of constructive dialogue. Following one such presentation it was a frivolous but perceptive listener who called out, 'Don't forget the Tetley's.' And how right he was.

But above all, let this book be about the possibility of change. Let us not subscribe to the futile notion that 'nothing will ever change'. Within this book you will read of unlikely people who made unlikely journeys in their own lives and on behalf of us all. In spite of our disbelief, the impossible became possible. To build a decent, tolerant, prosperous future for our children and their children we must believe in the possibility of change. Perhaps beginning with ourselves.

I would also like this book to contribute to a reflection on the role of clergy in situations of conflict and on the role of the institutional Churches in all their diversity in the light of what we did and what we failed to do during the Troubles and since.

In a later chapter I attempt to be honest as well as fair in my critique of the role of churches throughout our troubled past. But let us not forget that within all of our churches and communities there have been faithful under-shepherds who have given of themselves in selfless pastoral care of families and individuals in their darkest hours and who, in their pastoral practice as well as in their preaching, ensured that even when the candles flickered we did not lose hope.

For many this did not come without price. I think of my eldest brother, Peter, also a Methodist minister, and of his friend Father Kevin Mullan. They both ministered in Omagh when the town was bombed in August 1998, causing more deaths and injuries than in any other single atrocity during the Troubles. While Peter was deeply appreciated by most of those to whom he ministered, he suffered very public as well as private censure for his unflinching ministry of reconciliation, doubtless contributing to his sudden and untimely death at the age of sixty-six – a sad reminder of how pastors and counsellors in frontline pastoral and caring professions will absorb the pain of those whose stories are so easily forgotten.

As I write I am very aware of the now more public conversations on the future of this island. As a child of this realm and been twice honoured by Queen Elizabeth II, I am a content and respectful citizen of the United Kingdom.

But as a 'Derry boy with a West Cork father, a mother from Armagh and a Waterford wife, I have inherited a more than usual understanding of the whole of this island and its histories.[i] And as a minister of an all-Ireland Church, it has been my privilege to serve congregations in both jurisdictions. So, from childhood, I have grown up with a profoundly personal love for my island home. I love its landscapes and its people, its poetry, myths and legends. But, as with all true love affairs, one has to be honest about what hurts as well as what is pleasing. Having been closely involved in our peace process, I am very much aware of the deep hurt that we have inflicted upon one another, across the generations as well as in the more recent past.

As I listen to reasonable arguments emphasising the potential social and economic benefits of reunification I am reminded of conversations with estranged couples who have sought my pastoral counsel. If one or the other was serious about reconciliation would I begin by emphasising the obvious social and economic advantages of returning to share one house? Of course not. For a meaningful restoration of their relationship we would begin with the difficult, honest and at times painful conversation about the hurt and the history of their broken relationship, as well as what a return to a shared house would look like

---

[i] Our family and everyone I met well into my adulthood and the early years of the Troubles called the city of my birth Derry. I still call it Derry. But in this memoir I have added an apostrophe, 'Derry, out of respect for those who call it Londonderry to express their British identity.

and what it would demand of each if it were to be a meaningful and lasting relationship.

If nationalist Ireland, in its diversity north and south, is to invite large 'U' or small 'u' unionists into such a conversation they need to be very sensitive to the genuine fears and feelings of those with whom they wish to have an honest dialogue about the future. And conversely, I appeal to unionists and 'others' to be open to such a conversation. The alternative may well be to find ourselves in a situation which has come about by default rather than design. With the inevitable risk of a re-distribution of resentment and the repetition of history.

My hope is that this book will make a contribution to all of the honest, sensitive and respectful conversations that must take place if we are to have a more settled and shared future on the island of Ireland, in whatever mutually acceptable shape that might yet be.

For all of us peace is a challenge as well as a privilege.

Introduction

It has been one of the privileges of my life to have been invited by Rev. Harold Good to assist him in the writing of this memoir. To be entrusted with this task by such a distinguished pastor is an honour and I hope it is a responsibility I have discharged well. When Harold asked me to join him in this project in May 2019 I had already known him for many years through my work as a journalist and producer in religious affairs with the BBC in Belfast. I had also a pre-existing sense of his contribution to the peace process dating from his role in the decommissioning of IRA weapons. That well-publicised episode turned out to be just the tip of an iceberg. I was not aware of the depth, scale, variety and discreet intensity of Harold's work in making peace and creating goodwill over nearly six decades, both here at home and as far away as the Basque Country and Colombia – work that continues right up to the present and this 87-year-old's continuing unpublicised efforts to resolve issues around parades and bonfires in Belfast. I am pleased that readers will now get more than a glimpse not just into his peace ministry but into his remarkable life, beginning with his battle with bovine tuberculous that saw him strapped to a metal frame and on his back in a wooden trolley for years, unable to attend school until he was well over eight years of age.

Harold not only lives up to his surname; he is also a modest man, and I had to persevere at times to ascertain the extent of his contributions to the public good while respecting that which has to remain unsaid.

Over the years of interviewing, researching, writing and rewriting, which included the tribulations of the pandemic (which held us up for a bit), what was always a professional relationship deepened into friendship and thanksgiving for his giftedness.

The words of elder statesmen and women such as Tony Blair, Bertie Ahern and Mary McAleese that you will find emblazoned across this memoir speak for themselves. They echo what senior figures close to government in Belfast, Dublin and London, and a wide range of opinion throughout Ireland, have told me since I started this work. Harold has always sought to put his faith into practice in a concrete way, always discreet, impartial, independent-minded, never tribal or preachy, navigating the political space with skill and sensitivity, seeing beyond the present and not at the expense of others. As one person put it: 'There is something about Methodism that commands respect in a divided society. It doesn't represent a single constituency.' I believe that whatever the future holds, this and generations to come will find the path to necessary healing and reconciliation that bit smoother by following Harold's example and looking to his gentleness, his vision and his passionate belief in honest, sincere, inclusive and respectful dialogue.

That our enterprise has also had an ecumenical dimension – given our respective Christian traditions – has made it all the more fulfilling. I have been enriched by the insight this has given me into the Methodist charism.

I am forever grateful to all who have supported me in this endeavour over the past five years. And more recently, the inspirational Michael Brennan of Red Stripe Press, who took our project on board, along with the dynamic Eileen O'Brien and the rest of their team. I retain fondest memories of my many visits to the Good family home and Clodagh's hospitality, including her fabled tea and scones.

I am especially thankful to Katie, my wife, who has always been my rock and who somehow endured my prolonged absences in the study with continued loving support.

Martin O'Brien
August 2024

1

GOOD BEGINNINGS

'You can choose your friends but you sho' can't choose your family …'

Harper Lee, *To Kill a Mockingbird*

𝓘 do not have a perfectly formed family tree going back centuries, of the kind that might provide material for a non-celebrity version of *Who Do You Think You Are?* I have heard the suggestion that the Goods came with Cromwell's troops and did not return to Britain. Given my disdain for all things Cromwellian, particularly in relation to his bloody legacy in Ireland, I choose not to contemplate that as a serious possibility and there is no evidence to substantiate it.

I much prefer the unconfirmed but highly likely explanation that the Goods arrived in southwest Ireland in the late eighteenth century from another historically contested territory, Alsace-Lorraine – which had been part of the German territories during the Holy Roman Empire[1] – as part of a wave of Mennonite Christians fleeing religious persecution and seeking a new life in the New World. Those who may have been daunted by the prospect of an Atlantic crossing or who found Ireland and/or its colleens immediately appealing settled in the area around Skibbereen in West Cork, where my father was born and brought up.

But those who did not stay in southwest Ireland continued their journey to the New World, where a new life awaited them. It was while living in the US in the 1960s that I was told of a sleepy hamlet in Lancaster County, Pennsylvania, which bore my name. So it was that I made my personal pilgrimage to Goodville in Lancaster County, better known for its association with the Amish people. I must have become one of the few Irishmen to have crossed the Atlantic in reverse in search of his roots.

You can imagine my surprise as well as excitement when, on Pennsylvania Route 23, I read these words written on a large iron stand:

GOODVILLE
FOUNDED BY PETER GOOD
LANDOWNER AND FARMER
1812

Peter Good. My grandfather, my great-grandfather, my uncle, and my brother.

And in the adjoining cemetery of that traditional white wood-frame Mennonite church, I found several of our family names. Alongside Peter there were Henry Good, Anna Good, Alice Good and George Good, the latter of which is one of my own names.

While I have never got round to employing a genealogist who might be able to confirm a definite link between the founder of Goodville and his relatives and my own family, I have since revisited Goodville on several occasions and sensed an affinity with those I met, as well as those who rest there.

The name 'Good' is neither Irish nor English and was most likely derived from the German name 'Gud'. From a small number of people named 'Good' in West Cork in the late eighteenth and early nineteenth century, there have grown a considerable number of families with this name who have been fully integrated into Irish life and, interestingly, these include some Catholics, indicating incidences of 'mixed' or inter-Church marriages.

In southern Ireland 'Good' is a name commonly associated with farming, milling, business and Church life, with no evidence that anyone bearing this name was ever part of the establishment, either in Church or State. In Ireland this is something that I regard as a badge of honour, indicating a desire to be seen as independent, resulting in a capacity, I would suggest in all modesty, to be trusted and respected across society. As indeed my uncles and aunt were in their business life in several towns and cities.

Assuming my guess concerning the origins of the family is correct, one of the descendants of the first Goods to arrive was my paternal grandfather Peter Good, who was born in 1850, the sixth year of the Great Famine, in the parish of Kilmacabea, close to the small town of Leap, not far from Skibbereen.

The overwhelmingly agricultural area around Skibbereen suffered more from starvation and disease than virtually anywhere else in the country, something that was powerfully conveyed to the wider world in a drawing of 'a forlorn boy and girl searching for potatoes on the road to Drimoleague' at Caheragh by James Mahoney in *The Illustrated London News*.[2] As that is the parish where my grandmother was born and my grandparents were married, I do wonder how they avoided being decimated by the worst scourges of the famine.

Peter was one of five brothers and the family holding was too small to support them all, so the Good siblings inevitably scattered. Two emigrated to the United States, a third to New Zealand, and another remained in County Cork as a land steward to some big house. And my grandfather, Peter, embarked on a career in the Royal Irish Constabulary (RIC) at the age of eighteen in 1867, the year of the Fenian Rising. According to information supplied to me by the Royal Ulster Constabulary Historical Society at the Police Museum in Belfast, he was appointed on the recommendation of Sub-inspector Potter of Skibbereen on 16 September 1867 and moved to Tipperary (West Riding) on 3 March 1868. It was a colleague in ministry, Rev. Tom

Kingston, who told me that as a lad his father admired my grandfather for his refusal to take part in enforcing the evictions of his impoverished Catholic neighbours, which may have been the reason for his early departure from the RIC, which meant sacrificing his secure salary and pension. Interestingly, this was but a story from a third party until I read the records from the RUC Historical Society, which revealed under 'Punishments' that on 6 March 1871, my grandfather was fined £5, a substantial sum in those days, nearly £630 in today's money. We can only surmise that this was a punishment for insubordination, for refusing to enforce evictions. I discovered a separate document in an old trunk belonging to my father, signed by a Tipperary RIC County Inspector on 16 September 1876, which said: 'He was discharged on gratuity on account of ill health,' and he added, 'Conduct good'. He had served a mere nine years.

Following the death of his father, Grandfather Peter returned to the family home to look after the modest 10-acre tenant farm and two-and-a-half years after his discharge, on 25 February 1879, aged 29, he married Mary Patterson, known as Minnie, from the parish of Caheragh, near Skibbereen. Both were members of the Church of Ireland. As was common in those days they wasted no time in starting a family and responded enthusiastically to the biblical injunction to be fruitful and multiply. They had eleven children – six sons and five daughters – in the sixteen years between 1880 and 1896. Unusually for the time, ten of their children survived. Sadly, their seventh child, Thomas Albert, died when he was just two months old. But, movingly, he was never forgotten and always included when there was a recitation of the family names. Their ninth child and fifth son, Robert James, known within the family as Bob, born on 26 May 1892, was my father, who would in the fullness of time become a Methodist minister and President of the Methodist Church in Ireland.

Interestingly, neither my father nor any of his siblings spoke much about their childhood on that small tenant farm. But piecing together stories which we have extracted from the famous *Skibbereen Eagle*, we now realise how hard life must have been for Grandfather Peter and my grandmother Minnie. There is the record of a failed court case that Peter took against his landlord in an attempt to lower his rent, challenging the legality of the tenancy agreement. Not surprisingly, not long afterwards we find the auctioneer's notice of the sale of the tenancy, to include a compact dwelling, two young dairy cows due to calve the following April, a donkey with cart and harness and a furze machine, a cast iron device for chopping gorse into feed for the donkey.

There followed a brief relocation in Bantry during which my grandfather worked in the Biggs family mill before the family returned to Skibbereen and settled in 68 Upper Bridge Street, a modest four-roomed house with a privy in the yard where they brought up their large family. Two of the older boys, and in time my father, had to be boarded out with neighbours.

In the 1901 Census – a quarter of a century after he was discharged from the RIC – my grandfather was described as 'a retired farmer' aged just 50. And the 1911 Census revealed him to be a 'car-taker'! I was somewhat relieved to discover through my friend Tom Kingston that he was not the motorised version of a horse thief, rather that he was a 'caretaker' of both the Church of Ireland Abbeystrewry Parish Church and the Methodist Church.

From Tom Kingston I also learned that he spent much of his time sitting in the public square dispensing his wisdom and 'setting the world aright'. Tom's father was but one of the lads who sat at the feet of this man, for whom he and his friends had great respect, due to both his integrity and his earthy wisdom.

While he was a proud son of County Cork, and West Cork in particular, where he took us on a visit, my father did not take us to the house where he was brought up. My brothers and our cousins and I were only to discover that house many years later. Having grown up in spacious manses we wondered how a family of ten surviving children could have been accommodated in a two-bedroom house with a privy in the yard. Were he and his siblings rather embarrassed by their humbler origins, rather than rightly proud of what they had achieved in their own right?

In my memory my father and his brothers spoke about their mother in reverential terms but said little about their father. Minnie was a formidable woman. From her photograph and the mental images we have of her she had the appearance of a determined lady one would not wish to cross. But hers cannot have been an easy life. Imagine bearing eleven children in as rapid a succession as nature would permit. Like her comparatively easy-going husband, she was a person of principle. As a good Anglican, on Sunday mornings she would parade her brood to the parish church for morning worship. However, one evening, at the invitation of a friend, Minnie attended what was known as a Methodist 'cottage meeting' which was held in the home of a neighbour. Such meetings were a common feature of rural life in those times and gave the circuit preachers an opportunity to reach a wider audience than in their own local Methodist societies.

Whatever the preacher may have said on that night, as Mr Wesley would have put it, Minnie's heart was 'strangely warmed'.[i] From then on Minnie, as Mr Wesley would have wanted – he did not set out to found a denomination of his own but that is another story – continued to parade her family to the Church of Ireland parish church for morning prayer and their observance of the sacraments. But in the evening they were to be found in the more lively and less formal atmosphere of the Methodist preaching house. Not surprisingly, the rector was not impressed.

As the story goes, His Reverence, who was low on tolerance, asked Minnie's brood to wait behind after morning prayer and suggested that they should decide whether they belonged to his Church or to 'those Methodists'. Interpreting what was an obvious rebuke as a serious

---

[i] A phrase which John Wesley, also known as 'Mr Wesley', used to describe his personal religious experience. Wesley, along with his brother Charles, was the founder of Methodism. See Chapter 8.

question, the young Goods agreed. It was only fair to the rector that they should choose. They took a vote and the Methodists won.

This was to be a defining moment, not only for that generation, but for generations to come. For as a result of that impromptu vote, the Methodist Church was to be blessed, or otherwise, with several local (lay) preachers and five ordained ministers, four of whom were elected to be presidents of the Methodist Church in Ireland, and the fifth, my oldest brother, the late Peter Good, appointed a district superintendent, the Methodist equivalent of a bishop. The four presidents were my father, elected in 1958; my first cousin, George (1969), son of my Uncle John, known as Jack; and Winston (1991), son of my Uncle Richard; and me in 2001.

For Minnie, her responsibility for her children was temporal as well as spiritual. In those days, for families in their circumstances, there was little opportunity for second-level education, let alone third-level. So it was that, under Minnie's guidance, upon leaving school at fourteen, several of her children in turn were apprenticed to the retail drapery trade.

In the Ireland of the early twentieth century, many if not most of the large provincial retail stores were owned by Protestants, many of them Methodists. Names such as Shaws of Portlaoise and Athy, Burgess of Athlone, Boles of Boyle and Haddens of Carlow come to mind. Not forgetting Coad's of Waterford, my wife Clodagh's family shoe business, which we shall speak of later.

Securing an apprenticeship in one of these family firms was viewed the way third-level education might be seen today. So it was not unusual to see advertisements for some of these firms in Protestant church journals, inviting applications for such positions. Or the clergy might be asked to look out for suitable candidates. In today's world of equality and fair employment this would neither be tolerated nor considered legitimate. In those times it was simply seen as 'looking after your own' and not viewed as sectarian. And surprisingly, it did not adversely affect the custom given to these stores by a predominately Roman Catholic community. Before we rush in judgement, all of this needs to be understood in the context of the Ireland of that time – an Ireland that was in turmoil about its national identity and less obsessed with how people identified as individuals. In return for learning a trade and being given accommodation over the shop, these employees would provide cheap labour for their employer, who would give them a few shillings per week from the £30 or so that their mother had paid, perhaps in annual instalments of £10, for their three-year-apprenticeship.

In addition to this payment, Minnie would have had to provide them with a trunk full of suitable clothing for their new status behind the counter. I know of only one trunk other than my father's that has survived. It is made of a cheap pine, lined with striped cotton and, until it had to be removed, covered with a very cheap imitation black leather. It remains in an honoured position in my home and, appropriately, I have stored family records in it.

In time the young Goods who had served their apprenticeships bravely stepped out on their own and the name Good Brothers was to be added to the list of Protestant and Methodist family businesses, in towns as far apart as Youghal and Sligo, with others such as Kilkenny and Dungarvan in between. For these families it was a matter of gratitude as well as pride that they enjoyed the respect and confidence of the communities they served. I remember hearing stories of how their customers, many unable to afford solicitors, were known to entrust personal papers and wills to these families for safekeeping in their secure safes.

But being in business in the Ireland of the 1910s and 1920s brought its own challenges. Imagine the situation my uncle and aunt found themselves in when, on the night of 11 July 1922, a fortnight after the start of the Irish Civil War, a certain Commandant Whelan, of the Waterford IRA, entered the premises of Good Bros in Dungarvan with a list of requisites for his anti-Treaty fighters. In March of the previous year the same Commandant Whelan, known as Pax Whelan, had participated in the Flying Column's Burgery ambush just outside

Dungarvan, which had resulted in four killings; two were members of the IRA and two of the security forces.

I have a copy of the Good Bros billhead, detailing the orders he put on the counter and documenting the business of the night, which amounted to £70 worth of boots, laces, shirts and socks, the equivalent of more than £4,000 in today's money.

I can only imagine what was going through my uncle's mind when he carried out that lucrative transaction with Commandant Whelan and the IRA. He would have known who he was dealing with and his feelings must have been mixed, to say the least. Could he have dared to refuse to keep the IRA properly clothed and shod? Whatever the arguments for or against compliance with this request, given the circumstances of the time, did he have a choice?

Indeed, such stores as my uncle's would openly be referred to as a 'Protestant house'. Surprisingly, when many of the great houses, which were seen to represent 'the Establishment', were being burned to the ground, Protestant business houses were spared. Was it because these families, like my own, were not associated with the aristocratic overlords and landlords who were seen to be representative of the hated English establishment?

This was the Ireland my father grew up in. It is clear from a brief account of his life that he left to be typed up after his death in 1976, and from my recollection of conversations during my upbringing, that the principal focus of his life was his Christian faith and his responsibilities as a servant of Christ.

Initially, he was apprenticed to a draper/boot and shoemakers, Jabez Correll in Skibbereen, and, based on his own records, having served his time over the preceding three years he left Skibbereen on 11 November, 1911, to continue his career in Shaws of Maryborough (now Portlaoise) where he secured promotion to the post of 'charge and buyer in the shoe and boot department'. It was here that he succumbed to 'the call of God' and came north as a 'Lay Evangelist' on the Armagh circuit in June 1915, as a first step in his journey towards ordination in 1920.

Apart from a single year in Bunclody (formerly Newtownbarry) in County Wexford, his itinerant ministry brought him north and in time he was to meet and marry a young lady called Dorothy Mildred Allen, known as Doris, in County Armagh, and they were married in Cranagill Methodist Church on 17 November 1932.

This brings me nicely to my maternal forebears, whose history is more colourful than that of my paternal antecedents. Doris's mother was Elizabeth, known as Lizzie. She was of a strict Quaker family of apple orchard growers from the Grange, near Richhill, close to Ireland's ecclesiastical capital of Armagh. Tracing the branches of our family tree to more recent times, I find the name of my maternal great-grandfather, Ephraim Allen (1828–1916), whose extraordinary long life was bookended by the premiership of the Duke of Wellington and Catholic Emancipation at one end, and the Easter Rising and the Battle of the Somme at the other. As a young man, Ephraim spent some time travelling and gaining business experience in Dublin before returning to County Armagh, where he was to eventually inherit the family home and orchards.

In the minutes of the Richhill Friends' (Quaker) Meeting there is a fascinating account of a defining moment in Ephraim's life – and therefore our family's. Having heard of his romantic interest in a young woman called Eliza Robinson, who was not a Quaker, Ephraim was called before the elders of the Meeting. He was reminded of the strict rules of the Society of Friends. If he were to marry 'outside of the Meeting' he would forfeit his membership of it – an uncompromising approach to a 'mixed marriage'. As the minutes of the meeting confirm, someone in the Meeting had the courage to air his opinion. One can imagine what to us would be a quaint conversation.

'Methinks, we do Brother Ephraim an injustice,' said he. 'I happen to know the young lady concerned. If truth be told, Eliza Robinson is a young woman of much greater piety than Brother Ephraim. How can we ask him to leave the Meeting for marrying a woman of greater piety than he?'

His point was well taken, and a compromise was offered. If Eliza were to join the Meeting and agree to bring up her children as Quakers, Ephraim and she would be welcomed. As will be swiftly recognised, all of this was a mirror image of the now discredited *Ne Temere* decree, which indirectly enforced the pre-existing requirement of the Catholic Church that all the children of a mixed marriage be raised Catholics.[3] Apparently, this was the first known relaxation of the strict practice of the Society of Friends and the good faith of the elders was amply rewarded by Eliza's contribution to the Meeting through her piety and the addition of five more young Quakers.

Ephraim was not only a successful grower of apples. He was also a poet of no mean ability. In particular, he would write poems to commemorate and celebrate special moments in his family's life. For our family, the most interesting of his works is contained in a privately published volume entitled *The Song of the Cradle*. This is a remarkable record of his family, as told by the highly observant cradle which had 'nursed' more than one generation of the family and, as well as the happier events, hints at some of the family's darker secrets. For example, there is reference to one of Ephraim's brothers who brought scandal to the family and was 'exiled' to the United States and died a lonely death.

As well as being devout members of the Richhill Meeting, Ephraim and Eliza took an interest in the wider affairs of Quakerism. They were governors of the Friends School in Lisburn, to which they sent several of their children, including my grandmother Lizzie. In those days school and family were so very different from now. Going to a boarding school must have been an end to childhood as we know it. School holidays were few and far between and the relationship between child and parent must have become a distant one.

As a girl, Lizzie was amongst the more privileged of her sex to receive the kind of education provided by such a school. And as a result, she had something of an independent mind. I have a well-preserved copy of correspondence between her and her father in which she asked his permission to study French instead of what we would now refer to as Home Economics. Her father's reply is uncompromising – no. And that was that!

No less intriguing is another bough of the Allen family tree. For sitting on a shelf in my home is a porcelain replica of Dan Winter's cottage, situated near the site of the Battle of the Diamond in 1795. It was in this cottage where the decision was taken by Dan and others to form what became the Orange Order, thus opening another chapter in the sad sectarian history of Ireland. Attached to that porcelain cottage is authenticated evidence confirming that I am a fifth-generation grandson of the same Dan Winter and his wife, Hannah. Something that is a cause of interest to some and earns me credibility with others.

For Ephraim, who had been granted dispensation for his marriage outside of the Quaker Meeting, there must have been more than a touch of poetic irony when young Allen (same surname but of different stock) who was not a Quaker but a Methodist, came seeking the hand of Lizzie. However, consent was granted, and Isaac and Lizzie were married. The cradle must also have approved, for the same cradle that had rocked his daughter Lizzie recorded the births of her three children, the youngest of whom was my mother, Dorothy Mildred, the aforementioned Doris, born on 30 April 1905. Doris's father Isaac was born c. 1860, of Methodist farming stock from Drumharriff in the civil parish of Drumcree, County Armagh, now rather famous for all the wrong reasons.

In adulthood Isaac had a privileged life. He lived in a fine residence, by virtue of his position as Land Steward at The Argory, Moy, County Armagh, the neo-classical mansion now owned by the National Trust. Isaac was steward to the then Lord of the Manor, Captain Ralph MacGeough Bond-Shelton, famously the longest-living survivor of the HMS *Birkenhead*, which foundered on rocks off the Western Cape, South Africa, in 1852 with massive loss of life.

Having been brought up on stories of The Argory, Captain Bond-Shelton and the good ship *Birkenhead*, you can imagine my reaction when, while wandering through an unremarkable maritime museum near the isolated village of Arniston in South Africa, my eye lit on an amateurish but nonetheless striking oil painting of the ill-fated *Birkenhead* as she was sinking. From the signature I saw that the artist was none other than my grandfather's employer and close friend, the good Captain Bond-Shelton himself. He who had died in my grandfather's arms. For as his trusted steward it was Isaac for whom his master called from his death bed and in whose embrace he died in March 1916.

Isaac was a faithful member of his local Methodist church and a Freemason who, from what I know, was a charitable man who was respected by his neighbours of differing persuasions. But unlike his Quaker wife and her family, Isaac held passionate political and constitutional views. As a staunch unionist, Isaac was an Ulster Unionist Party county councillor, a Justice of the Peace, a vehement opponent of Home Rule who signed the Ulster Covenant in 1912, and a member of Carson's army, the original Ulster Volunteer Force (UVF).

As a man of action as well as a man of words and ideals, Isaac, like others, was prepared to fight Britain to stay British. So it was that, wearing his UVF armband – still in our possession – he was on the quayside at Larne on the night of 24–25 April 1914 when Colonel Crawford sailed into Larne harbour with his illegal consignment of German arms for the defence of the Union. It was on that night that nine-year-old Doris and her sister Muriel, two years older, huddled in their bed in the land steward's house, listening to heavy footsteps up and down the stairs as numerous guns and rounds of ammunition were placed in their roof space. In the morning they asked their mother what all the noise had been about and why there was all that straw on the stairs. 'Ask no questions and you will be told no lies,' they were told, or words to that effect. It was some years before she and her sister were to realise what that fateful night had been all about. I do not know how the guns were subsequently disposed of ... or should I say, decommissioned. I trust that they never caused harm to anyone.

Pondering these tales of my two grandfathers, from entirely different situations, with their differing perspectives on what was happening in the Ireland of their day, I like to think that running in my veins there may well be a little of the DNA of each. Which may in part account for my less adamant view of one side or the other in our yet divided community.

In 1967, nine years before his death, my father wrote of his marriage to Doris: 'The union was a very happy one. We were blessed with a family of three boys … they have brought us great joy, and we are grateful to them for their love and loyalty.'

My eldest brother was Peter, obviously chosen to carry on the name of our grandfather and our great-grandfather. Rather like our dad, following a promising career in business, and as a married man, Peter took the brave step in offering himself for a ministry into which he was ordained and served.

My brother Robin was a mere eleven months my senior. At school and in the years that followed he was to distinguish himself as no mean player on the rugby field and as a caring pharmacist in the pretty town of Alresford in Hampshire.

I have nothing but the happiest of memories of both of my brothers and their families, as children and into adulthood.

As the youngest of those three boys, I was born on 27 April 1937, in the room above the entrance hall of our 'Derry Manse at 3 Victoria Park, a spacious semi overlooking the river Foyle.

2

A Sickly but Privileged Child

'I am not what happened to me, I am what I choose to become.'
Carl Jung, psychiatrist and psychoanalyst

At a very early age I became a sickly child, struck down with bovine tuberculosis (TB), and as a result did not attend school until well into my ninth year. My earliest memories are from when I was a barely four-year-old, lying on my back strapped to a metal and leather frame in a hard, flat trolley in the garden of our manse in the Waterside area of wartime 'Derry, looking up at the clouds. And those clouds and all they conjured up in my four-year-old brain in 1941 were my stories. To this day I cannot look at wonderful cloud formations without seeing images that fire my imagination. We lived next door to the Austin family, and it was a kind carpenter on the staff of their iconic Austin's department store on the Diamond in 'Derry who made that fine trolley, especially for me.

In my earliest photographs with my two older brothers I looked like any other toddler. But all of that was to change. My earliest recollection of something being wrong with my walking was on a sunny afternoon when I was at the front of our then home, the 'stately' 'Derry Manse I had been born in. My father was washing our trusty pre-war

Austin 10, registration EZ 4662. For some inexplicable reason those numerals have imprinted themselves on my memory in such a way that, to this day, I am constantly spotting them or the nearest numbers above or below.

All of these years later, I could take you to the very spot on the raised edge of the grass where I sat down and announced to my father that I wasn't going to walk anymore. This, apparently, was the wake-up call which confirmed to my already anxious parents that there was something more seriously wrong than the growing pains with which they had previously been put off by the family doctor. There followed a series of further consultations with physicians, both general and specialist, all of whom offered differing but equally inconclusive diagnoses.

There were doctors my mother spoke of with less appreciation, but high on her list of those she spoke of with particular respect and gratitude was Dr Winifred Hadden of Portadown, one of a family of physicians noted for their devotion to Methodism as well as to their medical practice. In the strange sort of way that these things happen, I have to thank Mr Hitler for the events that brought me under the temporary care of the good Dr Winifred. For it was following one of the two relatively light bombings of 'Derry that my mother, brothers and I were dispatched as voluntary evacuees to our grandmother, who lived at Coragh Hill near Loughgall in County Armagh.

As well as her standard remedy of a rubbing with olive oil, of which I suspect there may yet be a lingering aroma from my limbs, Dr Winifred was known for her insistence on being taken seriously when she had an opinion that differed from other practitioners. Apparently it was she who first mentioned the then dreaded word, tuberculosis.

The chief suspect for this misfortune that had been inflicted upon me was an anonymous cow, last seen in the vicinity of our holiday cottage in Magilligan, County 'Derry. This was at a time when it was common practice for fresh and unpasteurised milk to be delivered in a tin can straight from the farm. The poor creature, who was constantly referred to as the cause of my misery, would have been totally unaware of the difficulties for which she was quite unreasonably held responsible. That said, I have to confess that for many years this did colour my perception of these gentle creatures, whose primary product is now so rigorously sanitised before it reaches our table.

Thanks to whoever or whatever, I was admitted to the Royal Belfast Hospital for Sick Children for specialist care and assessment. My only recollection of that institution was of the night when, to the soundtrack of air-raid sirens, we children were put under the beds to protect us from the dangerous deeds of the same Mr Hitler who in a funny sort of way was responsible for my being there in the first place.

Upon confirmation of Dr Winifred's tentative diagnosis, which was known as 'spinal caries' or Pott's disease, a form of bovine tuberculosis of the spine, it was decided that I needed to be admitted to Graymount, a specialist hospital for children suffering from tuberculosis.

However, following the raids in Belfast, Graymount had relocated to Greenisland, which in terms of time and means of transport was a much further journey from 'Derry then than it would be today. Especially in a time of strict rationing, when there was no petrol for anything other than essential journeys related to one's professional responsibilities.

In contrast to what happens today, visiting, even by parents, was restricted to Wednesday and Sunday afternoons. As a minister's wife, my mother was not free to travel from 'Derry on a Sunday. And for a minister's wife even the mid-week fare was expensive. So it was that, being of an independent disposition, my mother decided to take advantage of the reduced excursion fare on a Thursday. But it was not long before she received a formal letter from a Dr Clarke, the hospital superintendent, warning her that, should she persist, her visiting privileges would be withdrawn. And she also records how, on another day, having been seen to be in conversation with another mother, she was reminded by the matron that she was there to visit her own child and that conversation between visitors was not permitted.

My mother was a diligent diarist, which for the most part was recorded in Mr Pitman's shorthand, which was her particular skill from her time in the civil service from which, in those days, a young woman had to 'retire' upon marriage. But interestingly, her diary of events surrounding my illness at that time was in straightforward English. Obviously, she wished me to read of those events when I would be of an age to understand and appreciate what my parents had had to cope with in caring for their 'sickly' child.

While drafting this chapter I have been re-reading what my mother wrote in that diary. What she has written is so personal and at times painful for me to read that I hesitate to quote from it. As so often happens, I took it all so much for granted and deeply regret that I did not appreciate it while she was still alive. But apart from my mother's recorded stories, I have my own vivid memories of 'that place'. Nurses who threatened to put us in the basement with the rats if we did not conform to whatever it was we did not wish to do. And if we talked too much or cried too much, sticking plaster would be placed over our mouths, with strict instructions that it was not to be removed. I can still hear and feel the 'zip' of that sticking plaster being removed.

Unbelievable? When not taken seriously as a child I sometimes doubted my own memory of events. But almost twenty years later, in 1960 when I was hospitalised in the Musgrave Park Hospital in Belfast for surgery, following the re-awakening of my dormant tuberculosis, a young nurse came to my bedside and introduced herself as Winifred Magee. 'Are you the Harold Good who was in Greenisland Hospital as a little boy?' she asked. 'And are you the Winifred Magee whose mother and my mother wanted to be good friends but were not allowed to speak to one another?' I countered.

When we shared our memories as fellow patients in Greenisland, they were identical. To me, the wonder is that Winifred chose nursing as her vocation.

In today's more enlightened world of accountability, both Winifred and I would be chief witnesses in an inquiry into the abusive treatment of children in that hospital. One does not need an honours degree in psychology to understand the impact of trauma upon a child. I found my experiences of Greenisland Hospital were not lost on me when, many years later, in the mid-1960s I studied Pastoral Psychology in the USA. My mother recorded how timid and withdrawn I had become when I returned home from Greenisland.

The trauma from those days as a youngster in Greenisland Hospital in the early 1940s took time to leave me. For quite some time I was known to have shouted down the familiar and wondrous words of the doxology, 'Praise God from whom all blessings flow ...', the Grace that was sung each day before our not so blessed hospital meals. The sung Grace was probably a nod to the 'Prods' among us, while fish on a Friday was an acknowledgement of the dietary customs and spiritual practice of the Catholics. And as a result, for many years I had a stubborn aversion to any fish on any day of the week. Sadly, this is a reminder of how negative childhood experiences of religious custom and practice can distort what ought to be a happy and healthy experience of faith. Likewise, for many years, long after Greenisland, when it came to Christmas, the sight and taste of turkey revived the unhappiest of memories of 'stolen gifts' and a bed-ridden Christmas far from home.

So to compensate I would have my very own special duck or chicken, until a devious aunt served me a slice of turkey masquerading as chicken. When I devoured it and asked for more the game was up. And by now, as my family will confirm, my consumption of both fish and turkey has more than compensated for the years without.

It was not that my parents were uncaring, quite the contrary. But as helpless infants who did not know that all this was anything other than we might expect from adults, it never occurred to us to report it to our parents. If we had, we would probably have been dismissed as 'exaggerators'. But the positive side of reflecting on this childhood experience is that it has given me a very personal understanding of the plight of children who have been abused – physically, sexually or psychologically – and remain silent in the face of much worse treatment than we ever experienced in Greenisland.

For me, all of this was to change with the good news of the appointment of the first specialised orthopaedic nurse to Northern Ireland, entirely due to the generosity of the car-manufacturing giant Lord Nuffield, whose own child had suffered from a condition similar to mine. Coincidentally, as the manufacturer of the Morris car, it was Lord Nuffield's Trust that provided for the appointment of the newly qualified Gladys Morris to Northern Ireland. Her role was to be that of a peripatetic nurse, travelling across Northern Ireland to advise and support families caring for orthopaedic patients in their own homes. One can only imagine the joy of my parents on hearing of this opportunity to bring their child home from that dreadful hospital, about which at that time they only knew the half.

So it was that, on Sunday 25 January 1942, using his meagre ration of petrol, my father drove his car to Greenisland to collect me. It was dark by the time we came to the Glenshane Pass and the memory of that strange journey home to 'Derry is still vivid in my mind – lying on my back and counting the stars.

To immobilise my increasingly deformed spine I was strapped into a metal frame and under instruction from Gladys Morris a trolley was designed and constructed by the carpenter from Austin's Store, complete with wheels from a second-hand pram that my father brought home from Smithfield Market in Belfast. But for me it was my Rolls Royce, in which I was to sleep and eat and be wheeled around for as long as it was going to take for me to be allowed to walk again.

Miss Morris, for whom the whole of Northern Ireland was her 'parish', came regularly to check my progress and to advise my mother on how best to care for me. As well as a diet of raw eggs and carrots, I was to have as much fresh air as possible. This meant being wheeled out in the morning and only being brought in when it rained, whatever about snow and ice, of which I have vivid memories. But whatever, it worked! And in time I did walk again and made a significant recovery, psychologically as well as physically.

My continued enforced absence from school meant that my mother had to take responsibility for what is now known as home schooling, and teach me as best she could while I continued to lie on my back on the trolley.

As we were subjected to wartime food rationing my father had to obtain permission from the authorities to procure hens that would lay fresh eggs for his sickly child. And to avoid the risk of unpasteurised milk he bought a goat so that I could enjoy fresh, rather than boiled milk.

After serving for nine years as Superintendent Minister in 'Derry, my father was transferred to east Belfast in 1945. I still recall the drive into Belfast. We passed Bellevue Zoo on the Antrim Road and I saw a camel for the first time and thought I was in a foreign country. My father's immediate task was to build a new church on the Newtownards Road, to replace the one that had been destroyed in the Blitz of 1941. In recent years this fine new building has been replaced by the impressive Skainos Centre, encompassing the multi-faceted ministry of the East Belfast Mission.

My next challenge was to grapple with the mystery of school. I was already more than three years late in starting school and I had no idea what a normal formal education looked like. My local primary school was Strandtown, a short walk from Van Morrison's Cyprus Avenue, where we lived. 'We'll try him in the class for his age, and we'll see how he does, and move him down if necessary,' said the principal, Mr Martin.

I was blessed with the teacher whose class I was placed in – Mrs Cummings, an amply proportioned lady who arrived each morning on her bicycle. She had an intuitive understanding of the needs of a child entering a classroom for the first time, several years after his peers. To give me a sense of belonging and of purpose I was appointed to be the official 'puller off' of her wellington boots. A privileged responsibility that I took very seriously every morning. And to further my sense of belonging she paired me with a certain Reggie Henning to carry one end of the milk crate from which he and I distributed the then statutory bottle of milk to each child that helped us get the daily nutrients we needed. As a result, Reggie and I were to become the best of friends, graduating from the milk crate to the breeding of pet rabbits, which we sold to Mr Montgomery of Smithfield for 1s 6d each. Big money in those days.

As it turned out, my mother must have done a good job homeschooling me and I didn't require any demotion. Nothing exemplifies the esprit de corps of a primary school community more than the Nativity play and I enjoyed my first public performance, proudly performing as a shepherd.

'Do your best but don't worry if you don't pass' was the well-intentioned counsel from my parents and others when it came to facing 'the Quallie' or 11-plus exam which would determine whether or not I would earn my place in a grammar school. For them my physical recovery was much more important than academic achievement.

However, I surprised them and myself in passing this test and in September 1949, I entered Methodist College, Belfast, popularly known as Methody, a respected seat of learning founded in the 1860s to educate the children of Methodist ministers and others, situated on a prestigious site on Malone Road, opposite the main Queen's University campus.

I concluded my six years at Methodist College when I passed the Senior Certificate in June 1955. While I was at best a mediocre student (for which I of course blame my late start) and was limited in my participation in the extra-curricular and sporting activities, I have good memories of those years and of the friendships I formed. Two of my classmates, Archbishop Robin Eames and Professor Sir Desmond Rea, the first Chairman of the Northern Ireland Policing Board – one of the key bodies resulting from the Good Friday Agreement – remain good friends to this day.

In time I was pleased to serve as a Trustee Governor of the College and was, as a less-than-remarkable-student, much moved and honoured to be invited to be guest of honour at the annual Prize Day in 2018.

Sixty-three years earlier, in the summer of 1955 the Oxford-educated F.P. Rose, whom I admired mostly for his pastoral abilities, his sense of justice and innate fairness, spent much of his time writing references for departing students.

I still have the type-written words he said about me dated 19 August 1955. He chose his words carefully, noting that I had obtained both my Junior and Senior Certificates, had 'made steady progress' in my studies, that English was 'a strong subject' and that I had 'reached a satisfactory standard in Mathematics.' He continued:

> When his interest is aroused his ability is considerable, and he shows a mature approach in achieving his aims. Some lingering effects of an earlier illness have prevented him from taking part in strenuous games, but he has overcome them sufficiently to maintain a good school attendance, and he has participated in general activities to the best of his ability.
>
> There has been a pleasing development in his character and outlook, with a generous attitude to his friends and a willingness to take correction when he is wrong.

Mr Rose added:

> I believe him to be a sincere, upright and thoughtful young man, fit to undertake responsible work, and genuinely interested in the welfare of others. I support his application for suitable employment.

I mention this as a tribute to Methody and F.P. Rose in particular as it shows how he and the school saw a potential in this struggling late-starter that I did not recognise in myself. An affirmation which surprised me but for which I was truly grateful, as it gave me the confidence to think more seriously about my next steps.

I was now eighteen years old and for about a year I had been sensing what is often described as 'a call' to follow in my father's footsteps and serve as a minister in the Methodist tradition.

Interestingly, I was not alone, for between my year and the next there were nine of us who entered the ministry of different denominations. Two into the ministry of the Church of Ireland, three into the

Presbyterian Church and four of us into the ministry of the Methodist Church.

In the next chapter I will trace my steps to ordination. But first I will say a bit more about my parents and my early childhood, about their values and attitudes that influenced my formation.

Referring to the people of Israel, the Psalmist reminds us how all of us, whatever our history and culture, will hand on our stories 'from generation to generation.' (Ps. 78 v. 5–6). Invariably, if not inevitably, from our own perspective.

Like most Protestant children growing up in Northern Ireland, we had no lessons in Irish history other than what we heard from our parents. For most children this will have been from a single perspective. But my brothers and I were fortunate. From our apolitical West Cork father we inherited a perspective on Irish history that complemented the stories told to us by our County Armagh Unionist-supporting mother whose father had stored UVF guns in his roof space with the intention of going to war over Home Rule.

This, together with idyllic boyhood holidays with our southern cousins, gave us an understanding of both perspectives. An understanding which was not always appreciated or shared by our peers, north or south. For this I am grateful. Rather than confusing us, it freed us from the entirely false proposition that there can be only one interpretation of Irish history. Never having consciously adopted either a Nationalist or a Unionist identity, or felt constrained to die for either, has enabled me to feel entirely comfortable and at home with people of both traditions and, apparently, they with me. But that is for others to say.

Interestingly, in much later life both of our parents became founder members of the Alliance Party in 1970. When asked who or what had influenced her in moderating her political views my mother would reply, 'My children.' So perhaps this generation-to-generation dynamic works in more than one direction.

Having been born in West Cork and having remained very close to his siblings south of the border I think that my father could be aptly described as an 'All-Islander'.

Like the other main Churches on the island, the Methodist Church in Ireland – as evident in its official name – is an all-Ireland Church. In July 1936, after a two-year stint on Belfast's Shankill Road, a challenge for any Cork man, he was appointed Superintendent of the Derry City Mission, as it was officially called, and he and my mother took up residence in the manse with three-year-old Peter and two-month-old Robin, where ten months later I was born.

So, having been born in 'Derry I am a Northerner and a proud son of that city, as I would be had I been born in Dublin or Cork. While I left the Maiden City as a child of eight, I have retained a strong sense of belonging whenever I return, especially when I cross the Craigavon Bridge and walk up the ever-steepening Shipquay Street.

When the war at last ended, and petrol was once more available, we would set off for holidays with our relatives in southern towns and cities. So, Kilkenny, Sligo, Youghal and the less remarkable Dungarvan became for us very special places of annual pilgrimage. If not flowing with milk and honey, this was the land where you could buy the biggest HB ice cream slider for 4d; here were chocolate biscuits after every meal and whipped cream with puddings; here were generous uncles and aunts who would take us into their drapery stores and fit us out from top to toe before we left for home. This was their way of supporting their brother, who had exchanged a much more lucrative life in business to follow his calling into ministry. For us there was no sense of sacrificing the 'blue sky' of Ulster for the 'grey mists' of an Irish Republic. On the contrary, as for most of us in our memories of childhood holidays, the sun never ceased to shine.

Yet even as children we were aware of certain cultural and other differences between the two parts of Ireland. People played different music and flew a different flag. When we went to the cinema with our cousins we stood for a different song. They had different money, with horses and hares instead of kings and queens.

Of course our families and friends were also Methodists. On Saturday nights we were well scrubbed and our shoes shone for church the following morning. As we would make our way to the more modest Methodist church, we were very conscious of the multitudes in headscarves and cloth caps streaming into and out of local Roman Catholic churches, or chapels as they were called.

And why did the men stand outside when they should have been within? And why were they so anxious to get their services over early? And if, as we were told, it was to get to their afternoon Gaelic football or hurling game, did they not know it was Sunday?

By the welcome from pulpit and pew, we knew that our presence had boosted the local congregation by a significant percentage, which seemed to mean much to the preacher and the regular worshippers. All of this, together with other experiences and conversations, greatly contributed to our growing awareness of what it means to be a part of a minority community within a much larger community that may not share your views and values. But with whom you must live and move and trade with toleration and mutual respect.

My impression was that my family circle who lived in the south of Ireland did feel that they lived in a place where they were respected and shown tolerance, and where they reciprocated those values.

While of course there have been well-publicised stories from Ireland's bitter past, the experience of my wider family was contrary to the stories that I heard from concerned but ill-informed Northerners, many of whom had rarely, if ever, crossed the border.

I am forever grateful to my parents for nurturing us in a non-sectarian and openhearted kind of way. I never sensed any trace of anti-Catholicism or sectarianism within our family and that was a blessing. Though my mother, not surprisingly given her background, would have had a unionist outlook and was instinctively loyal to what she would have considered her British birth-right but not in an 'in-your-face' sort of way.

The only heated political discussion I ever remember in our home took place when I was about twelve. It was an animated exchange between my mother and a visiting Methodist minister from the south of Ireland who was staying with us for a few days, probably for Annual Conference.

My mother took a strong, predictable unionist position against our guest, who must have been arguing for what she would have regarded as the heresy of Irish unification. They had an ideological ding-dong during which my mother held her own quite forcibly. She had inherited her stance from her father, Isaac.

My father's understanding and practice of the Gospel extended to being liberal in his thinking in relation to Roman Catholics and Catholicism, decades before the winds of change of the Second Vatican Council.

At an evening meal he told us how on the golf course he had met 'this lovely priest' and they had 'a lovely conversation' before going into a little hut and praying together. Obviously, the fact that I still remember that casual conversation means it made an impression upon me and I am grateful that I was shielded from the raw, naked sectarianism that manifested itself in other parts of Belfast. It wasn't part of our story.

That said, I did not meet any Catholics when I was growing up, and that absence of social interaction reflected the reality of life in Belfast and in much of Northern Ireland generally.

There was only one Catholic family that I knew of when growing up in the predominantly middle-class Cyprus Avenue. They were the Lambe family, whose father, Paddy Lambe, owned pubs in nearby Ballyhackamore. If my father, a total abstainer and an embodiment of the temperance movement, had any difficulty with Paddy Lambe it would have been because he made a living out of selling alcohol, rather than anything to do with his religious persuasion.

The Lambe children were our age but we never played together and no one ever asked us not to play together. They went to a different school and had different sets of friends. It was assumed that we all lived separately and led essentially separate lives. So we co-existed without any social intercourse or interaction. If you were a Catholic in Belfast at that time and had questions about the governance of Northern Ireland, you would do as Protestants did in the Republic of Ireland, keep your head down and get on with your own life.

My father, Rev. R.J. Good, may have shied away from political discourse but that did not mean that he wasn't a man of strong moral conviction that was rooted in Scripture and in Wesleyan principles of social holiness. This was to be put to the test when serving in Enniskillen between 1955 and 1960, during the height of the IRA's Border Campaign.

On 4 July 1957, a matter of days after he was elected President-designate of the Methodist Church in Ireland, an RUC officer, Constable Thomas Cecil J. Gregg, aged 27, was killed by the IRA near Forkhill in County Armagh. My father was deeply affected by this callous murder, particularly as this was a young man he had baptised during his earlier appointment in Enniskillen. He was so deeply affected that when he became President of the Methodist Church he wrote to the other Church leaders to share his concern about what he sensed was the beginning of an intensified campaign of violence. In his letter he suggested that as people who carried particular responsibility for the good of society, they should meet to discuss what they might say and do jointly. This would have been an unprecedented, indeed historic, initiative by Ireland's Church leaders. He was deeply disappointed in their responses, with each of them saying in their own dismissive way, 'nice idea Mr President, but the time is not right.'

To his credit, my father's response was to make a solo run to meet with 'one of the leaders of the revolutionary movement' in Dublin, which he reported to the ensuing Methodist Conference in Portadown on 13 June 1959.[4] And the roof didn't fall in on him. The meeting had taken place in secret some weeks earlier. According to a newspaper report of his meeting, he and the Republican leadership had a frank and robust conversation in which he sought to persuade them that a united Ireland could not be attained by force. But even if it could be, they would then have serious moral and political questions to answer. Without knowing it, he was prefiguring similar approaches some years later by well-known Methodist figures, such as the Rev. Eric Gallagher with other Protestant churchmen at Feakle, County Clare, in 1974, and Gordon Wilson in 1993, and myself and others before as well as after the IRA broke their own ceasefire in 1996.

As I reflect back and admire my father's prophetic efforts in going where no Protestant Church leader had gone before, I also remain deeply fascinated by Peter Good and Isaac Allen, the grandfathers I never knew, whose DNA is somewhere in my genes. In lighter moments I imagine Peter and Isaac sitting on a cloud enjoying a fascinating exchange of their views on Ireland, past and present. I do have to say that the more I learn about the Ireland of 1912 and 1914 the better I understand the position of Grandfather Isaac.

As a postscript to the story of 'the sickly child' on the trolley who had to learn to walk again, I confess that as the years rolled by, and as a much too energetic and socially active student, my long-dormant tuberculosis re-awakened. When my doctors were unsure as to what to do, it was the perceptive Miss Morris, though retired, who I turned to. It was thanks to her intervention, and the respect she had earned from specialists who acted on her intuitive counsel, that I underwent major spinal surgery.

How would this sickly child ever repay the wonderful Gladys Morris, through whose professional and skilful care I was able to be released from Greenisland and in time be able to walk again? In a wholly unexpected way the opportunity to do so was granted when, in 1993, I was appointed to my final charge, which was in South Belfast. Amongst the good folk of that congregation, who was to be under my pastoral care? None other than the same Gladys Morris. What a joy that was for both of us.

And how moving it was for me and for her former medical and nursing colleagues who knew of her story and mine when I, who had known her longest and owed her so much, gave the final tribute and laid her tired body to her well-deserved rest.

3

BOY PREACHER

'Preach the Gospel at all times, and when necessary use words.'
Attributed to St Francis of Assisi

FIRST STEPS

A huge influence on my faith and my decision to think of ministry were two autobiographical books by remarkable men. While they would not be the kind of books that many – if any – teenage boys would read today, they are treasures that still occupy a special place in my library and in my thinking.

One was the autobiography of a Methodist minister, author and local politician known as Lax of Poplar, who pastored for more than 30 years until the mid-1930s in the East End of London, where the popular BBC drama *Call the Midwife* is set.[5] Lax was a man who got out of his pulpit and rolled up his sleeves, and his stories of social outreach to the excluded and marginalised made ministry sound like the best fun and the most satisfying job in the world.

I thought, if ministry is that much fun and you can make such a personal difference in ordinary people's lives, then count me in. So taken was I by Lax that many years later I went on a very personal pilgrimage to a rather rundown Poplar to get a sense of his legacy and honour his memory by viewing a portrait of him in his clerical and mayoral robes.

The other book that impacted me greatly was *Grenfell of Labrador: A Labrador Doctor* by Wilfrid Thomason Grenfell.[6] Grenfell was an evangelical Christian surgeon who turned his back on a comfortable and lucrative Harley Street career to embark on what he considered the more fulfilling mission of serving deep-sea fishermen and others in the icy conditions of Labrador in Newfoundland. Sir Wilfred, who was knighted for his medical missionary work, had a wholesome and inclusive evangelical approach and a practical understanding of the practice of his Christian faith.

Looking back over my life from my earliest days, I do not recall a moment when I had anything but a happy and trusting understanding of faith. So my childhood and upbringing were conducive to a serious consideration of ministry. The notion that growing up in a manse would turn off a young person from going into ministry was not true for me.

Whatever about those times in Greenisland Hospital, and being strapped in my trolley for much of my childhood, I am fortunate to have only happy memories of my teenage years at home in east Belfast. For me and my two older brothers, Peter and Robin, church was a natural and normal extension to our family and social life and this was where we made our out-of-school friends. But like many Protestant teenagers from that era who were not into dancing, my religious and social life was supplemented by the Saturday night rendezvous in the city centre's Wellington Hall or the film service at the old Grosvenor Hall, where we would often queue for an hour to get the best seats. But as it was for those who chose dancing, the interest was as much to do with catching the eye of a pretty girl as it was with whatever else the evening was about. After spirited singing of hymns and choruses and a word from an animated preacher we would go for coffee or a Coke at Isabeals city centre restaurant.

My father, a hard-working minister and my mother, his ever-supportive companion, were always busy people. It was obvious to me that their life together in that manse in Cyprus Avenue and later in Knock was one of great fulfilment. I never heard them complain. Indeed, I used to think what dull lives some of my friends' parents lived in comparison.

When I was around seventeen, during my penultimate year at Methody, I sensed the beginning of a call to ministry. There was no dramatic bolt of lightning. Simply a growing awareness that this could well be the next step in my journey of faith and providence.

Two years earlier, when I was fifteen, I had made a conscious and public commitment to be a follower of Christ. Alongside several other young people I attended the last of a series of classes in preparation for a public service of Confirmation in my father's Knock Methodist Church in Belfast on a spring evening in 1952. We were preparing to confirm for ourselves the promises made on our behalf by our parents in the sacrament of infant baptism many years before. To avoid the possibility of drifting into Confirmation without commitment, each of us was given a 'decision card' to take home to sign if we wished to proceed.

I remember asking of myself if I sincerely meant what I was saying or if I was just going through the motions. I assured myself that I did mean it and signed the card – which I still have. While the faith and example of my parents must have been a factor in determining my answer to that question, ultimately it was my decision and I made it without reservation or the feeling of any pressure. And while not dramatic, this was to be an important and defining moment in my life. And when thoughts about ministry came into my head I was in a particularly receptive frame of mind as to how I would respond. I was as yet an adolescent, so this was but a staging post on my journey as a novice in my discipleship. On that night I could not have anticipated where this journey was to take me, as will be recorded in this book.

Not long ago, exactly 70 years later, in the same church at Knock, I attended the Confirmation of five young members of our Church and poignantly recalled my own moment of Confirmation and commitment and other occasions when, as minister of that same church, I had the joy and privilege of confirming several of my own children at that same altar.

In terms of my choice of vocation, I do not recall having seriously considered other possible careers, although an unexpected stint at teaching (that I'll come to) did give me reason to pause for thought. Interestingly, looking through the careers of alumni of Methodist College over the years, a significant number of past pupils entered the ministry of different denominations. Amongst them I can count nine of my contemporaries as I recalled in the previous chapter. And not forgetting my brother Peter, a much later entrant to ministry.

For different reasons, Lax and Grenfell had an immense influence on my young mind and prompted me to seek the path of ministry. The year was now 1955, I was eighteen, and change was in the air for both me and my parents. In June, having completed my time at Methody, I left school with my Senior Certificate safely under my belt. For many school leavers it would be the time to leave home. For me, it was more a case of home leaving me, for at the same time my father was appointed to the Enniskillen Circuit in County Fermanagh.

Next steps

In preparation for my entrance exams for the Methodist ministry I would have several months of study, but having neither assets nor gainful employment, I had little option but to move with my parents to Enniskillen, leaving my brothers behind in Belfast. So it was that I, a Belfast lad, found myself to be something of an alien in what to me was a strange and unfamiliar land. Strange in so many ways, not least church-wise. Coming from the more theologically liberal, indifferent leafy suburbs of east Belfast I was unfamiliar with the conservative, close-on evangelical fundamentalist culture of Fermanagh. I had much to learn.

During our father's first week in his new parish, he suggested to my visiting brother Robin and me that, instead of our planned excursion to the one and only cinema in Enniskillen, it would avoid misunderstanding and be much appreciated if we would accompany him and my mother to the weekly Prayer Meeting at Darling Street Church. Our journey back in time was complete when with a megaphonic voice and passionate fervour a rather over-zealous participant prayed: 'And now Lord, about them dancing halls and picture houses … dens of iniquity, Lord. Burn them down, Lord. Tonight, Lord. Burn them down tonight, Lord …'. At this point my less pious brother dug me in the ribs and muttered, 'Didn't we have a lucky escape?' This was to be my introduction to a religious culture with which hitherto I had been quite unfamiliar.

Come September, knowing that studies for my entrance examinations would not consume all of my daylight hours, and driven by a desire for economic independence from my parents, I decided to seek employment. On advice from a newfound friend, I called at the offices of the Fermanagh County Education Committee in Enniskillen. Having been advised that they might be in a position to offer temporary employment on a part-time basis, I assumed that if successful I would be sweeping the school yard or washing the school buses. So, imagine my disbelief when I was offered the position of 'temporary, unqualified assistant teacher' at Brookeborough Primary School. Whatever the lowliness of the position, I could hardly believe that this eighteen-year-old who had just come from one side of a school desk would now be standing behind the other.

So it was, on the following Monday morning, that I met Charlie Kirkpatrick, the 'Master' of this two-roomed village school, who introduced me to my new charges for whose education I was to be responsible for the following school year! In my room, graced by a pot-bellied stove, were nineteen boys and girls divided between classes P2–P5, and the master had the older children in his adjoining room.

After his brief introduction to what he called his 'cowboys' and 'cuddies', I was left standing with nothing but my total lack of experience and an outline timetable for each day of the week. Having been warned that my services would no longer be required if and when a qualified teacher could be found, I quietly prayed that such a person would appear sooner rather than later. My prayer was not answered and I continued in post for the entirety of the ensuing school year.

As well as the conventional three 'Rs', the curriculum included predictable subjects such as Scripture, geography, drawing, crafts, and physical education. But apart from the timetable there was no guidebook or teaching material of any kind. Having been a Sunday school teacher, Scripture was no threat. But on that second day there was to be a period of geography, for which I had no outline lesson. It was entirely up to me. On my way home I noticed sheep in a field, which jogged my memory of a geography class in which we had studied New Zealand. That decided it – New Zealand it would be. On our shelves at home we had all ten volumes of Arthur Mee's *Children's Encyclopaedia*, the 1950s alternative to either Google or Wikipedia, which was to come to my aid and provide me with everything I needed to know for my lesson preparation during that year. With large tongue in cheek, I suggest to teachers today that Arthur Mee is all they need – and they should forget about all that Key Stage One, Two or even Three.

Once I got over the strangeness and sense of inadequacy regarding my new role, I came to enjoy it enormously: beautiful village children who were a joy to teach; perfect manners and total respect for their teenage teacher. I don't ever remember having to raise my voice or put any child in the corner. And I was so fortunate to have a patient, understanding and trusting master in the adjoining room. Charlie Kirkpatrick expected the best but allowed for my lack of experience and training.

Being an 'untrained, temporary, assistant teacher', I was overseen by an inspector from Stranmillis Teacher Training College who made regular unannounced drop-in visits. I remember him as a large man, fond of his pipe, which he puffed as he observed. As his specialist subject was art he took a particular interest in what I had produced in that area. Art having been the only subject in which I attained the highest grade at Advanced Level for my Senior Certificate, I apparently passed on my enthusiasm to my pupils.

I must have got something right, for one day the inspector called me to one side, seeking to persuade me to give up this silly notion of 'the Church'. According to him I was a 'born teacher' and at the end of the year I should go to Stranmillis and get properly trained and qualified. I confess that I was indeed tempted to take his advice. For a time I really thought that nothing could be more satisfying than the life of a master in a village school – if only such a position could be guaranteed. However, the call and the commitment to ministry prevailed.

What a contrast there was between this school and the two I had known, Strandtown in east Belfast and Methodist College, from which I had just come. Both were so large compared to this small village school, with its casual approach to learning and very special sense of community. A lad called Trevor was what would now be known as a boy with special needs. When I asked the master what I should do with and for Trevor, he suggested that I might occasionally turn the pages of his picture book to a different story. But when it came to games time and I asked for teams to be picked, Trevor was always first to be chosen. The other children were his neighbours and friends – some would have been family – and there was no way that Trevor was going to be left out or made to feel useless. Today he would be driven halfway around Fermanagh to a school for other children with special needs. I know all of the good reasons and the arguments for such provision, but I do sometimes wonder if the acceptance and inclusivity that Trevor enjoyed within his own community might have compensated for what he may have missed in what would be provided today.

From grammar school to village school; from city suburb to rural Ulster; from talking 'proper' to an appreciation of local dialect, it was all part of my further education. One morning I was greeted by an excited and excitable lad whose special privilege it was to boil a kettle for my tea. 'Please sir, the mens has had a stroke ...' It took me a little while to realise that because of industrial action on the part of the employees of the Northern Ireland Electricity Service, there was no power to boil my kettle.

Many years later I would meet some of those delightful children again, sometimes in unexpected places. Like Arlene, the little girl with jet-black hair adorned with a large white bow, in her role as the wife of the Rev. Russell Birney, Moderator of the Presbyterian Church. Or John, who after twenty-five years introduced himself with a flawless recitation of *The Donkey* by G.K. Chesterton, which he informed me I had taught him during that year. Obviously, since he is now a financial adviser, I must have taught him his sums well. What a delight and privilege it was for me when, 64 years later, the principal, Mrs Gardiner, invited Clodagh and me to be the special guests at the end of term prize-giving, to meet the grandchildren of those I had taught!

My year in Fermanagh ended successfully when I was accepted as a candidate for the Methodist ministry in 1956. However, as part of this process, prospective candidates were required to preach a trial sermon before the Synod. So it was that I found myself in front of a jury of seasoned preachers in the pulpit of Ballinamallard Methodist Church. Afterwards, one of them kindly offered his personal critique. 'Young man, that was three good sermons you preached. But may I suggest that in future you preach them one at a time.' My first and perhaps most important lesson in homiletics.

The next step was being selected as a pre-collegiate probationer for a period of three years. The powers that be had decreed that I should spend the first two years of my ministry in the border village of Bessbrook in County Armagh, to be followed by a third year in the Dublin Central Mission.

I was warmly welcomed in Bessbrook, where I made many long-lasting friendships. It is a model village just three miles from the mainly nationalist town of Newry, and less than eight miles from the border. It was founded in the mid-nineteenth century by the Richardsons, a Quaker family, who chose it as the location for their prosperous linen mill. Like their fellow Quakers, the Cadburys of Bourneville, they created a model village with no pubs, no police station, good quality housing for their employees and ample provision for wholesome recreational activities.

For my digs I was privileged to enjoy the warm and happy hospitality of the McCall family of Wakefield Terrace. From early morning the mill horn would blare out reminders of time to clock-in, lunchtime and end-of-working-day-time. When I see a Lowry painting of his matchstick factory workers, I am reminded of what for me was to be a familiar scene from my vantage point overlooking the main street. Sadly, in troubled times all of that was to change and the prosperous mill was converted into a huge army base. Now, having outlived its usefulness, it stands derelict.

While I was responsible for a second small Wesleyan chapel in the townland of Donaghmore I normally travelled my parish by bike or by scooter. But on my first Sunday, as I didn't know the way, my superintendent had kindly arranged for a retired missionary doctor to drive me to my afternoon service in Donaghmore. Having rehearsed my first sermon in the morning at Bessbrook, I was happy to repeat it with a measure of unwarranted confidence. On the return journey I was waiting for at least some encouragement, if not a compliment from the doctor. 'I'm sure what you had to say was very good but I didn't hear a word of it. You'll have to speak up!' was my driver's only comment. My second – not to be forgotten – lesson in homiletics.

My period in Bessbrook was an eye-opener for this boy preacher, at both the pastoral and political levels. There was the lady who informed me that she knew the cause of conflict in our then troubled world. 'It's all to do with them Sputniks', she proffered. I arrived just when the IRA had launched their border campaign of violence, which lasted from the end of 1956 until early 1962, and was at its most intense during my two years there. Just eight miles away, across the border at Edentubber in County Louth, an IRA bomb went off prematurely, killing four of their members and an accomplice. Understandably, people were anxious and fearful of what this might mean.

Having had a largely sheltered Protestant middle-class upbringing, I was ignorant of the legitimate grievances of the majority Catholic community in my home city of 'Derry, and indeed of the injustice felt by the Catholic minority generally under the then Stormont government, although nothing could justify the subsequent IRA campaign of violence and the suffering it inflicted, not least at Kingsmills, Co. Armagh, where ten Protestant workers were massacred in 1976.

Under the Special Powers Act, a 10.00 p.m. curfew was imposed, which was deeply resented by nationalists.[ii] But I was privileged to be issued with a pass for the purpose of attending to pastoral duties late at night. One night I was returning to Bessbrook from Donaghmore. It was well after 10.00 p.m. and as I approached Newry town centre I heard some kind of commotion. Curious, I parked my moped and walked down the street to find out what it was all about. Sitting in Margaret Square was a crowd of 100 to 150 people holding a peaceful protest against the curfew. It was a horrible scene, with the RUC hosing the crowd with a water cannon as if they were hosing vermin out of a farmyard. People were sliding and slithering all over the place. I thought to myself, 'This is the most degrading, inhuman, ghastly thing I've ever seen human beings do to one another. Whatever that's about, this is not the way to deal with each other.'

I was not politically aware or even interested in politics at the time but I found this display of how to deal with civil unrest so horrifying that it awakened me to a new understanding of political reality. The next day I heard people saying, 'That will cool them off and cool their ardour.' But instinctively I knew that this was not the way to deal with difficult situations or with conflict. It left an indelible impression on me and was one of the defining moments in my life.

I should stress that my revulsion at what I had seen did not mean for one moment that I had the slightest sympathy with IRA bombers and the enemies of the State. But young and politically naïve as I was,

---

[ii] The Civil Authorities (Special Powers) Act 1922, which was made permanent in 1933 and not repealed until 1973, gave sweeping powers to the Unionist government and the police throughout 50 years of one-party rule at Stormont. Repeal of the Act was one of the key demands of the Northern Ireland civil rights movement.

I realised that this kind of response to public protest was pouring petrol on the fire of Catholic grievances, which I was only beginning to understand.

At the same time I was confronted with the challenge of pastoral care and having to learn what it really means to sit with and literally hold the hands of people who have experienced unconscionable loss. In this first case, I was working with a family dealing with the death of their child. For me this also meant meeting a 'mixed' family for the first time. These parents came from a Protestant and a Roman Catholic family. Normally, handling such a situation would require great sensitivity and skills I had not yet been taught. Perhaps it was my naivety that enabled me to share in this family's grief without recourse to muttering expected but often hollow words of comfort.

In a newspaper interview not that long ago I was asked where I felt closest to God. I responded, 'I know I am expected to say on the beach at Ballycastle. But actually it is when I sit at a fireside or a bedside with an anxious or troubled soul.' Perhaps in making that remark I was unconsciously travelling back in time to that first of so many deeply defining pastoral moments – for me as well as for those to whom I sought to minister.

Not long after I arrived in Bessbrook I was approached by a small group of then youngish men following an evening service. Had I ever thought about joining the Orange Order? And could they discuss this possibility with me? As they had no minister in the membership of their Orange District it would be greatly appreciated if I would give it serious consideration. And, if I did, I would instantly be installed as district chaplain. Prior to this I had had neither interest nor inclination in this direction, but in the interests of recognition and instant promotion I agreed. I imagine my grandfather Isaac and my illustrious ancestor Dan Winter would both have been highly pleased. The installation ceremony was brief and painless.

There was a mixture of ages, with an extremely pleasant and respectful group of decent men in whom I neither heard nor saw any evidence of sectarianism, in attitude or conversation. These were church-going folk, some farming folk, others worked at the Mill, and they lived and worked happily with their neighbours, Catholic and Protestant. Looking back, this lodge was to the working men of the village what the Rotary Club would be to the suburban professional. A lot of camaraderie and raising charitable funds for good causes. Interestingly, what was most memorable for me was a series of lectures given by the respected English-born, Cambridge-educated Orange historian Canon Dewer of Scarva. To me it was totally objective and as a Protestant schoolboy who had studied only English and European history these were to be the very first lessons I ever received in Irish history.

As we approached the Twelfth there were plans to be made for the parade to the Field, which I had no particular interest in attending.[iii] As this was a temperance lodge, there would have to be an ample supply of soft drinks. One member said he had a good friend in that business who would let them have what they wanted at the right price – so he was encouraged to pursue this. When the lodge next met there were the crates of orange neatly stacked, ready for the journey to the Field. But there was a problem. Each crate had the name of the supplier stamped on it in large letters – a name that was instantly recognisable as 'not one of us'. It was readily agreed that it would be discourteous and unappreciative to send the consignment back, and it would cause unnecessary embarrassment to a fellow member to have to explain to his friend. So the crates were quietly emptied into cardboard cartons and ferried to the Field incognito. While I was amused, it was also a reminder of what lay under the surface of our otherwise reasonable relationships.

[iii] The Twelfth refers to 12 July, when members of the Orange Order annually celebrate the victory of Protestant King William III of Orange over Catholic King James II at the Battle of the Boyne in 1690. On the day Orangemen and bands all over Northern Ireland march to a demonstration field where a religious service is held and resolutions are passed.

On a particular Sunday I was asked to preach the sermon at an Orange service in another place. I had never been to an Orange service, so I was not sure what to expect or what to say. However, while it had not invaded our village life, I had become aware of growing disquiet across our province, and in certain areas this disquiet was expressing itself in ways that were creating fear and division within communities. Sam Thompson's timely drama *Over the Bridge* had not only brought some of these unspoken issues on to the stage – but also into private conversation and public debate.[iv] In my innocence – or was it enlightenment? – I picked out one sentence from Thompson's script: 'There's a hell of a lot of religion in this place, for all the good it does!' This service and my quote were the banner headline in a local paper the following week. Not surprisingly, this was to be my first and last invitation to preach at an Orange service.

Not long before I was to move on to my next appointment there came before the lodge an application for some kind of loan or grant to make it possible for a farm to be sold to a lower bidder – to prevent it going 'the wrong way'. This time two bells rang within me and when I naively shared my concern it was kindly explained to me that this was simply to protect 'our' interests. It was at this moment that I knew this was not where I belonged, and I did not return. To this day nobody has come looking for me. I think they understood and respected my position and when the time came for me to move to my next posting in Dublin I left with the blessing and good wishes of the brethren in the lodge, as well as my friends in the village and in my congregation.

My third year as a probationer in Dublin Central Mission was an eye-opener in another way. Much of my pastoral work was conducted among the poor and deprived in the Coombe area of the south inner city. Until then I had been totally unaware of the grinding poverty that stared me in the face – overcrowding, homelessness, hunger, sickness, alcohol addiction, domestic violence and debt. So it was that I found myself a member of a small but effective Methodist team responding to

---

[iv] A controversial play about sectarianism in Belfast shipyard.

Christ's command to feed the hungry and clothe the naked, under the leadership of the Rev. Hugh Allen, who for me reflected the ministry of my other role model, Lax of Poplar. One unforgettable experience for me was the excitement on the faces of hugely socially deprived children who, with their mothers, were treated to a wonderful seaside break at the Mission's holiday home, 'Somerholme' in Laytown, Co. Meath.

While I was one of the last students for ministry to be placed in a parish ministry prior to our more formal college education, I would argue that this had its merits. We were young men discovering what it was to which we had felt called and were now committed. So it was, after three years of introduction and entirely practical preparation for ministry, that I headed for Edgehill Theological College, located in the leafy suburbs of Belfast's posh Malone Road for three years of study, following in the footsteps of scores of Irish Methodist seminarians who had studied there since it had been transferred out of the theological department of Methodist College (Methody) in 1926.

How different it was then, in terms of training for ministry in most if not all of our churches. To begin with, we were mostly young. Many of us were not long out of school. And we were certainly single. Indeed, in our Methodist discipline, as well as agreeing to abstain from the use of alcohol and tobacco, we could only seek permission to be married *after* ordination. And as well as the discipline of study, we were required to share responsibilities for the care of the hens who provided us with fresh eggs and for the enormous garden which – along with the autumn produce from country harvest festivals – provided us with an ample supply of vegetables. The upside of this was that for three years we shared a common life of fun and friendship as well as prayer and study. This camaraderie was very special and remains with those of us who are still standing to this day.

Having completed my studies in Edgehill College, and my three years of probation, the way was now clear for my ordination, along with ten other ordinands at the Methodist Conference in Cork's historic Wesley

Chapel on Monday, 18 June 1962.ᵛ All the years of prayer, study and preparation had led to that memorable moment when the President and several other ministers, including my father, laid their hands upon me. Ordaining me to a ministry of Word and Sacrament and the 'cure of souls' – filling me with much youthful zeal to change the world into which I was now stepping. In professional ministerial terms, the 'boy preacher' had finally come of age.

ᵛ Each of my ten fellow ordinands had remarkable and varied ministries, in Ireland and across the world. Very sadly, at the time of writing only three of us are still alive.

4

An American Journey

'The world is a book and those who never travel read only one page.'

St Augustine

I was disappointed when immediately after my ordination the Methodist 'powers that be' posted me to Waterford for what was to be a two-year appointment.

In fairness, it was a last minute 'swap' in response to the request of a fellow ordinand who for personal reasons wished to remain in Belfast. But as in my recent ordination vow, we had promised 'to go where we are sent', who was I to protest? Nor could I have anticipated the outcome for me personally of that decision. Whatever about the good Lord's intentions, there is no doubt that there are times when the governance of the church moves in very mysterious ways.

Although Waterford is the oldest city in Ireland, founded by the Vikings, its small Protestant population of which the Methodists were a tiny fraction made it something of a sleepy backwater more suited to a minister on the brink of retirement rather than one at the outset of his calling, with the world at his feet, impatient to change that world.

I confess that I was out of my comfort zone, removed from the world I knew in the North with little prospect of the spiritual and psychological stimulation that my young mind craved. My arrival, on what was one of the wettest twelfth of Julys ever, did nothing to kindle my now smouldering enthusiasm.

However, I was not to know that eventually within it there would be compensation for what at best I considered to be an inconsiderate decision of those responsible for our postings. For in time this diversion turned out to be fateful: as it was to transform and enrich my life in the most romantic and beautiful way imaginable.

Nor was it to be an 'unproductive' period of ministry. As in any worshipping community there were pastoral needs and relationships of which obviously, I cannot speak but which were confirming for me in the essential nature of ministry, whatever the size, location, or status of a congregation.

Also, among the churches there were a number of single young adults, many of whom had come to the city for apprenticeships or employment. Together with the Church of Ireland curate and the young Baptist minister we re-opened the splendid but rather neglected premises of the YMCA and formed a lively and much appreciated youth club. With weekend house events, experiments with drama, summer camping holidays in Scotland and England, my time was fully occupied. While in no way was there a 'sectarian agenda' in all this activity, it has to be admitted that it was welcomed as an opportunity for young people from a dwindling Protestant minority to meet potential life partners from the same background. As a result, there was more than one couple for whom this led to marriage, including for a young woman called Clodagh Coad who belonged to a well-known family in the business community of Waterford and second-generation Methodists.

During our courtship we exchanged stories about our respective families. And I heard how her family had been impacted by the troubled times of the 'teens and the twenties' in Irish history.

As well as his well-known boot and shoe business in the centre of Waterford, Clodagh's paternal grandfather Richard Coad had a large house and farm known as Blenheim, outside of the city where he reared his eleven children. From a newspaper cutting I read of how on the night of Friday, 10 December 1920, the night before the catastrophic burning of Cork City, unnamed persons set fire to his barns destroying 'a large quantity of grain'. From the family I have heard of how in trying to put out the flames her grandfather had a serious heart attack from which he never fully recovered. As a result Clodagh's father, who was barely thirteen years old on that night, had to leave school prematurely to share responsibility for the family business and the farm.

Later, during the Irish Civil War when Michael Collins and Éamon de Valera took opposing positions on the Anglo-Irish Treaty of 1921, her grandfather Richard refused to sign a protest against the Treaty, insisting that as a businessman he did not wish to get involved in something so politically divisive. As a result, for a considerable period, his business was 'boycotted', and no customer was permitted to cross the threshold of his shop. But such was the respect that her grandfather had earned from the Roman Catholic schools and convents that in response to their 'undercover requests' he carried on a discreet after-dark business supplying boots and shoes in all sizes and shapes.

Clodagh's family stories and mine underline how so many of us, in our different ways, have been impacted by the history of Ireland. Consciously or unconsciously, we all have to work out how we have been influenced in our attitudes and in our interpretation of that history.

Ohio (1964–1966)

As I had looked forward to the end of my two-year term in Waterford, I felt ready for a new challenge. Having spent my entire life within the relatively small island of Ireland and the limited confines of the Methodist Church in Ireland, I felt the need to explore the wider world, to satisfy my 'wanderlust' and to expand my experience. Having access to some personal contacts in the United Methodist Church in North America, I was offered and had accepted the position of 'Minister to Youth' in a large Church in a town called Warren in what is known as 'The Buckeye' state of Ohio, now the perennial 'swing state' in US presidential elections.

As I shared my US plans with Clodagh we were faced with a difficult decision. Would I go to the US and see how we felt upon my return after two years? Or were we ready to commit ourselves to one another, get married and head off across the Atlantic, to the New World and a new life together? The more we thought and talked and prayed we agreed that there was no good reason to delay. Why not? And so it was following a short engagement we were married on 11 August 1964 and set sail for America a week later. It was a big 'ask' of Clodagh, who could not have imagined the eventful and at times demanding life to which that journey was but a beginning. I will be forever grateful to her for her unconditional trust and love over the past, at times very challenging, 60 years.

We had booked our passage from Cobh, on the good ship SS *America*, not knowing that this was to be its last voyage before being tied up and eventually scrapped. So, it was a bit shabby and run-down. Any preconceived expectations we may have had of a 'glitzy' life on a luxury liner were soon shattered. Having existed on a modest stipend it was as much as I could afford to book a second-class cabin. I was not to know that it was situated below the waterline with neither window nor porthole, let alone a balcony which one might expect on a modern-day cruise ship. Instead, there was a noisy hosepipe which was to be our air supply. Neither before nor since have I been given to claustrophobia, but for most of the nights on that voyage I deserted my bride and was to be found with a night security officer on a 'steamer chair' on the upper deck.

During the voyage we met and conversed with fellow passengers, many of whom were curious as to why we wanted to come to America. Did we not know that politically the nation was in a mess?

Frankly we did not, although it was not so long after the assassination of President Kennedy and the battle between Lyndon B. Johnson and his deeply conservative Republican challenger Barry Goldwater, with Johnson winning by a landslide.

Our almost total ignorance of American politics was soon to be rectified. We were fascinated by the number of younger Americans who informed us that if Barry Goldwater were elected, they would leave America. I was reminded of that during the 2020 presidential election upon hearing a new generation of young Americans saying the same thing concerning a certain Donald Trump. On the Sunday morning during our voyage we were made particularly aware of our 'steerage' status when we were afforded the opportunity to attend 'Divine Worship' in the first class lounge. With fellow 'second classers' we queued at the gate which separated us from the more privileged passengers until at precisely five minutes before the starting time a burly member of the crew called out, 'Ze gates to heaven are open!' and we meekly trotted through to the opulent world that awaited us.

The rather traditional and dignified service was conducted by an Anglican priest from New York. For the last hymn we were invited to sing the familiar 'Onward, Christian Soldiers'. A strange choice I thought for a service on the ocean wave. While we were not exactly 'In peril on the sea,' would that hymn not have been more appropriate? Following the penultimate verse, during which we had intoned 'We are not divided, all one body we …', there was a pause during which the celebrant announced that he had been asked to remind all second-class passengers that following the Benediction we were to return to our end of the ship. So much for '… all one body we.'

However, for me the indignity was worth it as the story has provided me with an attention-grabbing introduction to the many sermons I have been asked to preach at annual services of prayer for Christian unity.

Upon our arrival in New York there was a problem. The immigration officers were not satisfied with the x-rays and medical reports of my history of spinal tuberculosis and corrective surgery. Obviously, there was a fear that I might infect the nation – so under armed guard, together with Dave Lynn, the young minister who had come to drive us to Ohio, we were escorted to Staten Island Hospital where 'waifs and strays', suspects and illegal immigrants are clustered and interrogated. This is where we awaited our fate, sitting on hard seats in a 90-degree Fahrenheit non-air-conditioned room for four hours and more. When informed that I was to be quarantined for seven days before they would be satisfied that I would not infect the nation, or with words to that effect, I protested.

Surely in this great city of New York there were good physicians who could read my x-rays and understand my medical records. When taken to another room I feared the worst. I need not have worried. Without looking up from the papers on his desk the officer asked me did I know anybody from County 'Tie-rowan', as he pronounced it. While I was thinking of whose name I might suggest he informed me that this was where his great-grandmother had come from, signed the release papers, wished me well for my stay in America and told me I was free to go. After a 400-mile six-hour drive through the night we arrived at our destination. Thus beginning our new life together and a new life in the New World.

The contrast between First Methodist Church in Warren Ohio and Waterford could not have been greater. A congregation of over 3,000 members, five ministers and three robed choirs within which, as Minister to Youth, I had a very particular and well-defined responsibility.

Conspicuous within the congregation was the presence of two Black families. I found it as curious as I found it disturbing to hear that there had been a special meeting of the Church board before these families were admitted to membership. Particularly as I knew my senior pastor, Ted Meyer, to be a most liberal man. It was he who explained that for these two men and their families this was something of a political test of the attitude of this congregation – and therefore it was necessary to make clear that they would be made welcome. As, happily, they were.

This was mid-60s America and this was to be our introduction to living in what at that time was a very divided nation with largely segregated communities, schools and churches and states such as Alabama in the deep South breaching the Constitution by denying Black people the right to vote. The struggle for civil rights, under the inspirational leadership of Baptist minister and 1964 Nobel Peace Prize winner Rev. Martin Luther King Jr, had become central to US politics and dominated the news. On 25 March 1965, the Selma to Montgomery civil rights march in Alabama was finally completed and King delivered his remarkable 'How Long, Not Long' speech to thousands of supporters including church groups, some of whom had travelled from all over the country. We in Warren found the prospect of an 800-mile journey a bit daunting so the Rev. Ted and I joined a march and rally in our city in solidarity with the marchers in Selma.

In August the landmark Voting Rights Act enforcing the constitutional right to vote was signed into law by LBJ but as with our Good Friday Agreement that was to be but a beginning. Now the challenge for church as well as society was to embrace and incarnate it into the life of the nation. And as in every divided society there was a legacy of the past which overshadowed much of the progress that had been made and was further anticipated. Northeast Ohio was a particularly conservative Republican stronghold so life was not always easy for my more liberal senior pastor who was subjected to much criticism from a politically conservative community, as well as from some within his congregation.

It was at this time that I began to connect what I was hearing in the US with words and phrases with which I was familiar back home, and I began to understand how racism and sectarianism were but two sides of the one coin. This was also in the middle of the Vietnam War, with the grief and division that it had inflicted upon America. Again, not an easy call for a liberal preacher. Being Irish protected me from much of the debate. When I cautiously expressed what I thought, I soon realised that I was being given something of a fool's pardon. I was an outsider and 'a bird of passage' – so not to be taken too seriously. And of course, being Irish, I received a lot of attention on St Patrick's Day, with interviews on local radio. But I was rather puzzled when as a Protestant I was expected to wear something orange rather than green.

It was while we were still in the city of Warren that our first child was born. A beautiful baby girl who we named Carolyn Anne. What a fuss was made of her. And how loving and generous was the congregation – especially towards Clodagh so far from her Irish family at such a special time as this. Hard to realise that Carolyn Anne is herself now a granny – to Patrick, Eden and Tom.

INDIANA (1966–1968)

Having completed my two-year 'contract' with First Church, Warren, we were due to return to Ireland. Those two years had passed so swiftly and I yearned for an opportunity to see and learn more in America when happily such an opportunity did present itself for 'going back to school,' as they say in the US. To study for a Master's degree in 'Pastoral Psychology and Counselling' at the Christian Theological Seminary (CTS) in Indianapolis, in the neighbouring state of Indiana. It was to be a huge privilege to have as my supervisor of studies the pioneering Prof. Paul E. Johnson, who was known as 'the father of professional CPE, or Clinical Pastoral Education' and with whose writings I was familiar from my studies at Edgehill College.

I was very fortunate to be granted an Eli Lilley scholarship which covered my college fees and carried a modest living allowance. But for additional income and a place to live we were interviewed and offered the position of house parents in a Methodist residential home for emotionally disturbed children. This was quite a challenge and especially so for Clodagh – already caring for Carolyn Anne – to whom the lion's share of the responsibility fell as I was out most days attending lectures from 8.00 a.m. at the seminary which was a 60-mile round trip in the car each day.

Clodagh's professional qualifications in 'Institutional Management' and her motherly disposition especially equipped her for the task over the next year when we gave much, but received more in return and learned a lot.

While not without its challenges, there was a warm family atmosphere in that house enhanced to no end by the presence of Carolyn, now a toddler, who added greatly to the sense of family. We never harboured any fears about her safety as every one of those boys were so caring and protective towards her. Pity the lad who would cause her any hurt. When we left it took Carolyn some time to recover from her grief at the loss of her 'brothers'.

My fourth and final year there came in the form of an internship in Pastoral Care in the Methodist Hospital, Indianapolis. This was a large teaching hospital affiliated to Indiana University with a highly specialised pastoral care department providing a unique partnership between the pastoral and medical interns with shared hands-on experience on the wards and, in particular, in intensive care and emergency services. In addition to the hospital setting, I also underwent a secondment to a community-based pastoral counselling centre where, under supervision, I was to be disabused of simplistic pietistic approaches to the real needs of hurting individuals often in broken relationships.

All of this provided me with experience and learning for which I am forever grateful and which – without realising it – was preparing me for a future ministry in a very different Ireland. In particular, I was to carry with me a totally new and lasting understanding of what my teachers emphasised as the need for 'non-judgmental, empathetic and unconditional acceptance' in pastoral ministry. I could not have realised at the time how key all of this was to be in my ministry in the years to follow upon my return to a disturbingly different Northern Ireland.

For Clodagh life in the hospital complex was to be much less demanding than caring for her greatly extended family of troubled teenagers. Like Carolyn, Clodagh and I missed those teenage boys who had for a year been in our care and integral to our family. We enjoyed it when they were allowed to visit us in our hospital apartment. However, the move to the Methodist hospital and being relieved of responsibility for those boys turned out to be all for the best because shortly after our move to Indianapolis in early 1966 we found we were expecting our second child, Sharon Ruth, who arrived the following November.

All this domestic excitement, our growing family and my academic adventure with its valuable grounding in pastoral studies was playing out in the mid-sixties post the assassination of JFK, with America now experiencing the twin convulsions of the civil rights movement and the Vietnam War.

It was during this period that we were to come to understand more fully the correlation between racism and sectarianism. Racist comments, even those considered to be relatively inoffensive, sounded familiar and we came to recognise the parallels. Again, without realising it this was part of our preparation for future ministry in what at that time was a highly sectarian Northern Ireland.

However, our more personal experience and understanding of race relations and racism was yet to be bettered in unexpected ways. It was on a public holiday weekend, Memorial Day, that we planned a camping weekend break in Kentucky's Mammoth Cave Park. It was getting dark by the time we arrived and as we set about unpacking the tent, we were not having much success in assembling the many poles that went along with it. To our rescue, from the next tent site came an extremely handsome young Black man – a Sidney Poitier lookalike. His name was Duane and behind him was an equally attractive young white woman, whose name has slipped my memory, who took Clodagh and the now hungry Carolyn Anne to their tent to warm the bottle while Duane and I struggled with the tent poles. We shared a hot drink with our new neighbours, who were on a weekend trip from Chicago, before settling down to sleep in our by now securely erected and cosy tent. A real joy as I have always loved sleeping under canvas.

The next day, as we walked and wheeled our stroller through the Mammoth Cave Park, we met the couple, walking hand in hand. Knowing something of the attitudes towards inter-racial relationships at that time, particularly in a Southern state, we did wonder about their wisdom, whatever about their courage.

We were puzzled when they did not appear back to their tent by our bedtime. We went to bed and after quietening our crying baby settled down for our second night's sleep. It was about midnight when we heard a tapping on our tent pole. It was Duane, telling me of the dreadful day they had and asking for my help. As they had gone exploring the small towns around the park they had been followed and harassed by the state troopers, resulting in two speeding fines and a third fine for something like abuse towards a police officer. They had no money left for their third fine so their car had been impounded and the young lady had been taken into custody with the prospect of a court appearance unless and until they paid their fine.

To get back to the campsite Duane had given his transistor radio (something of a luxury item in those days) to a stranger in return for a lift. Would I/could I help? Would I lend them the necessary money for their fine and drive him back to the police station to pay the fine so that his girlfriend could be released?

There was no way I would leave Clodagh and our little one at midnight in a strange place in those circumstances but promised that I would go with him first thing in the morning. Which I did – to a small town some ten miles away. What I saw there was much too close to a re-enactment of a scene from the film *In the Heat of the Night*. A police station staffed by heavily-built scowling deputies or troopers who revelled in the hostile environment they had created for Blacks and those who forged relationships with them. In a cell in front of the desk (more like a cage) was Duane's hapless white girlfriend.

She was in a very distressed and terrified state, having been taunted by the troopers throughout the night. It seemed that her real 'crime', in the eyes of the police, was having a Black beau. I had a cheque book and without questioning other than 'how much' I paid the fine. I was not questioned – perhaps the printed 'Rev.' on the cheque may have helped. But before she was released Duane and I had to go to the garage where their car had been impounded. But before the proprietor would speak to me he demanded, 'tell that n----r get off my lot'. He then took my cheque on the understanding that I would retrieve the car and drive it off his lot but 'NOT that n----r'.

We collected the young woman from her cell and, having agreed that Duane would stay silent and I would say only what was necessary, we drove back to the campsite. Both they and we decided that we would pack up and return to our respective homes in Indianapolis and Chicago. I had cautioned Duane not to exceed 30 miles per hour until we crossed the state line and we followed them at a discreet distance. It was wise counsel for until we had crossed the state line we were followed and observed by at least three police cars, obviously watching for the slightest reason to pounce once again.

Within a few days, we received a full return of what we had paid on their behalf with a fulsome apology and profound gratitude. We have often wondered whether that relationship continued and if so, how did the story end. Whatever, it was yet another story – sadly not the last – of raw racism which was all too common in those days in the mid-sixties.

As a 'Lilley Fellow' we had benefited from a scholarship from The Eli Lilley Foundation and had been generously treated by both the seminary and the Methodist Hospital. But halfway through my final year and anticipating the cost of travelling home to Ireland, we were aware of our need for some extra funds.

So, I offered my services to the district superintendent of the Methodist Church for any part-time services to a local congregation, particularly at weekends. The day after I had contacted his office, the DS (as known in Methodist circles) called me and asked to see me that day. Yes, he had work for me to do. It was a sad story of an inner-city Black congregation whose pastor had become so totally obsessed with the struggle for civil rights that apparently he had transferred his excessive anger at authority of any kind to the elders of his congregation.

So it was, that at a meeting of the Church Council the elders informed him that they had advised the bishop that in everyone's interests there should be a change of minister. However, the next day a neighbour of the church called the police to say that someone was smashing the windows in the church. The state troopers arrived in time to apprehend the pastor as he was about to put a chair through the beautiful Gethsemane stained-glass window above the altar. In the circumstances no charges were brought against him, instead he was admitted to the state mental hospital.

So, would I look after this congregation until the annual conference when a new minister would be appointed, I was asked. I suggested that since I was not Black I might not be the right person. 'That's why I thought of you', he said. 'You're Irish – you are neither Black nor white.'

'Are you suggesting I am green?' I joked, suggesting that I might be seen to be 'green' in more senses than one.

We will not easily forget that first Sunday morning. With the smashed windows covered with large Frigidaire refrigerator cardboard cartons, a totally unfamiliar scene for me and for Clodagh in every possible way. Other than ourselves there was only one white face, a woman. As the ethnicity of the inner-city community and congregation had changed all other white members had transferred to suburban congregations – but this lady was not for moving. As a result she was much loved and revered and was treated as the Queen Mother of the congregation.

I preached on a text from Philippians Chapter 3 in which St Paul writes: 'But one thing I do: Forgetting what is behind and reaching forward to what is ahead.' In my view, this is one of the most powerful verses in all of Scripture. It is an exhortation to let go of what is in the past and to embrace the possibilities of a new and brighter future. I have preached to this text on more than one occasion in different but not dissimilar circumstances in Irish churches where congregations have experienced hurt and conflict.

The service concluded with the Sacrament of Holy Communion. Unforgettable was the spontaneous singing across the congregation of 'There is a balm in Gilead'. As people came forward to receive the bread and the wine the sense of healing was palpable. Here was a people of 'Amazing "GRACE"', as we were just beginning to understand.

On another evening we had been to see the film *Guess Who's Coming to Dinner?* Those who have seen this classic film will remember one of the scenes. The 'Black mama', who had helped to raise the pretty daughter of the prominent white judge (Spencer Tracy) and his wife (Katherine Hepburn) was as upset as her parents when she appeared home with the handsome Sidney Poitier at her side. Dropping the tea tray she exclaimed, 'next they will be telling me that Martin Luther King Jr is coming to dinner'. We chuckled with the rest of the audience. We came home, switched on the TV to hear the dreadful news that Martin Luther King Jr had been assassinated while we had been enjoying this film. The nation and the world was in shock.

There was deep anger with riots and the threat of more riots across the country. How was I expected to handle this situation on the following Sunday? A congregation and a community in deep grief, grieving for the loss of their hopes and dreams as well as the death of the one to whom they had looked as their 'saviour' and deliverer.

As a stranger in a very strange land, how was I to handle the emotions and preach to this situation in an appropriate and sensitive way? I felt myself to be totally inadequate. I met with the church leaders and suggested that they invite someone who would resonate with their situation and emotions in a way that I feared I might not. They responded: 'No Reverend, you are our pastor, you minister to us.' And so I did.

It was an unforgettable service, on that Sunday morning, 7 April 1968. Not so much for what I may have been given to say but for the amazing response of a grieving and deeply hurt community. As I have so often said – having read and studied many books on 'GRACE' – once more it was these people who helped me more than any to understand what really is so amazing about GRACE.

The day of Martin Luther King Jr's funeral was a day of national mourning and I, together I am sure with the vast majority of the nation, just wanted to sit and watch the funeral on television, an old black-and-white television, and to observe and identify with the people who had lost their leader. We'd all got caught up in this, or so I thought.

However, while we were watching the TV most of our white neighbours, middle-class professionals, were having a noisy barbeque at the swimming pool. 'Will you not come down and join us?', they asked. When I explained that we were watching the funeral they replied, 'You're not watching that, are you? That communist, what's all the fuss about?' As much as to say he deserved to be shot. I was particularly confused as some of these people had been medical missionaries in other countries and yet had this deep ingrained racism within them. And not for the first time I recognised the parallels between raw racism and naked sectarianism.

On the night of Martin Luther King Jr's assassination Robert F. Kennedy made a memorable speech in Indianapolis and his words of love and compassion are credited with ensuring that the riots which disfigured 100 American cities did not break out in our city.

Memorable also was the Sunday when our second child, Sharon Ruth, was baptised by my mentor, Paul Johnson, and welcomed into the global Christian family by this very loving people. As we left them for our return to Ireland, they showered us with gifts as well as their love and blessings.

Having been a late starter and an unremarkable student at school and college it was a proud moment when I graduated with my Master in Theology degree, 'Summa Cum Laude'. Having committed ourselves to return to Ireland I resisted the temptation to continue in a doctoral programme. Imagine my emotions when almost 50 years later, in 2015, I was to cross that same platform to receive an honorary doctorate from my alma mater with the citation delivered by the South African anti-apartheid activist Rev. Dr Allan Boesak, in his role as director of the Desmond Tutu Centre for Peace, Reconciliation, and Global Justice which is partnered with the seminary at nearby Butler University.

This summary of those four years in the USA would not be complete without reference to the wonderful people who welcomed us and cared for us in so many ways. The family we met on our voyage to New York, families in all our churches and in seminary as well as those we met through other friendships. They have remained lifetime friends, welcoming us back to their homes as we have so joyfully welcomed them to ours. Sadly, some of them have passed away but those who read this will know who we mean and to them we send our love and gratitude.

Having completed our time and achieved even more than we had dared to hope, the time had come for our return to Ireland – with an undisclosed personal plan to return to the US after five years. With work and study and the bearing of two lovely daughters it had been a busy four years, and we were looking forward to a quieter and more settled life in our homeland and to give our parents an opportunity to enjoy their grandchildren.

Hearing that a new minister was to be appointed to Cloughjordan in County Tipperary, we thought what an ideal place this would be for us – and asked a friend to suggest this to the Methodist powers that be. But the Conference had other ideas and we were informed that I was to be 'stationed' in Agnes Street, on the Shankill Road, the predominately Protestant and economically neglected area of Belfast's inner city.

So it was that in early August 1968, having sailed to America on the final voyage of the SS *America*, we sailed home on the penultimate voyage of RMS *Queen Elizabeth*. Given that 'penultimate' refers to the last but one before what is to follow, could this have been a sign?

5

Home Again

'There is nothing like returning to a place that remains unchanged to find the ways in which you yourself have altered.'
Nelson Mandela

The Northern Ireland that I returned to in the summer of 1968 was about to change utterly and I was not to know that this would, as we shall see, impact upon our plans for returning to the States. We were on the cusp of an era of great darkness and missed opportunities. I took up my new post in Agnes Street Methodist Church on the Shankill Road in August 1968, the month that saw the first civil rights march, from Coalisland to Dungannon, when what we were to call 'The Troubles' was about to unfold.

One of the great 'ifs' of our history is whether an openhearted and generous response by the Unionist Party and the Stormont Cabinet to the just demands of the civil rights movement, with resolute leadership and united vocal support from the Protestant Churches, drowning out the 'Not an Inch', 'No Surrender' and 'O'Neill Must Go' rants of Rev. Ian Paisley, would have secured a very different outcome.

No one, and certainly not I, could envision that decades of continued sectarianism, intransigence, and the most unconscionable violence lay ahead bequeathing a legacy of loss, suffering and mistrust with which we continue to contend today, notwithstanding the epic achievement of the Good Friday Agreement.

I took up my duties in Agnes Street with not a little trepidation, mindful that I was expected to fill the shoes of the legendary Sydney Callaghan, a much-loved pastor, big in heart and stature, whose transfer to Donegall Square in the city centre caused dismay among parishioners, and whose ministry reminded me of my role model, Lax of Poplar. Upon his appointment the then single Sydney had dispensed with a large suburban manse and moved into a modest 'two up and two down' house next door to the church which became known simply as '168'.

A house and an address which was to prove to be a God-given lifeline for the community during some terrible days and nights ahead. For us and our family there was to be a new home in a quieter area, but there were times when Clodagh could be forgiven for thinking that, like my predecessor I actually lived in '168' rather than at the manse.

I was also cognisant of the history of this huge Victorian church and its adjoining Methodist national school's pivotal place in the community since they were built in the 1880s. It had once boasted of overflowing congregations but by the time I arrived church attendance was more modest with the move of upwardly mobile families to the suburbs. Interestingly, part of this grand old church has been immortalised in John Hewitt's poem 'Going to church': Hewitt's father Robert had been the 'Master' of the Methodist school.

> A preaching house, its galleon-pulpit held the dominant position over all;
> the organ pipes, the choir behind it tiered,
> roared out the anthems only choirs can sing.[7]

Recounting those lines remind me of my first funeral in Agnes Street, that of Miss Thompson, assistant teacher to the poet's father where Hewitt himself was taught by this lady of whom he wrote:

… and Maggie Thompson, lean with greying hair,
by Uncle Willie courted for a time;
he married someone else, a heinous crime,
the guilt for which I felt she made me share.[8]

I have clear memories of my first Sunday evening in Agnes Street and its immediate aftermath. When I came out of church after the evening service a small group of parents were waiting to see me outside the church gates. I was acutely aware that whatever they wanted my response would be measured against the record of Sydney Callaghan and I couldn't be sure how I would 'perform'. It turned out that a few of their boys had got in trouble for 'breaking and entering' a local sweetie shop and helping themselves to confectionery and money from the till. They had actually entered the shop through the roof and were to appear in court the next morning. The request to me was simple and direct: would I be there 'to speak for them?'

Obviously I did not know the lads but the parents of one told me about their boy. He was in our Boys Brigade, had won badges and the top Scripture prize and so on. And his granny played the piano at the meetings of our church women's group!

I wasn't sure just what I could say or do to be helpful but welcoming this immediate opportunity to connect with the local community beyond my congregation, I assured them I would indeed be in court to do whatever I could do. Next day I arrived in the courthouse to be introduced to our local Stormont Member of Parliament, later to be elected as Westminster MP for North Belfast, the redoubtable Johnny McQuade. It was well known that Johnny's contribution to politics was limited – but in himself he represented the people of 'The Road'. He is perhaps best remembered for his standard response to every question from the media: 'No com-ment'. Whatever about his intellectual capacity, Johnny dressed the part with his black jacket, pinstriped trousers, rolled umbrella and bowler hat.

He confided that he did not know the boys either and was just there to support the parents and suggested that if asked by the judge I should speak for him as well as for myself. When the judge asked had I anything to say in defence of the boys I repeated what I had been told about the lad from our Boys Brigade and emphasised all the positives that his parents had shared with me as well as my impression of his parents as being caring and responsible citizens.

As soon as I finished, the judge without either hesitation or further enquiry gave his judgement. If in spite of all these good influences in his life this boy had done what he was charged with he must be a very bad boy indeed and sentenced him to six months in Rathgael, the boys' borstal. Sadly I had failed my first test and opportunity to earn some street 'cred'. Obviously I did not have the reputation and powers of persuasion that 'our Syd' had, but I redeemed myself to some extent by visiting the poor lad in borstal.

But out of this story were lessons to be learned and some good to come. Compared to the lawlessness that was soon to engulf this community the sweetie shop break-in was as nothing. Nevertheless, it was agreed that the renowned Satan – or his representatives on earth – had no difficulty in finding alternative activities for 'idle hands'. Obviously this did not justify even petty theft, but in the absence of youth clubs and recreational activities – which all closed for the summer months – it was easy to see how vulnerable it left youngsters of the area. So, a sequel to the court case was the bringing together of our church and the local YMCA in a joint effort to see how we might better provide for those idle vulnerable young lads, especially during the summer months.

Some time later a group of angry residents knocked on the door of '168'. They were incensed by what was happening on the 'Hammer Playground', the 'Hammer' being the name by which this part of the Lower Shankill was known.

The playground was owned and operated by the old Unionist-dominated Belfast City Corporation and a squad of corporation workmen had been deployed to dismantle all the swings, slides and roundabouts. Upon enquiry I was told that this was in response to damage to the playground equipment and that the appropriate department in City Hall had unilaterally decided, for the want of a better word, to decommission the whole playground. There had been no consultation and there were no plans to replace it. As an angry coalition of parents, the church, the YMCA and others from the local community, inspired in particular by our church youth committee chairman, the popular local butcher Andy Ross, we channelled our rage into raising enough money to replace the equipment. And with expert help from engineering students from Queen's University the playground was back in business.

Around the same time, we had a visit from some church folk from the USA. Would we be able to use the services of a volunteer or even two? So it was that the playground was not only re-built but had two wonderful volunteers from the US Church of the Brethren to staff it and provide imaginative programmes for the children. All this was to be a further contribution to my political education.

Sadly, there was an absence of political awareness of how little the establishment seemed to care about the people who voted for them. I found it curious, if not ironic, that in spite of the way the residents had been treated by their local political representatives in City Hall they still spent many laborious hours repainting the red, white and blue railings.

The people of the area were unaware that they were as deprived as any nationalists or Catholics. Their housing conditions with the not-so-proverbial outside toilets were no better than those in the Catholic Falls Road. Behind our church were the remains of a terrace of derelict houses that had been allowed to fall into disrepair. On what was left of the gable wall in bold letters was the ironical statement, 'WHERE THERE'S POPERY THERE'S POVERTY'!

We had arrived back from America in the early summer of 1968 with the sound of Joan Baez singing 'We Shall Overcome', the US civil rights anthem still ringing in my ears. Without knowing it, that anthem which had become the soundtrack to civil rights marches around Northern Ireland had its origins in a hymn composed by an American Methodist minister, Charles Albert Tindley (1851–1933).

What had been simmering under the political surface was beginning to erupt. Sadly, the would-be reformist Captain Terence O'Neill was forced to resign as Stormont Prime Minister under pressure from extremists from within his own Ulster Unionist Party and from without, led by Rev. Ian Paisley, who had run him close in his own Bannside constituency in a general election in February 1969.

Tensions continued to rise and when in mid-August of 1969 'Derry and Belfast were convulsed by the worst violence since the 1920s, necessitating the urgent dispatch of British soldiers to keep the peace, I was on a family holiday in the sandhills of Portnoo in Co. Donegal. Alongside me, also on holiday with his wife and young family was Eric Carson, a fellow Methodist minister from the neighbouring North Belfast Mission based in York Street.

As we listened to the hourly news bulletins on our transistor radios with growing concern, the 'Battle of the Bogside' in 'Derry had been followed by serious disturbances in Belfast and elsewhere. We were torn between the commitment to our families in our seaside idyll and our responsibility for our respective congregations back in a city 130 miles away that seemed to be tearing itself apart.

Communication with Belfast was very limited, something hard to grasp in these days of mobile phones, WhatsApp and instant emails. Phoning home was not straightforward. In a queue at the only public telephone in Portnoo I stood with coins in hand behind George Otto Simms, the saintly and scholarly Church of Ireland Archbishop of Dublin and Primate of Ireland. He told me he had been asked to comment on the situation, showed me some scribbled notes of what he intended to say and asked me, a clerical 'nobody', to advise him further. I remember suggesting something that I have long since forgotten, and he thanked me graciously.

By the night of Thursday, 14 August, the situation had deteriorated considerably and Eric and I knew that we had no option but to leave our families behind and drive through the night back to Belfast. It was a journey that took the better part of three hours. I did not realise that it was to be the beginning of a journey that was to change the direction of the rest of my life and my ministry.

When I returned from Donegal to Belfast one of the first things I was to see for myself was the devastation in Bombay Street close to Clonard Monastery where an invading loyalist mob had set fire to numerous houses, driving a whole street of Catholics out of their homes in one of the worst sectarian attacks in living memory. The fact that the police were either unable or unwilling to protect the residents, despite repeated phone calls from a Fr Egan, a Catholic priest in Clonard, seriously damaged relations between Catholics and the RUC in west Belfast and elsewhere, as did the belief that members of the B-Specials colluded with the attackers. And the failure of the IRA to offer any effective defence of the community in the face of the loyalist onslaught later played a huge part in the birth of what became known as the Provisional IRA.

Following that dreadful attack in Bombay Street I decided to visit the scene and was deeply affected by what I saw. Accompanied by Fr Des Wilson, a local priest, who was to become a good friend, I was taken to St Thomas's secondary school, which had been turned into a refugee centre for the scores of families who had been forced to flee their homes without any time to take their possessions. All they had was what they had left with.

I expressed my horror and my sympathy and asked if there was anything I could do to help. I was told that there was a particular need for clothing and other things necessary for the care and comfort of babies and children.

The following morning at our Sunday worship in Agnes Street I reported on my visit and the need for clothes and 'baby things'. I would be returning to the school in the next few days and if anybody had gifts they would like me to bring I would be grateful if they left them at the Church office in '168'. As people were leaving some said they did not have baby clothes and nappies but pressed money into my hand hoping that this would be helpful. When counted I was given £70, well over £1,000 in today's money. And this from a largely modest income Shankill Road Protestant congregation.

Mrs Bell, the local chemist, asked me to call down to her pharmacy where she had several boxes of baby 'things' which she asked me to deliver. In no time I had a full carload of clothing and baby gear plus the cash which I took to the school, where I was welcomed with appreciation for bringing such a tangible expression of care and concern from a Protestant congregation on the Shankill.

By their generosity my parishioners were saying that they were appalled by what had happened, totally disagreed with such hatred and wanted to show this in a practical way.

The outbreak of violence of 12–16 August 1969 (viewed by many as the start of the Troubles) had left eight people dead, more than 150 homes destroyed, 1,820 families evacuated, the deployment of the British Army and the erection of 'peace lines' or 'peace walls'.

Prior to the wars in former Yugoslavia and Ukraine, the expulsion of so many people from their homes has often been described as being the greatest population displacement in Europe since the Second World War.

Any hope that the streets would return to calm were quickly dashed in October 1969 during a night of violence on the Shankill Road triggered by the publication of the Hunt Report which recommended the disbandment of the B-Specials. As I relate more fully in Chapter 10, three people would be killed, including Constable Victor Arbuckle, the first RUC victim of the Troubles. And the bloodstained bodies of the other two deceased would be carried from the streets into our church hall just hours before it had to be made ready for Sunday School.

The violence of mid-August 1969 made headlines around the world and shocked the British political establishment. Less than a fortnight later I received a telephone call informing me that the then British Home Secretary James Callaghan was coming on an urgent fact-finding mission to Northern Ireland. And that he was anxious to include a Protestant working-class community in his programme. Would I arrange for that? Of course I agreed and I invited some of the local ministers to join us. For the wife of our superintendent this meant 'afternoon tea' and the homely mugs had to give way to the best manse bone china which she went home to fetch. The plan was that Rev. Donald Gillies, a local Presbyterian minister, and I would take the Home Secretary on a walkabout. However, word got out and by the time Mr Callaghan arrived a huge crowd had gathered and we had to forge a way to the door of '168.' But not before an articulate and angry Shankill woman had left him in no doubt about her fears and feelings, very largely reflecting the mood of the crowd. A 'conversation' which we were able to build on over the china teacups. I had long forgotten that my walkabout with the Home Secretary made the local and national TV news until archive footage recently emerged on the excellent BBC *Pop Goes Northern Ireland* series and on the extensive RTÉ archive website.

The shock of August 1969 and the upsurge in community tensions posed an acute challenge for local clergy. In the wake of what we had just been through, the Rev. Eric Gallagher, elder statesman and former President of Irish Methodism, convened a meeting of Methodist ministers to reflect on what was happening and on our response to it. There was much discussion and debate but for me one contribution stood out above all others.

The Rev. Wilfred Stafford, an elderly retired minister, asked permission to speak. In tones of humility and honesty, he shared with us his deep and personal regret for those times in his ministry when he remained silent when he should have spoken and those times when he had retreated from difficult decisions and actions for fear of confrontation. I remember his impassioned plea which had a deep and lasting effect upon me. 'I plead with you, don't come to my stage in life and ministry regretting that which you did not have the courage to say and to do. About which you can now do nothing.'

Those words are still with me and I have never ceased to marvel at their wisdom and simplicity. They have helped me stay on what I believe to be the right track and emboldened me when I have needed encouragement to do the right thing. And at the time they helped galvanise me into action of my own.

Already several of us as Protestant ministers – Methodist, Presbyterian and Church of Ireland – were going on joint nightly patrols which had proven highly helpful in defusing potentially combustible situations.

But these patrols were not without risk, as we were to discover. Such as the night when my Church of Ireland colleague Ian Patterson and I sought to dissuade some loyalists from using a crate of petrol bombs at a particular street corner. Their intended targets were not Catholics or republicans, but British soldiers who were patrolling nearby. When Ian and I rounded the next corner we were fired upon by soldiers who in self-defence had assumed us to be the petrol bombers they knew to be targeting them. Fortunately they appeared to be 'tracer bullets' or warning shots, which gave us time to bang furiously on the door of one of my parishioners where we 'hid' until daybreak.

Prior to these joint patrols we had not really known each other and had been working diligently in our own patches and parishes without sensing any need to meet on any regular or formal footing. But now our joint connecting with the community and with each other was reaping a dividend.

However, I personally sensed a need for us to go a step further and make connections with our neighbouring Roman Catholic clergy, whose parish boundaries were only a few hundred yards across the then invisible peace line which separated us.

My first call was to Father Des Wilson in Ballymurphy, who had accompanied me to Bombay Street, and whose independent style of ministry had got him into trouble with his bishop, William Philbin, to the extent that eventually his 'licence' to conduct public Masses was removed. However, he continued with an unobtrusive but highly effective ministry from a house in the estate.

It was my privilege to visit Fr Des in a nursing home shortly before his death in December 2019. We shared friendship, memories and prayer. As I said my farewell I knew that he was a man totally at peace with himself, his neighbours and his God. Shortly after this I attended his funeral. For a priest who had been censured for his style of ministry it was as significant as it was moving to see not one but three bishops sharing their tributes in the service.

I invited Fr Des to meet with myself and some of my fellow ministers from the Shankill in 168 Agnes Street. I remember him coming with his priestly collar well hidden behind a scarf. How sad I thought. But on reflection I don't think he needed to hide his identity. People had a respect for the 'cloth', of whatever colour.

My next 'port of call' was to Canon Pádraig Murphy, a parish priest on the Falls Road. Pádraig and I had not met before but found we had been thinking along similar lines. 'Let's spin a thread', I said, 'which might become a string which might become a rope with which we could build a bridge'. So we agreed to jointly convene a meeting with clergy from both sides.

The first of these was in Pádraig's presbytery. A spacious room where we were warmly welcomed with tea and biscuits. The conversation was serious but cordial and it was agreed that we should meet again, but this time we should bring some lay people with us.

However, the Rev. Donald Gillies, the arch anti-ecumenical Presbyterian minister from the other end of Agnes Street who had joined me with the Home Secretary on our Shankill 'walkabout', wanted further assurance. In his distinctive Scottish intonation he demanded, 'We may drink tea together, but there must be no praying together.'

I remember how Canon Pádraig couldn't get his head around this 'drink tea but no praying'. And with the compromise that there would be no praying, where might we meet?

In the atmosphere of the times, there was a shared concern that whichever venue, Protestant or Catholic, there would be those who would not feel comfortable out of their own zone. It was then that I remembered a conversation with a Mr Alex Jaffe from the synagogue on the Somerton Road. As a minority community the Jewish community would like to be helpful, he had told me, but couldn't think of what they might have to offer. So, stepping out of the meeting I phoned Mr Jaffe. Of course they would be delighted to host such a gathering. So it was that the Jews brought Belfast Christians together.

It's important to recall that despite our theological differences on the virtues of ecumenism, I found Donald Gillies a very brotherly person as we patrolled the streets together seeking to dissuade Protestant youths from following a violent path. He had earlier written a book that contributed to the decision of the Presbyterian General Assembly to withdraw from the World Council of Churches. Later, he was to change his mind and wrote a second book arguing for the unity of *all* Christians. The 'slender thread' had indeed become a bridge.

Amongst the positive outcomes of these interdenominational conversations in the synagogue was a way to deal with rumours. Often unfounded but which generated fear and brought people onto the streets. However, it was not always possible to dispel a rumour at a time when fear stalked the streets. One weekend I recall word going round that 'they' (being the Catholics/IRA) were reportedly coming to get 'us' and burn 'us' out. After church on the Sunday morning my stewards said they would organise the boarding up of windows to protect the church. I suggested that if there was so much fear the people would need a safe place or sanctuary. I suggested we keep the doors open and the lights blazing. Understandably there was some resistance to my suggestion. I said that whatever the circumstances I would undertake responsibility for opening up the church and that I would be there in event of trouble or anybody needing help – of whatever kind I did not know.

One of the women said: 'If you are there on your own you will need someone to make a cup of tea and I will be there with you.' Then one of the men suggested that we would need a man or two around the place to keep us safe. So it was that a group of us found ourselves in the church not knowing what might happen to the church or indeed to ourselves.

We were not to know it, but that was to be the first night of many weeks when we kept the church and the adjacent hall open with 'the lights blazing' as 'a safe house' for whoever needed emergency accommodation with blankets and camp beds that had been provided by the social services.

Many people, Catholics and Protestants, had been forced to leave their homes to become refugees in their own country, either through varying degrees of intimidation ranging from extreme physical attacks with petrol bombs and bricks through to a fear for the safety of themselves and their children. So it was that both traditions found temporary accommodation in our premises until the authorities were able to find them a permanent home.

With wonderful volunteers, from our congregation as well as others who just arrived, we provided bed and breakfast and loving, unconditional care and friendship. We were deeply moved by the many stories of conversations with our helpers, one of which was of the little Catholic girl ending her rosary in a Methodist Church hall with her impromptu prayer, 'Please God don't let them burn down our house so that we can go home and be happy again.' Sadly, she was not to know that her home had already been destroyed.

One afternoon – in an incident right out of Kenneth Branagh's recent movie *Belfast*, which depicted that period – a group of distressed neighbours from adjacent Richmond Street ran into '168' crying 'They're putting out the Hannas!'

Thomas Hanna and his wife Jean were an elderly couple who lived quietly in Richmond Street with their two grandchildren whose mother was unable to look after them. They were well known on the Shankill, he who was blind and she who led him was quite bent over, possibly with the burden of responsibility as well as some physical disability. Their 'crime' was that they were a 'mixed' couple, one a Catholic, one a Protestant, living in a staunchly Protestant area. Before this, their 'mixed' status had not been an issue, but now with sectarianism rearing its ugly head it suddenly mattered a lot, not to their neighbours but to loyalists from outside the area who pushed their way into their home shouting 'No Taigs here'.

I ran to the Hanna's home with their furious anguished neighbours to find that their attackers were putting the last of the couple's furniture on the street. They also opened Thomas's bird cage and his beloved budgie flew away, adding to his already extreme distress.

When I protested vehemently I was told 'We need this house for Prods'. With the help of neighbours we gathered up their possessions and cared for the family in our church hall until a house was found for them in a safer area.

One day many years later, around the mid-1980s, I received a letter from a lady who had been visiting her elderly aunt in Clifton House, a residential care home slightly north of Belfast City Centre. For some reason the word Methodist came into the conversation whereupon the lady in the next bed asked her if she had heard of a Methodist minister called Harold Good and if so could she get a message to him. And so it was, after all of these years I was reunited with the now even more elderly and much frailer Mrs Hanna.

She told me of all that had happened over the years but felt she had never properly thanked me for what we had done for them at that dreadful time. It was a moving moment when I held those frail hands in mine and we prayed for peace of heart and mind as well as for our land and our world.

Many years later a professional counsellor gave me the name of a man called Tony who wished to contact me. I phoned the number given, to discover that this was one of the two grandsons who would very much like to meet me. He gave me his address and I suggested that I would call for him and take him out for lunch. When I knocked his door I was welcomed in and there before me was a splendid lunch. Sandwiches with every kind of filling and pastries and cakes galore. Yes, he too wanted to say 'thank you' after all those years. Over his generous lunch he shared the saddest of stories of what had happened to him and to his brother.

When social services became involved the grandparents had been judged to be incapable of properly looking after the lads, so they were taken into care. There followed a horrendous story of institutional abuse and of inevitable personal tragedy. 'They call me "Del boy,"' he explained, 'because I buy and sell bits and pieces of bric-a-brac' [like the character in the BBC sitcom *Only Fools and Horses*]. 'And when I saw this, I thought of you.' There now sits on my desk a most unusual but treasured gift from Tony. A sort of paper weight with the word 'Believe' standing out in shiny chrome lettering.

The next time I was to see 'Del Boy' was on television on the evening news. As himself a victim, Tony was now the chosen spokesperson for victims of institutional abuse at the time of the public inquiry chaired by the late Sir Anthony Hart.

On the afternoon of 11 November 2022, I was in the Tesco store at Knocknagoney when a man came up to me said: 'Hello! Are you Rev. Good?' It was David, the second Hanna grandson. Meeting him after half a century was deeply moving. 'Where have all the years gone?' he cried. He just wanted to thank me for all that I had done for his family during the terrible events of his childhood and we both promised to have a proper catch-up.

I relate this as yet one more unrecorded story of personal tragedy and loss, not included amongst the official records of victims of the Troubles. And how many more could be told. A huge number, I suspect, perhaps well in excess of the 3,720 victims who are recorded as being killed as a result of the conflict and the 47,541 physically injured.[9]

Another such story follows from a night of rioting at Peter's Hill, at the bottom of the Shankill. Another minister and I had gone down the road to see if there was anything we might do or say. From within the shouting and mayhem we heard a yell for help. There was a man being gripped in the hold of angry men who clearly were intending him no good. Later we were to find out that the victim was a Dublin journalist who had been on the Falls Road in search of a story and had then made his way over to the Shankill. When stopped and challenged his Southern brogue gave him away and his captors and interrogators suspected that he might be a republican infiltrator. Having no idea what this was all about we appealed to his captors to let him go. Things got nasty and as he cried out for help he was thrown to the ground and subjected to a vicious kicking. Without thinking I threw myself on top of him assuming that my clerical collar would provide all the protection that I would need. But the kicking continued until mercifully, and providentially, soldiers appeared and took the poor man away to a place of safety and helped him on his way back to Dublin.

It was many years later that Clodagh was to take a phone call from a stranger who wished to speak to me, to thank me for saving his life. While I had a vivid memory of the incident, it was only when I returned his call that I realised more fully what a terrifying experience it had been for him. When we met, he told me the very sad story of how following that experience he had suffered a nervous breakdown, lost his job as a journalist, later as a teacher and finally his marriage. In recent years we have met several times and on my wall is a picture he painted for me as a tangible 'thank you', not just for what happened on that fateful night, but for giving him the opportunity to tell me his story which he had suppressed for many years, at the price of his mental health and well-being. Once more, another victim of our troubled years not recorded in the statistics.

Meanwhile, Canon Pádraig and I began to be invited to address various groups, such as the fledgling PACE [Protestant and Catholic Encounter] organisation. Given the significant difference in our physical frames, it was not surprising that someone dubbed us as Laurel and Hardy. Or was it because they thought what we were doing was more comical than serious? I particularly remember a meeting we were asked to address in Denvir's Hotel in Downpatrick. It had been organised by the then Clerk of the local council, the remarkable Maurice Hayes. This was to be the beginning of a long friendship with Maurice. I felt honoured to be one of the two Protestant ministers he particularly requested to take part in his funeral Mass in his beloved Downpatrick, the other being my Presbyterian friend, John Dunlop.

In November 1969 I received a letter marked from Downing Street. *The* Downing Street, as distinct from the one which was adjacent to our church on Agnes Street. It was from the Prime Minister's Office informing me that he was minded to submit my name for inclusion in Her Majesty's New Year Honours list 'for relief work to the community'. I was embarrassed as well as surprised. I was but one of many who had spent their days and nights on the street and responding to what was happening around us. And was I not doing what I and others were called to do ? Having been assured that others, including a priest from the Falls Road, were being included, I accepted on behalf of the 'team' of clergy of which I by chance more than choice was the leader. So it was that Clodagh and I and our first-born daughter, Carolyn, had our day at the Palace, in the presence of the Queen herself, from whom I received an MBE. Many years later, in the 1985 Queen's Birthday Honours I was pleased to receive an OBE in recognition of my contribution as a member of UK and more local voluntary and statutory bodies.

Further recognition of what we had been attempting came by way of a telephone call from Stormont, from the office of the newly appointed Minister for Community Relations, Dr Robert Simpson, inviting me to come to see him in his office. His Department had been established in a hurry as part of the reform package insisted on by the government in the person of James Callaghan.

When I was seated Dr Simpson asked me a question that surprised me: 'If I were to give you £10,000 what would you do with it?' In today's money he was asking me what would I do with £155,000. I asked for time to consult and was later to return with a proposition that I had agreed with my church officials. We would do two things. Firstly, spend money on developing our church halls and school rooms into premises more suitable for more broadly based youth and community activities. Secondly, we would seek to secure and employ a suitably qualified person to lead the project and develop programmes as appropriate. Dr Simpson and his advisors readily agreed and thus came into being the 'Agnes Street Youth and Community Centre'.

This was to be managed by a committee comprised of church representatives with the required percentage of representatives from the wider community. We were entirely fortunate in the appointment of Mr Jack Montgomery, a well-qualified youth and community leader who had been working with the YMCA in Scotland but was anxious to return to his native Belfast.

The stories surrounding that centre and its work would easily fill the pages of another book with the names of sadly forgotten helpers like Alf and Minnie Midgley to the fore.

The significance of such hands-on community work can never be overstated if we are not to condemn another generation of our children and young people to a repetition of our sad history. The shocking involvement of children as young as five or six in rioting – as recently as the summer of 2024 – should serve as a wake-up call for all of us.

Speaking of which, I share a story from the part of the community with which I was most involved but I am fully aware of similar stories from both sides of our community.

One evening, following earlier disturbances, the Army set up a cordon to prevent an altercation between residents from the Shankill Road and their Catholic neighbours in Unity Flats down Peter's Hill. Not surprisingly, this was not appreciated and led to rioting and attacks on the troops who were holding the line.

In the 'excitement' of the moment, and being much too young to understand the potentially lethal consequences of their actions, a large group of youngsters commandeered a milk float, and, with a youth at the wheel, were determined to drive down the road to break through the heavily armed cordon of troops.

Given that for the soldiers this could well have been viewed as a lethal weapon hurtling in their direction, totally unaware of the 'cargo' of children for whom it was the most exciting of adventures, it would not have been surprising if they had opened fire with the most tragic of circumstances.

In an attempt to prevent this from happening, some of us stood in front of the vehicle. But the youngster at the wheel was not for persuasion and revved up the engine in preparation for a deadly 'take-off'. Fortuitously, when something diverted his attention I seized my moment, reached into the cab and removed the key from the ignition, averting a potential tragedy. Upon reflection, this is but one example of how fear and hysteria can eclipse reason and responsibility in any part of a community at war with itself. While but one example of what lay behind much of what happened on all sides during those dark years, let it alert us to the ongoing challenge of ensuring that succeeding generations do not inherit the consequences of our tormented history.

Imagine my distress during a period of particularly high tension when on rounding the back of the church I came across the scene of children being instructed in the art of making petrol bombs. To them it was a game of sorts, but for those instructing them it was a much more sinister enterprise. I had seen what petrol bombs had done elsewhere. And here were children from our neighbourhood, many of them in our Sunday school and our church activities, being exploited in such a shameful manner.

I was horrified by what I was seeing and I broke up the gathering as quickly as possible, urging the youngsters to go home while those giving the instruction quickly made themselves scarce. A friendly eyewitness said it was like 'the cleansing of the temple'.

Later that evening I was interviewed by a BBC TV reporter who asked me what upset me most. Being so fresh in my mind I recounted how the sight of the children making petrol bombs had deeply affected me. I expressed my condemnation of *all* acts of violence, especially those that involved and exploited children. My comments gave him a story and headline, both local and national. Which was fine by me but not by some of the people of the area. I was accused of 'revealing military secrets' and of letting our side down. 'You never hear their priests letting their people down like that,' I was told by locals.

The night that followed saw further destruction and mayhem with buses burned and strewn over many roads. Much of the city had come to a standstill and on the next morning there was no public transport. Imagine my surprise when a man came seeking me with an outstretched hand. He had just walked from Glengormley – a distance of six miles – specifically to find me to say 'thank you' for being honest and for saying what needed to be said on the TV. Obviously a most welcome approval for my course of action in contrast to the abuse I had received. But next morning, when we discovered an unlit petrol bomb sitting symbolically at the back door of our manse, I suggested to Clodagh that perhaps it was time for a visit to Granny in Waterford. She readily agreed.

Sadly, there were more horrors to follow as the rapidly escalating 'Troubles' came to dominate my ministry and the lives of so many people throughout our province.

Such as what happened in the immediate aftermath of the introduction of internment without trial by the old Stormont government on 9 August 1971, a wrong-headed initiative that made things immeasurably worse in terms of the death toll, galvanised republicans, outraged moderate nationalists, and – along with Bloody Sunday in 'Derry the following January – sounded the death knell for 50 years of one-party Unionist rule.

This time it was residents of Velsheda Park and Farrington Gardens, a traditionally Protestant area, who were to be the targets of sectarian attacks. This seemed to mirror what had happened in Bombay Street two years earlier.

Reportedly, a van with loudspeaker had toured the area warning Protestant families to leave or risk being burned out of their homes. This resulted in hurried exits by families under threat who were desperate to save their possessions as they left. It is recorded that about 240 homes were destroyed in the Farrington Gardens, Velsheda Park and Cranbrook Park areas.[10]

There remain confusing reports as to whether the houses were set alight by republicans who wanted to clear the area of Protestants; or by Protestants as they fled, to ensure that those who had 'evicted' them would not have the benefit of the homes they were forced to leave.

Whatever the precise details, it was another tragic episode in the growing tension and breakdown of community. Once again I found myself walking streets strewn with debris and viewing rows of burnt-out homes, in my mind a 'mirror image' of Bombay Street. As I walked past what was left of one home I met a youngish couple with an elderly woman, the mother of the younger man. They were carrying some bags with items they had gathered from the charred remains of what had been the old lady's home. She had lost the two most precious of her possessions. Her budgie – her much loved companion – and the framed photograph of her late husband, which could not be replaced.

I did not even try to think of something of comfort to say as I took her arm and walked with them to her son's car at the top of the street. As I opened the car door to help her she took her seat, looked at me with saddened eyes, thanked me and said, 'Reverend, isn't it wonderful to know that we have a house that is not made with hands.' She was quoting from Paul's Second Letter to the Corinthians (5:1) referring to our habitation of this life as an 'earthly tent'. That dear lady was not to know it, but what she shared with me that day I have shared with many congregations and audiences in the years that have followed. Yet another story of incredible grace coming, literally, out of the debris of those dark days and nights.

I was not to know that for me one of the darkest days would come just four months later. On Saturday 11 December 1971. I had conducted a marriage service in my church and as the newlyweds were signing the register we heard a huge explosion. It was so close that it felt as if the church had been lifted up and set down again. As soon as the couple walked back down the aisle I headed down the road with many others. A no-warning bomb had gone off at the showrooms of the nearby Balmoral Furniture Company on the Shankill Road. It was heart-breaking, a scene of utter devastation. With others I started digging through the rubble and the wreckage with our bare hands. We recovered four bodies, including two young children and two men, one barely an adult and the other a middle-aged gentleman.

One of the most enduring images of the Troubles, graphically portrayed on a Shankill Road gable, is that of a fireman carrying out the body of the youngest victim, seventeen-month-old Colin Nicholl.

The others to die were two-year-old Tracey Munn, twenty-year-old Harold King, an auctioneer's assistant, and Hugh Bruce, who was 50, a commissionaire who had been employed by the owners to check on visitors to the store.

They had been brutally murdered by the IRA. Another nineteen people were injured, many seriously. After the bodies were recovered I dusted myself down and headed for the Royal Victoria Hospital, to where the injured had been taken, to see what pastoral assistance I might offer.

In the corridor I met Nursing Sister Betty, a fellow Methodist from Fermanagh, who recognised me and asked if I could speak to Helen Munn, who was the mother of one of the children who had been killed. She had been seriously injured in the bombing and it transpired that she had been caring for both of the children who had been killed, her little daughter Tracey and baby Colin, who was the son of her good friend who had gone to England for the weekend to comfort her sister who had lost a child in a car accident.

I found Helen deeply distressed at the loss of her child and at the loss of her friend's child, for whose death she felt responsible. But her distress was compounded by her anguish that Tracey had not been baptised and she worried what might happen to her as a result. I was able to spend time in reassuring her of God's all-embracing, inclusive, unconditional and welcoming love and grace from which none would be excluded, and particularly the most innocent of children.

The years roll by and one day I find myself seeking to explain to a group of visiting American Methodists something of our troubled story and our search for peace. Also invited to tell his story was a well-known loyalist, Billy McQuiston, known to his friends as 'Twister'.

Billy told his story. Of being on the Shankill Road on the day of the bomb attack on the Balmoral Furnishing Company, minding his own business having neither interest nor part in any paramilitary activity. But upon hearing the explosion he rushed down the road to see what was happening and as a youth, two weeks from his fifteenth birthday, found himself digging with his bare hands alongside me and others.

While I went to the hospital to offer comfort, Billy went up the road to the HQ of the paramilitary UDA and signed up. That walk up the road took him on a journey to prison where he was to spend a precious twelve years of his young life. I now know that his was but one of four such stories that unfolded out of this particular atrocity.

On 30 January 1972, less than two months after that horrific bomb explosion on the Shankill Road, came the horror of Bloody Sunday in my native 'Derry. An outrage that would alter the course of our history, with the fall of Stormont, a running sore of grievance for the bereaved families and the wider Catholic community and a boost in recruitment for the IRA that their leadership could not have dreamt of. It was to be many years before the long-awaited Saville Report and Prime Minister David Cameron's apology in the House of Commons 38 years later.

On that fateful Sunday I was in Bristol as a guest of Rev. Mervyn Wilshaw of the Victoria Methodist Church and their neighbours of other churches. Months earlier I had written an article for the English *Methodist Recorder* about the challenges of pastoring during the Troubles which Mervyn had followed up with a phone call asking how his church and fellow Christian denominations might assist. I had no hesitation in saying that we could do with a mini-bus for the multi-faceted work of our community centre. He invited me to Bristol to make my case to a concerned and united group of Anglican, Roman Catholic and Methodist congregations.

On the Sunday morning I had preached in Victoria Methodist Church ahead of an evening event at which I would be introduced to the three congregations to explain and make my 'pitch' for the mini-bus. But before the event, as we were watching the TV evening news, we heard the initial reports of the shootings by the Army.

Coming from my background and as a person who supports law and order my instinctive inward response was to give the Army the benefit of any doubt. And to believe that their intervention must have been entirely justified in response to gunmen and bombers who had posed a lethal threat to them and to the public.

I was quite prepared to say as much in my presentation as I anticipated I would be expected to explain this grim news from home. But before my turn to speak the local Catholic curate, who like myself had been born in 'Derry, spoke openly with unrestrained anger and condemnation of the actions of the Parachute Regiment.

So, by the time I came to speak I had sufficient wisdom to refrain from making any public comment about what I thought had happened. In the fullness of time the reaction of the young curate was entirely vindicated.

Home again, one evening I was alarmed to see scores of young men being marshalled on the Shankill Road wearing balaclavas and carrying cudgels. They were marching in disciplined military style. I stood watching at a discreet distance with the captain of my Boys Brigade who was groaning, 'to think that I taught some of those lads to march like that.'

Then two familiar figures appeared, the former Ulster Unionist Stormont MP Austin Ardill, a retired Captain of the British Army, and Bill Craig, who until his dismissal by Terence O'Neill had been the Minister for Home Affairs in the Stormont government. It transpired that they were there as founding members and leaders of the right-wing Ulster Vanguard which was closely affiliated with the loyalist UDA. As they 'inspected' what would now be called a 'pop-up' army their presence and their 'rank' would have given those young men good reason to believe that they were being enlisted to serve and protect their community in a time of crisis.

I saw it all very differently and sought to persuade some of these youngsters not to be drawn into they knew not what. Some years later as a prison chaplain I found myself in a prison cell with two of those young men. They were William Moore and Robert Bates, both now deceased, who following that parade had gone on to join the UVF and were subsequently recruited to the loyalist murder gang known as 'the Shankill Butchers'.

I was waiting for them when they returned to their cell from the court, having just received a full-life sentence for their crimes. They reminded me of that night on the Shankill Road when we first met. Behind their balaclavas I would not have recognised to whom I was pleading, but they had remembered and told me how they wished to God they had listened to me instead of those who persuaded them to go in another direction.

'We thought we would get medals,' they said, 'but instead we've got life!'

When I concluded my term as chaplain these same young men presented me with a beautifully hand-tooled leather cover for my Bible, portraying the well-known image of praying hands. Speaking to young people I have often shown this cover to illustrate how hands can be used to both create and destroy.

By 1973 there was no let-up in the daily litany of bombings and shootings and general mayhem. By now I had been back from the US for nearly five years and four of those years I had been pastoring in a war zone. To be honest, without realising it, I was probably experiencing what is now known as 'burnout'. And there was still the intention and attraction of a return to America and with those five years almost up I had already received permission to resume a ministry in the US where I had been promised an attractive appointment in Indiana to which a large part of me was looking forward to returning.

However, one day I received a call summoning me to a high-powered meeting with the President of the Church, the District Superintendent and the Secretary of the Methodist Conference in Ireland, who wanted to meet me that evening. What trouble have I got myself into? I wondered.

They greeted me warmly but came quickly to the point.

We understand that you have applied for permission to return to the States. We have granted you permission to do that and we are not going to withdraw that permission. However, we are asking you to reconsider your plans because we feel that you have a ministry here.

I was a bit taken aback. It was not what I had expected but I was relieved that I wasn't in any 'trouble'. And in my heart I felt that it was a reasonable request in the circumstances.

'I'll reconsider my plans,' I replied.

A few days later I was holding a meeting with the leaders of my congregation in Agnes Street when I took a phone call from the District Superintendent of the Methodist Church in Indiana. The fact that he had gone to the trouble and expense of phoning me – not an easy procedure in those days – rather than writing a letter, indicated that something urgent and important had arisen.

Like the leadership of my Church a few days earlier, he came straight to the point. 'I have been holding this post for you here in Indiana for quite some time. But now I need an answer, Yes or No.'

'I'll let you know very quickly,' I promised.

It did not take me long to make up my mind.

I thought of all the good people in the other room at an incredibly difficult time in the history of our city and our province.

I thought of the request from my own Church leaders to reconsider America.

Although I felt tired, I said to myself I cannot possibly walk away from my ministry right here.

So within days I told my friend in Indiana that I was extremely grateful for his kind offer and his patience with me but that I had to decline in order to serve my people here at home amid so much disorder and chaos.

A short time later the Methodist Conference approved my transfer the short distance north to the largely Protestant community of Greenisland by the shores of Belfast Lough, where you will recall I had spent an unhappy time in hospital as a sickly child. This time was going to be very different.

6

PASTURES NEW AND LESS FAMILIAR

'A ship in a harbour is safe but that is not what ships are built for.'
John A. Shedd, author and businessman

Having reconsidered our plans to return to an appointment in America, I had assumed we would remain in Agnes Street. However, those responsible for appointments in the Methodist Church decided otherwise. Perhaps it was thought that after those tense years on the Shankill Clodagh and I and our growing family deserved a less stressful appointment.

So it was that we found ourselves in greener pastures in Greenisland which was one of several relatively new housing estates built to accommodate the many families who, due to redevelopment, had moved out of the inner city. As something of a social experiment it was a 'mixed' community in which Catholics and Protestants were living well together, in spite of the efforts of some who had not yet shaken off their sectarian shackles. But thanks to a strong ecumenical commitment on the part of local churches and the influence of the then ground-breaking movement of 'Women Together', it was a world apart from the parish I had left behind.

So it was that Clodagh and I found ourselves within a much younger and hugely welcoming community and a supportive congregation. If, as I surmise, the intention of the 'Stationing Committee' was to offer me a 'respite' from the 24/7 demands of ministry on the Shankill, this was most certainly it.

Having said that, having experienced the horrors, the killings, the injuries, the intolerance, the in-your-face sectarianism at the heart of our civil conflict, there remained within me a desire to continue in a more hands-on ministry of healing and reconciliation.

This was 1972, the death toll was spiralling and that year was to see 497 killings. More than any other year in the Troubles.

While seeking to be faithful in my ministry to my new congregation, I was conscious of this tension within me when I received an invitation to attend an international conference organised by the World Council of Churches (WCC) in Bangkok that December.

The theme of this event was 'Salvation Today', calling upon the member churches of the WCC to a serious international engagement on the relevance of the Gospel in a world sadly divided by internal and global conflict. Within which there was to be a session on Northern Ireland.

I had obviously been selected because of my most recent first-hand experience of conflict in 'Protestant'/loyalist Belfast. My fellow traveller was a then little-known young lady called Mairead Corrigan (now Mairead Maguire) from Catholic/nationalist West Belfast.

Our brief was to help our fellow delegates from around the world to understand our conflict, its history, its impact upon the communities we represented and the role of the Churches within a bitterly divided society. What a challenge!

On our first day we were divided into small groups, within which we were introduced to a diminutive in stature Black Anglican priest from South Africa whose name was Desmond. Unfortunately, his luggage had been lost in transit but his secretary took his measurements into the city and returned within a few hours with a perfectly made-to-measure suit.

Little did I realise that I was in the presence of two future Nobel Peace Laureates. For as well as Desmond Tutu there was Mairead who some time later, together with Betty Williams, was also to be awarded the Nobel Prize.

It was following one of the most tragic incidents involving the IRA and the deaths of her niece and two nephews, one but six weeks old, and their mother being critically injured that Mairead and Betty founded 'The Peace People' for which they were to be honoured in Oslo.

And while I have long forgotten what we said and have no way of knowing whether my own presentation or Mairead's made much of an impression, I do recall the impact that the conference as a whole had on me and how it came to influence my ministry. For it came at that time of 'restlessness' and helped me focus on what I sensed was to be the focus of my ministry.

In the plenary sessions we listened to a range of internationally renowned theologians, preachers and activists in church and community. One such was the renowned German Reformed theologian Jürgen Moltmann.

I have to confess that being a pastor rather than an academic, much of what he and others were offering from the lofty podium went above my 'Norn' Iron' head. But one phrase which Moltmann was to offer struck me by its simplicity and yet its profundity. Coming from a Northern Ireland where the level of violence and political intransigence had seriously dented our theology of hope, I grasped his closing comments which concluded with his compelling voice declaring: 'Never forget, Jesus takes the inevitability out of history.' For me, a defining and affirming moment. Never again would I accept for myself or let go unchallenged the all too frequently declared and much too readily accepted: 'Things will never change. It will always be like this.'

Amongst the other speakers were people who themselves had at some time been members of underground and resistance movements, such as an Angolan freedom fighter and a former Indonesian general who was involved in the overthrow of President Sukarno. Their stories sounded familiar to those of us who had come from any part of these islands in the early seventies as well as other places of communal conflict, such as South Africa, Colombia, Cambodia, Uganda and the Middle East, from where many of our fellow delegates had come.

I was particularly challenged by the story of one former combatant who spoke of the formation of an inclusive government in which he now served as a minister. As I listened, I came to understand how a political policy of 'exclusion', such as had operated in Northern Ireland, would take us nowhere. 'Exclusion' was at the heart of every conflict, past and present. Surely we needed to find ways of bringing people in rather than keeping people out.

Reflecting on all that I had heard in these presentations, I knew that challenging the policy of exclusion and replacing it with an inclusive approach would come to define and affirm my ministry.

Within a few days of my return from Bangkok I was interviewed by a 'rookie' reporter from my local paper, the *East Antrim Times*. His name was David McKittrick. David was to become one of the most perceptive and respected authors and journalists in Northern Ireland and beyond. I shared what I felt I had learned in Bangkok and the paper carried a front-page banner headline:

A MOVE TO LEAD EXTREMISTS "TO THE TABLE"[11]

In the article David quoted me as saying that I thought a visit from some of those I had heard speak would be valuable. 'I don't think I could ever understand the mentality of people who place bombs in a crowded street,' I said, 'but some of those who had spoken could, though they had since come to see that ongoing violence could destroy political progress and things already achieved'.

The article concluded with my being quoted as saying that I was still considering whether to get in touch with both the IRA and extreme Protestant organisations, 'to get the ball rolling.'

Almost two years later Protestant Church leaders, including my senior Methodist colleague and mentor Eric Gallagher, did so with the IRA at Feakle, Co. Clare. Another story that should be re-told, a story of inclusivity and engagement rather than fruitless condemnation which stuck with me and informed my whole approach to the resolution of conflict and the fostering of reconciliation.

Sadly, Bangkok was also memorable for very personal and tragic reasons. On my first night I got the shattering news that Bruce Powell, a schoolboy from Belfast, the grandson of one of my most faithful members in Agnes Street, and who often worshipped with his gran, had died in a water-skiing accident near Bangkok while on a Christmas visit with his brother to their ex-pat parents, Joan and Roy, whom I had looked forward to visiting.

So, instead of enjoying a planned visit to their home following the conference, I found myself giving the address at Bruce's funeral in the Anglican church in Bangkok prior to a Thai-style cremation ceremony. How was it that I should have travelled to Bangkok to be there to minister to my friends from Belfast in the most tragic of circumstances?

Now in my mid-thirties, I was not seriously questioning my vocation as a minister of 'Word and Sacrament', but I felt a bit unsettled, drawn to a more discernible ministry of inter-community reconciliation of some kind.

So it was that I had a conversation with the Rev. Ray Davey, the inspirational visionary who in 1965 had founded the Corrymeela Community, a movement dedicated to reconciliation within Northern Ireland and beyond.

'Corrymeela', for which one suggested translation means 'hill of harmony', is based on a clifftop site on the beautiful north Antrim coast just outside Ballycastle. Davey had prophetically anticipated the need for reconciliation in our divided community many years before the outbreak of the Troubles and was determined to do something concrete about it. He and others had been influenced by their visits to the Iona Community in Scotland, by Taizé in France and Agape in Italy and hoped to find such a site in Northern Ireland. Upon hearing of the sale of the Holiday Fellowship house in Ballycastle they knew that this was where they were meant to be. And the rest is history.

The contemplative life of Corrymeela had been dramatically changed and challenged when following the fiasco of internment there was an exodus of families from west Belfast, many of them finding a temporary refuge at Corrymeela.

Ray surprised me by telling me that there was now a need for a director of the Ballycastle Centre and that they were presently looking for someone 'like you'. As I told Alf McCreary in the first of his books about Corrymeela: 'I thought about it, and it seemed to make sense. Maybe I was not led but looking back I think I was placed.'

And so it was that with the blessing of the generous folk of Greenisland, we moved to the north coast, transformed a rather unpromising looking cottage into what was to become a very lovely home called 'Treetops' and opened a new chapter in our lives – and that of our four children. We fell in love with the area and have retained a 'bolt hole' not far from Corrymeela for over 40 years.

The story of the founding and development of the Corrymeela Community has been well documented in more than one book by Alf McCreary.[vi] In the seven years since purchasing and opening what had been the Holiday Fellowship Centre, Ray Davey and his volunteer visionaries had done a remarkable job in developing the site and renovating and furnishing the building. But it had now come to a point where there was a need for more 'hands-on' direction.

This proved to be an exacting as well as an exciting challenge. But one that I relished while acknowledging my indebtedness to remarkable colleagues such as Billy McAllister and Desi McLernon (wardens), Gerry McCambridge (bursar), Kathleen Bakewell (secretary), Anna Glass our cook and a succession of volunteers from around the world as well as from closer to home.

I soon identified three priorities in my new role of centre director.

- Upgrading the accommodation to a standard which would provide for serious residential conversations and conferences – as well as a place of sanctuary for those who needed a place of care and protection.

[vi] See, for example, *Corrymeela: Hill of Harmony in Northern Ireland*, Hawthorn Books, 1976; *In War and Peace: The Story of Corrymeela*, Brehon Press, 2007.

- With members of the Community, to identify, plan and manage residential conferences on fundamental themes relevant to the situation in which we found ourselves in the Northern Ireland of that time.
- To develop the volunteer programme so that it became more selective and focused – in contrast to the 'drop-in' approach to volunteering which I had inherited. This was to lay the foundations for what was to become known as our 'Serve and Learn' programme with international volunteers being carefully selected for what they would take home from the experience as well as what they would bring to the Centre.

All of this was to prove to be a busy and demanding role. At times I would look at my imaginary 'hat rack' with the various hats that this 24/7 role demanded: 'inn-keeper'; 'site manager'; 'personnel manager'; 'programme manager'; 'worship leader'; 'pastor'; 'community relations officer'; 'problem solver'; 'fund raiser'.

Obviously, as in any situation of challenge and change there were those for whom my style of leadership was not what they either expected or desired. Corrymeela is a large and disparate community with strong views as well as commitment. Amongst the members there were those who did want a director but did not always welcome direction. An ongoing tension which is by no means unfamiliar within the voluntary sector.

The demands of the job were such that it was difficult to balance work and family time. A lot was left to Clodagh in that respect.

Having said that, for me personally, this was to be an extremely important period in my life – and I would like to think it also was for those whom we sought to serve in those dark days of the seventies.

I remember getting a letter from a senior minister, regretting that I had left the ministry. Of course it was very different to a settled parish ministry, but ministry it was. With daily worship (not just on Sundays) and pastoral care and counselling on demand.

But worship was to be much more interactive than that to which I was accustomed. In the busy spring to autumn months our worship centre was an ex-Army tent. While the tent has an important biblical precedence (tabernacle) with many of those who came we certainly did not mention the association with the Army. But in time – and given Irish weather – a most fitting legacy of my time at Corrymeela was the building of 'An Croí', meaning 'the Heart', a place of meeting and of prayer at the 'heart' of the Centre. An achievement of which I remain rather proud.

On one occasion, we were hosting a cross-community group from the Falls and the Shankill. As ever, there were those who stood out more than others. One called Mary from the Falls Road and the other called Martha from the Shankill. A wonderful coincidence from the biblical story of two women with the same names. Both had identical stories to tell. Of being put out of their homes and of the challenge of bringing up their children in riot-torn streets.

When I asked for volunteers who might wish to share in the leading of worship, Martha was quick to respond. She who could not remember the last time she had been in Church. When it came to her moment Martha leaned forward … as did we all in anticipation of what was to follow:

> I want to tell you something that I can't tell my neighbours. They wouldn't understand. I have twelve grandchildren. Six of them are Protestants and six of them are being brought up Catholics. But I want to tell you, I love them all equally, and do you know what? That's how God loves us. He makes no difference between us. He loves us all the same.

As Martha straightened up, having made her 'confession', I thought she had put so plainly and in a way that everyone in that tent/tabernacle could understand the timeless message of Jesus in a way of which he, the master of simplicity, would heartily approve. A message which theologians across the ages have spent tireless hours in mountains of manuscripts helping us understand that which is so fundamental and timeless at the heart of the Gospel.

Another memorable worship was conducted by Bernard Brett, a quadriplegic totally dependent upon non-verbal limited communication. He had a certain charisma which drew people to him. Even children gathered around him – and not just out of curiosity. One evening he indicated that he would like to lead worship. His helper shared his prepared thoughts and readings. But what was most memorable was his choice of song – 'Lord of the Dance'. As we all sang with new understanding of the message of that song, Bernard 'danced' with the movement of his head, accompanied by his sadly distorted but beaming grin.

A key committee of the Community was given responsibility for the planning of residential conferences and conversations addressing some of the most relevant and difficult issues affecting life in Northern Ireland at that time.

One member – from her own very personal experience – suggested a weekend during which we would invite couples who were already in or contemplating a 'mixed marriage' – which in our context meant a marriage or intended marriage between Roman Catholic and Protestant partners.

I confess, I wondered what response there might be to such an invitation. But to ensure that it was made as widely known as possible we placed paid advertisements in daily papers. Within days, the weekend was fully booked.

And come they did. Married couples, some for many years. Engaged couples and couples who had not yet committed themselves to one another. There was the sharing of many stories. Stories of pain. Stories of families that were broken, of parents who were unaccepting or downright hostile to the choices of their children. Others who had been threatened with 'disownment' should they persist in the relationship.

But there were those who had come through such experiences with positive outcomes. Those who had managed to preserve their personal integrity, balancing their commitment to one another with patience and understanding of the fear and prejudice of parents and families.

Those who had helped to plan the programme felt it to be important that there be opportunity for shared worship in the form of an ecumenical service and for those who wished it, a celebration of Holy Communion in a Protestant tradition as well as a Mass. It was extremely moving to see couples attending both. It was left to people to choose for themselves how they wished to participate, whether to partake fully by receiving Communion or by asking for a blessing.

I will not forget one couple returning to their seats in tears, tears of joy. Having been married for several years this was the first time they had shared bread and wine at the altar. 'Now', they exclaimed, 'our marriage has finally been fully consummated.' Shame, I thought, and a judgement upon our churches.

In our closing conversation it became very clear that there had been a very strong bonding between all of these couples. And yes, they were determined to keep together, to support each other and be available to others who were looking for guidance and counsel. Thus was born, in 1974, an amazing organisation known as NIMMA, the Northern Ireland Mixed Marriage Association which for 50 years has pioneered new thinking and practice between the churches as well as supporting and encouraging countless couples. Work which by its very nature has been sensitive and discreet. I am pleased to have been involved in its foundation. Further details are available at nimma.org.uk.

Other weekends included 'Troubles and the Media', chaired by John Cole, the distinguished Belfast-born journalist then deputy editor of *The Observer*. This was a conversation well ahead of its time, bringing together some of the most influential journalists in Northern Ireland and beyond to discuss their role and responsibility in the reporting of the Troubles.

Perhaps the one that was particularly trail-blazing was a weekend event entitled 'Policing and Community'. The plan was to bring people from areas which were known as difficult if not 'no-go' areas for the Royal Ulster Constabulary (RUC) to engage with senior police personnel in a safe and neutral setting. This was a particularly challenging and sensitive undertaking. Policing was one of the most divisive issues within an already deeply polarised society where there were very different perceptions of the RUC, depending on what part of the community you came from.

To many Protestants and unionists they were a bulwark against a ruthless terrorist organisation, the IRA, who murdered or attempted to murder police officers daily in their campaign to destroy the State. On the other hand, many Catholics and nationalists saw an overwhelmingly Protestant and unionist-supporting force that had propped up a discredited one-party state and batoned and water-cannoned peaceful civil rights marchers off the streets.

Sadly, the chief constable of the day, Sir Jamie Flanagan, was not supportive of our suggestion. The RUC had its own Community Relations Branch and this was their responsibility, not ours, was his argument. But not to be deterred from what we knew to be an imaginative initiative and a necessary conversation, we went ahead with the idea. Pooling all of our individual contacts with police officers and with people from the communities with whom we wished to engage, we made very personal approaches. And so they came! Police officers, not representing anybody but themselves, they said. Community representatives from some of the most troubled areas of Belfast and elsewhere. Others self-describing as 'community workers' to hide their more sinister identities. Ensuring that the voices of republicans and loyalists were heard in that room, along with voices from the RUC.

There were formal introductions with obvious suspicions, spoken and unspoken. And there were honest but respectful debates and disagreements.

At Corrymeela one of the great levellers is the communal dishwashing, with tables taking it in turn. I knew we were getting something right when I saw a housewife from the Bogside waving her tea towel in the face of the Superintendent from Strand Road 'Derry police station. Not intending to insult but making her point in the way she knew best. Around that sink she was on 'home ground'. Clearly, he was not. But he heard her loud and clear.

Within the relaxed and non-threatening atmosphere of Corrymeela 'ice' began to melt. In 'down-time' there were excursions to a local hostelry where real ice began to melt in a different kind of 'spirit'. With people regardless of so-called 'rank', from the most different backgrounds imaginable sharing frank conversation and camaraderie.

Resulting from one of those conversations between senior police and representatives of an erstwhile extreme republican group (the recently unproscribed Republican Clubs), leaflets carrying photographs of police officers which had been edited to make them look like Nazi officers were withdrawn and voluntarily re-printed without the slur. An example of what can happen when people actually meet and engage in a non-confrontational setting.

An active participant in all of this was a certain Jack Hermon, an assistant chief constable later to become chief constable of the RUC. He told me that he had come against the wishes of his chief constable but that he would meet with him on Monday morning to impress upon him the tremendous value it had been and the potential for further such events.

Not long after, I was invited to meet Jack Hermon at RUC HQ in Brooklyn. He had secured permission and funding for a series of similar weekends to which I had no hesitation in agreeing. Jack was now responsible for community relations and we worked together very happily in the planning of a series of residential weekends.

For one of these weekends it was planned to bring together young lads from East Belfast and West Belfast. This was organised by Police Community Relations liaison officers who worked with some of the most challenging young people in these troubled areas.

I had stipulated that as Corrymeela was a 'gun free' area any police officers carrying weapons for personal protection must surrender them for safe keeping in our locked safe. Unfortunately, on this occasion one young police officer did not do so. Very unwisely he had 'hidden' (or so he thought) his gun under his mattress.

Imagine the panic. A police officer's gun had gone missing amid a houseful of young lads, chosen to be there as they were seen to be at risk to themselves as well as to others. We gathered them together, explained the seriousness of the situation and appealed to their individual and collective conscience to help us to retrieve the 'lost' weapon. I gave them my word that if the weapon was returned to me personally this would be between me and whoever was responsible and promised that there would be no repercussion. Bedtime came – with no response and no return.

Jack Hermon explained to me that he could only allow a limited time for the gun to be returned. If it were not returned before daybreak he would have no option but to call in Special Branch to take control of the situation. I knew that should this happen it would lead to a total breakdown in trust between Corrymeela and the communities that we so anxiously needed to retain. A relationship which had taken much time and effort to establish was now at serious risk.

Midnight came and passed. We could not go to our beds and leave the house and its occupants in such a volatile situation. So sustained by yet more caffeine we sat in the lounge hoping against hope that by some 'miracle' the weapon would yet be found and returned. It was in the early hours that the lounge door opened, one of the lads beckoned to me and into my ear he whispered, 'Room 16'.

Not knowing what to expect, I entered the room to be met by the sight of two young lads, one from the East and one from the West, both of them holding out to me what I hardly dared to hope was the missing weapon – wrapped in a towel. I assured them of my profound appreciation and reassured them that I would keep to my word and there would be no repercussion. What I had not realised was that up the road were the Special Branch vehicles which Jack was able to send back to base. Phew!

Next morning we gathered the total group and I commended them in as positive words as I could muster. I suggested that we must never forget the significance of what between them they had achieved that night. If only others in our community could emulate their example and together, as had they, find a way to deal with the weapons that were responsible for so much death and fear, we would be in an infinitely better place.

I refer to this incident as the second of four acts of decommissioning I have personally witnessed. The first in my church in Agnes Street when a loyalist handed the Rev. Eric Gallagher a parcel containing a gun, saying he just wanted rid of it and what it represented. The third was the final conclusive act of IRA decommissioning in 2005 and the fourth my participation in the decommissioning of arms by the Basque separatist group ETA in 2017, about which I will write more fully in Chapter 15.

The Corrymeela post was demanding but immensely fulfilling, though its particular responsibilities and challenges ensured that no one could please all of the people all of the time. One had to manage and accommodate as best one could the conflicting expectations of a very diverse membership. It also had a cost in terms of family life.

So, having achieved a great deal and having brought the work of Corrymeela to a new level, I accepted that it was time for me to move on. I did so not fully realising what an important period this had been for me personally in preparing me for what was yet to come.

Over the main door there is a sign which declares 'Corrymeela begins when you leave.' This, as I was to discover was certainly true for me as for all those who have had the privilege and the opportunity to serve within it. From my time in Corrymeela I carried with me the access as well as the mutual trust with many people which I had come to value during that period and to this day.

7

Return to Parish

'Nothing is real until it is local.'

Anon

But what and where next? I was encouraged to apply for and was offered the post of director-designate of the Belfast Voluntary Welfare Society at Bryson House, one of the oldest and largest charities in Northern Ireland. Although secular, its commitment to social justice and provision for the deprived and its comprehensive family support services resonated with my Methodist principles and John Wesley's concept of social holiness.

However, after several sleepless nights I concluded it was not for me. After all, I was called to be a pastor and a preacher in the Methodist tradition, not an administrator. So it was with regret but with understanding that Denis Barritt, the person I was to succeed, 'released' me to return to local ministry.

I was very pleased that, at my suggestion, the very talented, liberally minded former pro-power sharing unionist politician Peter McLachlan was successful in his application for the now vacant post at Bryson House, to which he made an enormous contribution. Much later and very tragically Peter died of a terminal cancer. I was humbled but privileged when he asked me to share his journey during those last months of his remarkable life and was at his bedside when he passed from us. To keep faith with Peter's wishes, his family and I carried his ashes to the top of Cavehill and released them to a powerful wind which carried them away and beyond over his beloved Belfast. The significance of it being Pentecost Sunday did not escape us.

For me, it was hugely important that my return to local church ministry was by choice, and not because I had no alternative.

In the year that followed I had an 'interim' ministry, caring for two declining congregations in North Belfast together with a part-time chaplaincy in Crumlin Road prison. Ironically, from behind closed doors this was to open new doors in my desire for a ministry of reconciliation.

When ready for a permanent appointment, it was decided that Ballynahinch, a small provincial town south of Belfast, was where I should be placed. I was not expecting this, as to me it appeared to be an out-of-the-way place about which I knew nothing. And I did wonder if after Corrymeela I could cope with life in a small town considered to be culturally conservative in both the political and the church sense. I could not have been more wrong. A lesson learned which I constantly pass on to those younger in ministry who may be unsure or resistant to where they may be sent.

The profile of the town of Ballynahinch was changing. With the arrival of new and younger families to be cared for there was a need for a new church building, and apparently I was a guy with a reputation for 'getting things done'.

The quaint but rather outdated Wesleyan Chapel with uncomfortable wooden pews with fastening doors was a relic of by-gone days. Privately, Clodagh and I wondered if this was a sign for us to think again about returning to the States.

On our first Sunday service I looked down upon my new congregation, the majority of them young families with children of similar ages to ours. They looked up at me with faces that shone with eager anticipation. Even at 42 years of age I was the youngest minister they had ever had and could have ever hoped for. By the end of the second hymn I knew this was where I was meant to be and by the last handshake at the church door we knew that we were going to be a happy family within our new church family. Nothing in the five years that followed gave us any reason to doubt our first impressions.

We were not to know it but these were to be amongst the happiest and most fruitful years of our ministry. Within two years we were to lay the foundation for a most beautiful new Sanctuary with the existing building being transformed into a happy space for activities for all ages.

This is not to say there were not challenges within the wider community.

I soon discovered that inter-church relationships between Protestant churches were virtually non-existent, let alone with Father Smyth and his congregation. When I suggested that we should think about this the response was positive. 'It's just that nobody ever suggested it,' was the reaction.

Soon we were to break new ground, particularly in the development of the happiest of relationships with Rev. Jim Lamont and his congregation of the First Presbyterian Church and Sister Jarlath McKenna, principal of the Catholic Assumption Girls Grammar School.

Inevitably there were those who did leave us for other churches. But with but one exception, they did so with good grace.

One couple had been missing for several Sundays. Thinking there might be illness I called to see them. After customary conversation about the weather, I mentioned that their friends at church had missed them, and hoped they were both well. The husband explained that since I had come, church was not quite the same, and not as he expected church to be. After assuring me that there was nothing personal in it he said: 'I was brought up to believe that if you didn't come home from church more miserable than when you went, it wasn't worth your while going.' Wondering if I heard aright I asked him to repeat what he had just said. 'Don't worry', he said, 'I have found a church that makes me feel like that and now I'm much happier.'

Another couple who had been life-long members asked me to call and at their fireside explained: 'The way you say and do things is not for us. But it seems to have meaning for others who are returning to church and getting involved. So we are not going to stand in their way and we have somewhere else that we can go where we will be more comfortable.'

It turned out that this was to be the local Free Presbyterian Church. Later they confessed to being shocked and upset when the first sermon they heard was essentially a very personal attack upon that 'apostate', the Methodist Harold Good! But, sadly, having declared that they were leaving, they felt they could not return. I was much moved when many years later, the good lady was to call me to her husband's bedside when he was leaving this world for the next. For me yet another example of how in church, as well as in community, we can differ with respect without fracturing relationships.

We began to be known as the 'ecumenical' church with new members saying they had joined us because they wanted to belong to a more open church for themselves and their families. Sadly all too often we assume the 'dissenters' represent the rest and allow ourselves to travel at their speed.

The opening of our new church was a red-letter day in the history of our congregation that we wished to share with a wide representation from the local community. Unfortunately, Ballynahinch Free Presbyterian Church wrote back thanking me for the invite but stating they could not attend 'because of the apostasy of the Methodist Church in Ireland and its total failure to oppose the visit of the Antichrist, the Pope, to our Nation.' A reference to John Paul II's visit to Britain when he was warmly welcomed to Buckingham Palace by the Queen.

I was pleasantly surprised when ITV/UTV honoured our new church by inviting us to provide the 'live' morning service on national television for the Sunday before Christmas. An honour indeed for a small-town congregation and one to which they rose with joyful song, happy faces and best feet forward.

On the morning of the service I woke up to the news of the IRA bombing of Harrods and found myself adjusting my script to include prayers for the victims and their relatives. A moment of reality for a service being broadcast from a bomb-weary Northern Ireland.

I was very conscious of the responsibility on my shoulders – and even more so when just before we were to go 'on air' the producer whispered to me that in the next hour I would be preaching to more people than John Wesley would have preached to in his entire lifetime. No pressure!

The TV service went without a hitch and I was as pleased as I was relieved. But on that evening, for the Fourth Sunday in Advent, we had organised a carol service to which we had invited local schools under the banner of 'Let the Children Sing'. There was a ready acceptance of our invitation from the Spa Primary School and from the Catholic Assumption Convent Grammar School, which we advertised in the local press and on the billboard outside our church.

Such an ecumenical carol service was breaking new ground in Ballynahinch. But for some local loyalists it was a step too far. Both Sister Jarlath and I were receiving nasty phone calls, threatening disruption – and more – if the participation of the choir from the Assumption school was not cancelled. After the television service we had a meeting with my church leaders and the good sisters from the Assumption Convent.

It was agreed that we should not allow ourselves to be dictated to by faceless threats. But Sister Jarlath explained she would need to inform parents and leave it to them to decide if in the circumstances they were prepared to bring their girls. So it was that, following phone calls from the good sister and her staff, almost all of the parents of the girls promised that they would be there. Some said that having watched our morning service on TV there was no way that they would let us down.

A senior police officer in our congregation said, 'leave security to me.' It must have been a rare situation, even in Northern Ireland, to have armed officers in the shadows to enable us to sing of the birth of the Prince of Peace. It was a memorable evening, concluding with the baptism of a baby boy. As I held the little one at the font, the convent school girls could resist no longer – and crept up and around me and his parents. It was a joyful opportunity for a very visible celebration of 'one faith, one baptism and one Lord'.

The worst that happened was a flag-bedecked car driving up and down past our church playing loud and offensive songs which were drowned out by wonderful singing from inside. For the next eighteen years Mr Bob Leonard, the head of music in Assumption, brought his choir to sing during Holy Week services in whatever church I happened to be.

One summer we enjoyed a pastoral exchange with a minister in Ohio. On my first Sunday back an anxious mother drew my attention to offensive graffiti on the wall opposite our church door with the much too familiar slogan linking the 'F' word with the Pope. Her little girl had asked her what that meant. Was there not something I could do about it?

From previous requests I knew that for reasons of safety the local council were reluctant to send workers to delete sectarian graffiti. So next day, with a half tin of red lead paint I armed myself with a ladder and a brush and started work on the offensive slogan.

Passersby commented on the weather and asked me had I enjoyed my 'holiday'. But nobody wanted to know what on earth I was doing up that ladder! Next day when I arrived at the church someone had re-directed the sentiment from the Holy Father to myself, for on the church door in bold letters was painted 'F… Rev. Good'.

Later, just before 'the Twelfth', the notice board bearing my name and phone number outside the church disappeared without trace or explanation. Until one evening a young loyalist with whom I had built a relationship on an occasional jog came to my door. Apologetically he produced the missing sign which he had rescued from the local bonfire. 'Bad and all as you are,' said he, 'I wouldn't let them do that to you!' High praise indeed!

While 'jogging' was not really my thing it had paid dividends in the building of an unlikely relationship of trust and respect.

Much to the distress of our children who had been so happy in Ballynahinch, it was decided that I should move to 'pastures new'. At our farewell the senior steward of the congregation confessed that when my name had been suggested for Ballynahinch the leadership protested that they had requested an 'evangelical' rather than an 'ecumenical' preacher. Turning to me he said, 'Thank you for being both, and helping us to discover that these terms are not mutually exclusive.'

I have often said if I got no other bouquet in my life, this is one that I will most cherish. For my understanding of 'evangelical' is from the Greek word *'euangelion'* which means 'the sharing of good news'. Which should never be confused with an unwholesome and divisive fundamentalism.

So in 1984 we were on the move again, this time to the leafy suburb of Knock in east Belfast, where my father had ministered in the early fifties and where I had spent several of my formative years.

This was a congregation that was largely untouched by the Troubles until a July morning in 1991 when the IPLO, a faction of the INLA, shot dead John McMaster, one of my parishioners, in his well-known tool shop in the centre of Belfast. It was a despicable murder, 'a barbarous act' as I described it at his funeral.

I told the media on the day of the murder that I wished I could take his killers to the McMaster family home where they would see that they had not only taken the life of a businessman 'but also the life of a family.' Like so many victims of our violent past, to this day John's widow, Muriel, bears her silent grief with dignity and with grace.

His killers claimed that John was in the security forces. In fact he was a member of the part-time Royal Naval Reserve that was in no way involved in dealing with the security situation. John would have worn his naval uniform on his way to and from the Reserve's headquarters on HMS *Caroline* in Belfast Harbour and it is thought that may have sealed his fate.

For me, following such atrocities too many had previously confused the political and the pastoral. So, at the funeral I first made an impassioned plea to the politicians 'to resume talks to find a new way which will allow us all to live together in peace'. And then, following a period of silent reflection, I made the call to worship. My separation of the two was appreciated by the family and other mourners.

Each congregation has its own distinctive features.

In Knock I recall truly wonderful Sunday morning worship enhanced by a splendid, robed choir that offered splendid anthems and led enthusiastic congregational singing of Wesleyan and other timeless hymns.

At that time it was largely a much younger community that we served. While challenging, I always enjoyed the enthusiastic participation by youngsters in our 'Time with the Children'. For me this weekly challenge was as important as the more adult sermon. No one can keep you on your toes like children! And frequent baptisms were also a source of hope and joy.

In response to concerns shared by some that many members of our large congregation were not more involved in mid-week activities, I noted how many of our members were making vital contributions to our wider society. Physicians, in practice and in academia, public servants, police officers of the highest rank and calibre, nurses, teachers, lawyers, dentists, business people sustaining commerce in the most difficult of circumstances, carers for the vulnerable in the voluntary as well as the public sector. They were all here. These were the people who having heard the Word on Sunday morning were the 'doers' of the Word in the real and very demanding world of Monday to Sunday.

This for me was the challenge as I prepared my sermons for each Sunday, not because my congregation was critical but because of the sense of responsibility I felt on my shoulders. Ever conscious of those lines from Milton who in his reference to preachers and sermons wrote of 'hungry sheep who look up, and are not fed …'.

One Sunday morning I looked down and noticed the familiar face of Norman Dugdale, Permanent Secretary of the Department of Health and Social Services. I had come to know Norman in the statutory and voluntary sectors on which I had served or chaired. As well as one of the most highly respected and formidable civil servants, Norman was a classical Greek scholar, a thinker and a poet of no mean standing.

It was a rare Sunday when Norman and his wife, the gifted artist Mary Dugdale, were not in their pew. Knowing of his intellect and his high expectations of his colleagues and staff within the DHSS, could I fulfil his expectations from the pulpit? I was truly humbled when invariably Norman would pause on the church steps to thank me for what he had found to be particularly helpful in the service. Again, confirming my realisation that this was a congregation committed to putting their faith to work rather than 'wearing it on their sleeves' or spending time in wearisome discussion and debate.

While there were obvious socio-economic differences from previous communities I had served, the pastoral needs and opportunities were no different. No less demanding but no less satisfying, only much greater numbers.

Of course there were challenges and at times disagreements. But the remarkable and ever wise Sydney Callaghan, who tutored us in our pastoral practice, counselled 'when you find yourself in a difficult relationship, see it as a pastoral opportunity rather than an invitation to a third world war'.

I am greatly saddened when I hear stories of ministerial stress and strain. I can only say that for me every day was a joy and a privilege. But as I am so often reminded, back then was a different day. With rare exception we were not 'competing' in the ecclesiastical marketplace with new and alternative expressions of church. Nor with the expectations of a younger generation for what is known as 'contemporary' worship.

For me every act of worship must be contemporary, whatever about its style of music. Sadly what so often goes under the heading of 'contemporary' majors on individual salvation with scant reference to the world to which we return after church. I very much like the wording I noted on the notice board of a Methodist church in Texas, inviting people to share in 'Timeless worship for a contemporary world'.

In addition to my pastoral responsibilities within my congregations, since my time in Corrymeela I found myself serving or chairing committees in the statutory or voluntary sectors. I accepted invitations to do so because I believed such public service enabled me to descend from my pulpit to gain a deeper understanding of the community to which I desired to speak and serve.

Realising that much of my time was devoted to some of these 'extra-curricular' responsibilities I asked my Leaders in Knock to tell me if they felt I was devoting too much time outside of my strictly 'parish' duties. Their response was: 'We are pleased that you are involved in all of these things. For we know that this helps you better understand the world in which we live and work.' I found this to be as affirming as it was gratifying.

One of my most pleasant memories in Knock is of renewing my friendship with Chris Patten, (now Lord Patten of Barnes), arguably the best prime minister the UK never had. Nor did he get the chance to shine as Secretary of State for Northern Ireland.

I first got to know Chris at a very personal level when he was a splendid direct rule minister responsible for health and social services. We enjoyed opportunities for conversation on many themes and topics. As a practising Christian in the Roman Catholic tradition we shared an understanding of the relationship of faith to public policy and practice.

It was following his time in the Northern Ireland Office that Chris was appointed Minister for International Development and then to the Cabinet as Environment Secretary. I was delighted when he accepted my invitation to return to Northern Ireland to preach at our annual Methodist World Development Service. In thanking him for his address I presented him with mine: a carved wooden sign reading 'No. 1 on the Green Road', the postal address of our Knock Manse. He assured me that as Secretary of State for the Environment he would proudly hang it on his office wall.

For us, Chris Patten's lasting legacy must surely be his report which laid the basis for necessary and fundamental policing reform in Northern Ireland. I find it interesting how police services and justice departments from other countries look to the Patten Report for inspiration and as a model for good policing, not least in America. As I write I am deeply concerned by the crisis in policing following the leaks of sensitive data and the impact this may have on the religious composition of the service, as well as community confidence.

In keeping with Methodist practice at that time, eight years was the normal maximum stay for a 'circuit' minister. So after a moving farewell service in Knock we packed once more and headed for my next appointment, to the Belfast South Circuit, which consisted of two churches. The historic mid-Victorian grade B listed University Road church designed by William J. Barre with its distinctive Italian bell tower and the 'daughter' church on the Lisburn Road which had been built to provide for the new community which came to that part of Belfast at the height of the industrial boom.

With the changing demography of south Belfast our congregations were declining, as were other Protestant denominations. However, in my new congregations we found the most wonderfully faithful, welcoming and thoughtful people. But there were few younger families and no sign of new arrivals to replace those going to their eternal reward.

It became increasingly obvious to me and to leadership in both churches that the future of these congregations lay together. So it was that we began to build a positive and trusting relationship between the two congregations that laid the foundation for a united congregation.

Not an easy transition for a loyal and loving people in both places. But the University Road church with its fine architectural design and honourable history was in a poor state of repair with an estimate of £1m to properly restore it. So it was, that after much soul-searching it was decided to build a new complex and worship centre on the Lisburn Road site which came happily to fruition in my successor's time with the development and opening of the imaginative and multi-functional Agápē Centre.

The University Road church was sold to a developer prior to the 'property crash' and sadly remains unoccupied. A sad sight which I try not to look at when I drive past.

With smaller congregations and a part-time chaplaincy at the City Hospital there was plenty to do, but I still found time to be involved in the developing 'peace and reconciliation' focus of my ministry which I describe elsewhere in these pages. And what happy relationships we enjoyed with local congregations of other denominations, with united services to celebrate major Christian festivals and events. It was a particularly special occasion when, along with the clergy of Fisherwick Presbyterian and St Thomas's parish churches and others, we presented gifts on behalf of our congregations to Monsignor Ambrose Macaulay, parish priest of St Brigid's, and his congregation at the opening of their beautiful new sanctuary on Derryvolgie Avenue. As Methodists, our gift was a beautiful red leather-bound lectern Bible.

It was in my penultimate year on this circuit that I was honoured by my election as the President of the Methodist Church in Ireland. And what a privileged as well as an exacting year that proved to be.

8

'A People Called Methodists': Who and What We Seek To Be

'Be friends of everyone. Be enemies of no-one.'
Charles Wesley

Following the IRA ceasefire of 31 August 1994, the Methodist Church was the first of the main churches to meet openly with Gerry Adams. As a member of our church's Council on Social Responsibility I was part of that meeting, which took place on 22 November 1994 in the Methodist Chaplaincy in Elmwood Avenue. If passers-by were curious, Adams' 'trademark' black taxi would have provided a clue as to with whom we were meeting.

In furtherance of our commitment to engage with people and parties across the political spectrum this meeting was followed by further conversations with David Ervine of the Progressive Unionist Party and Peter Smyth of the Political Affairs Division of the Northern Ireland Office. In his minute of our meeting with him, Peter Smyth records: 'In Good's account, it was clear that Adams automatically identified the churchmen as unionists red tooth and claw, and as Paisleyites under a slightly different flag.'¹² Whilst I don't recall Gerry Adams using these words, this is Smyth's account of my conversation with him.

And while we are somewhat surprised at Gerry Adams' interpretation of our conversation on that day we note that fifteen years later in a discussion with Gay Byrne on RTÉ's *The Meaning of Life* programme Adams said, 'I think the Methodists are the best.'¹³

These meetings with Gerry Adams and David Ervine are merely examples of the multitude of meetings and conversations which we held at all levels at various stages, including with Senator George Mitchell and General John de Chastelain – on the decommissioning issue – and with the perceptive and innovative Dr Majorie 'Mo' Mowlam, during her time both as opposition Northern Ireland spokesperson and as Secretary of State. The official minute of one of our early meetings with Mowlam as Secretary of State for Northern Ireland, in August 1997, records her appreciation for 'the day-to-day work carried out by all of the Methodist representatives and their honesty and positive contribution.'¹⁴

In Chapter 10 I refer to a letter I received from the Rev. Ian Paisley in response to our Methodist 'Open Letter' with a plea to party leaders to 'urgently seek a mutually acceptable way of working together to secure the peace.' In his unexpected reply Paisley wrote on 1 March 1996 , 'I should be grateful if you could give some explanation and clarification of this statement. Do you suggest that democratic constitutional politicians should work together with Sinn Féin/IRA and if so how would you suggest this should be done?' Perhaps this was the first indication that he was prepared to listen to any of the churches of which he was entirely critical.

In quoting these examples of our 'outreach', I must stress that we were by no means the only church or faith community involved in such conversations. Nor would I wish to suggest any sense of spiritual or ecclesiastical superiority. I am acutely conscious of those times when we as Methodists, individually and as a denomination, have failed to live up to what we declare ourselves to have been called to be. For such moments in our history and in our personal witness we ask forgiveness.

But I am often asked what, if anything, makes Methodism different from other Christian traditions and why were we taken so seriously by players as diverse as Adams and Paisley?

For those who wonder who and what we are and from where we have come, historically and theologically, let me seek to shine some light on the characteristics which have shaped our thinking and our particular contribution in our shared efforts to make this corner of the world a better, more just and more peaceful place.

As with all other movements and organisations, ecclesiastical or secular, to understand Methodism requires an understanding of the historical context into which it was born. For that was in mid-eighteenth century England with its widening social gaps accelerated by the industrial revolution and the alienation of the masses from the established Church as well as the state.

It was into this social and spiritual vacuum that there rode a horseback preacher by the name of John Wesley. He was an ordained minister of the Church of England who, following a long period of spiritual doubt and disillusionment, had a very personal and profound experience of spiritual renewal which he could only describe as having had his heart 'strangely warmed'.

Originally the label 'Methodists' was a nickname given to Wesley and his friends at Oxford who were observed to be meticulously 'methodical' in their practice of prayer and study. And the label stuck.

A study of the extraordinary life and ministry of Wesley reveals how 'methodical' this man must have been to have accomplished what he did. Rising each day at 4.30 a.m., it is recorded that he travelled on average 4,500 miles per year, preached 42,000 sermons in market squares and churches and wrote or edited 450 books, many of them quite literally 'on the hoof'.

This was the beginning of a movement within and well beyond the boundaries of England and the established Church from which Wesley and his brother Charles did not wish to separate. It was only after his death that the Methodist movement separated from the Church of England and became a denomination in its own right. While a minority in Ireland, it is part of a worldwide communion of 80 million adherents.

It is an ongoing and remarkable story, well recorded in volumes of secular as well as Church history. For it was as Wesley and his preachers travelled across these islands with their message of God's unbounded grace for all that the 'disregarded' people of that time began to find a new confidence in themselves and a new purpose in living. All of which had a dramatic impact on eighteenth century society as well as upon the transformed lives of individuals and their families.

But first and foremost, Wesley was an unapologetic evangelist, proclaiming the 'unsearchable riches of Christ' as understood in the reformed tradition. When speaking of this period of history as the evangelical revival of the eighteenth century, the term 'evangelical' must not be confused with negative and potentially destructive 'fundamentalism' as preached and practised by ultra-conservative right-wing extremists in the United States and elsewhere. Fundamentalism in any form, be it religious or political, is one of the most serious threats to the good ordering of society as well as to a proper understanding of the joyful 'good news' as revealed to us in the life and teaching of Christ. The two must never be confused. For in its purest form 'evangelical' is derived from the Greek word *euangelion*, which literally means 'good news', as I explained in the previous chapter.

It was this good news that Wesley and his preachers sought to proclaim, travelling by horseback and by coach across these islands he took this good news out of the protected sanctuary of the church building to wherever people would gather. Be it at a crossroads, in a market square or under an old oak tree. As a meticulous and disciplined diarist Wesley's journals contain a remarkable record of those journeys as well as a commentary on the social and religious context in which he preached.

As was said of Jesus, 'the common people heard him gladly' and in spite of opposition from predictable sections of both church and society the movement grew with the formation of 'societies' where people would gather for 'methodical' study of the scriptures, prayer and fellowship, while at Wesley's insistence remaining within the Anglican Church, particularly for their attendance at the sacraments.

'A People Called Methodists': Who and What We Seek To Be

The message was simple. It can be summarised into what Wesley himself described as 'The Four Alls' of Methodism. Not to be confused with a public house by that name in County Cork!

These 'Four Alls' can be summarised as:

1. The need of ALL people for personal salvation
2. Which is freely offered and available to ALL
3. Of which ALL can be personally assured
4. With no limitations as to what God can do in the life of ALL

To understand the radical, all-embracing, transforming impact of this message we need to imagine how it would have been received in mid-eighteenth century Britain. Particularly among the much less privileged classes who felt themselves to be excluded by the establishment in both church and society.

As the late Rev. Norman Taggart, a former President of the Irish Methodist Church, once wrote:

> They [the 'Four Alls'] provide a popular and useful summary of Methodist belief … The repeated word 'all' is a code word in Methodism, occurring frequently in a variety of settings as a reminder that openness and inclusiveness are central elements in the movement's mission. The use of 'all' in connection with the need, acceptance, knowledge, and quality of salvation, draws attention to God's grace at every turning.

It is this inclusive understanding of 'grace' which is at the heart of Wesleyan/Methodist theology. Influenced by the seventeenth century Dutch theologian Jacobus Arminius, the basic doctrines of Arminianism stand in contrast to the restrictive tenets of strict Calvinism with its emphasis on 'election' and 'pre-destination'.[vii] These beliefs,

---

[vii] Arminianism is described in *Encyclopaedia Britannica* as 'a theological movement in Protestant Christianity that arose as a liberal reaction to the Calvinist doctrine of predestination.'

together with what reputable theologians will claim to be a mis-reading of biblical references to a 'chosen people', have had negative social and political consequences in places as geographically distant as South Africa, the Southern States of America and Northern Ireland.

But as well as an *evangelist*, Wesley was a *radical social reformer*. Emphatic in his assertion that 'The gospel of Christ knows of no religion but social religion; no holiness but social holiness', his passion for social justice extended from the founding of schools for the poorest to his vigorous opposition to slavery. As an ardent supporter of abolition, he argued his case in his book *Thoughts Upon Slavery*, in which he exposed and denounced the evils of slavery upon which was built so much of the wealth of the British Empire. And as a prolific writer of letters, the last recorded letter Wesley wrote was to William Wilberforce, in which he denounced slavery as 'the sum of all villainies' and 'the vilest that ever saw the sun'.

The impact of this 'twin approach' to the gospel upon the social life of England is regarded by many secular historians as one of the factors which saved England from a similar fate as that which engulfed neighbouring France in the Revolution of 1789.

For an empowered, socially disenfranchised people, having learned how to preach and pray and sing lustily the hymns of Charles Wesley, were now finding a 'political' voice for the first time.

This is well illustrated in the history of Christian socialism, the founding of the Trade Union movement and in stories such as that of the Tolpuddle Martyrs in Dorset. It was former Prime Minister Harold Wilson who argued that the Labour movement owed more to Methodism than to Marxism.

And to this day the working out of Wesley's emphasis on social holiness is seen in the Methodist city missions established in towns and cities on these islands and around the world. Such as the Dublin Central Mission, the North Belfast Mission, the pioneering work of the Grosvenor Hall in central Belfast, the East Belfast Skainos Centre and the North West Mission in 'Derry.

Not forgetting that it was a Methodist preacher by the name of William Booth who was to become the founder of the now global ministry of the Salvation Army. And it was in 1869 that a Methodist minister, the Rev. Thomas Stephenson, founded The National Children's Home, now Action for Children, to become one of the first and still among the largest children's charities across these islands.

And for our founder the provision of education was also a priority, with his first school in Bath to provide for the underprivileged children of miners. In Ireland our schools and colleges include Methodist College Belfast, Wesley College in Dublin and the much acclaimed Gurteen College in Co. Tipperary, which encourages young people to stay on the land by providing them with the most up-to-date knowledge and expertise. While children and young people who attend these schools may not be underprivileged as were the miners' children at Kingswood, Methodist schools, colleges and universities are to be found across the globe with a strong commitment to provide opportunity for education for both rich and poor.

It was John Wesley's brother Charles, the prolific writer of hymns, who exhorted the Methodist people to be 'the friends of all and the enemies of no-one.' In other words, faith must not be confined to the pulpit or thought of as a solitary pursuit but as a demonstration of one's love of God and one's neighbour by striving for the good of those in need and in places of conflict advocating for peace.

Historically, that anti or non-establishment facet of Methodism invested it with a certain independence which at one time put distance between it and the established Anglican Church. While that has now radically changed, as seen in the happy formal covenant between the Methodist Church in Ireland and the Church of Ireland, Methodists have a particular understanding of what it means to be excluded from establishments, political and ecclesiastical.

And as a smaller church in Ireland, Methodism has also an understanding of what it means to be a minority, having an empathy with the feelings and fears of other minorities and those who have felt excluded, marginalised or misunderstood. And as a minority we are not perceived as a threat by larger denominations or indeed by political interests.

Another defining characteristic of Methodism is its embrace of ecumenism, both in its outreach to other Reformed denominations and, crucially, to Roman Catholics.

This ecumenical outreach to our Catholic sisters and brothers owes much to John Wesley's historic *Letter to a Roman Catholic*, written in Dublin in July 1749. This was during the anti-Methodist riots in Cork fomented by a Roman Catholic attention-seeker with at best the acquiescence of senior Anglicans hostile to Methodist preachers and some 80 years before the seminal Roman Catholic Relief or Emancipation Act of 1829.

Notwithstanding his long-held criticism of aspects of Catholic theology his *Letter* is rightly regarded as one of the most daring ecumenical gestures in history, coming as it did long before either the word or the idea of ecumenism took hold.

In this letter he speaks of the 'true, primitive Christianity' that Methodists and Catholics share, asking 'can nothing be done, even allowing us on both sides to retain our own opinions, for the softening of our hearts towards each other, the giving a check to this flood of unkindness, and restoring at least some small degree of love among our neighbours and countrymen?'

He said that 'God being our helper' Catholics and Methodists should resolve 'to speak nothing harsh or unkind of each other'. He told Catholics: 'I hope to see you in heaven.' And 'If your heart be as my heart, give me your hand.'

In his homily in the Methodist Church in Rome marking the 300th anniversary of Wesley's birth, Cardinal Walter Kasper reminded his hearers of Wesley's invitation to Methodists and Catholics 'to help each other on in whatever we are agreed leads to the Kingdom' and his proposal that 'if we cannot as yet think alike in all things, at least we may love alike.'

What is distinctive about that letter is that it is totally free of party-political interpretation and therefore cannot be used to underpin or justify the religious and/or political fundamentalism which plagues our world of today. Like most of Wesley's homilies and writings it reflects the essential Gospel, pure and simple, which is about building God's kingdom of love and justice on this earth.

Objective observers have suggested that it is this combination of historical factors and a ministry based on an uncomplicated Gospel that has enabled a minority Church to be trusted as 'ice breakers', mediators and peacemakers. As has been said by some commentators, 'to punch above our weight.'

In 1966 our Methodist Conference was held in Dublin, against the background of growing tension in Northern Ireland and growing opposition to the reforming inclinations of Prime Minister Terence O'Neill, with republican celebrations marking the fiftieth anniversary of the Easter Rising and Ian Paisley's anti-ecumenical protest outside the Presbyterian General Assembly that resulted in his imprisonment.

Some historians have identified 1966 as the onset of the Troubles. The early summer of that year saw three killings by the UVF in Belfast and the unprecedented use of the Special Powers Act (heretofore only deployed against nationalists) by O'Neill to proscribe that organisation.

Significantly, in that year our Conference rose to the occasion in unanimously passing a detailed and comprehensive biblically based resolution entitled 'A Call to the Methodist People – The Present Situation in Ireland'.

How different our subsequent history could have been had the words of that resolution been heeded by all involved in our conflict.

It spoke *inter alia* of how the New Testament draws attention to:

- 'The necessity to safeguard and witness to the faith'
- 'The obligation to maintain and live out the Christian doctrine of love and reconciliation'
- 'The call to promote the just society'
- 'The onus on the civil powers to uphold justice and righteousness'

The resolution went on to declare that 'the obligation to love demands that we demonstrate to our neighbours of whatever faith, to our opponents as well as to our friends, those qualities of love which were found in Christ.'

And that 'any form of injustice, inequality or discrimination, based on creed, race, or colour is contrary to God's Will,' stressing 'the requirement for everyone to obey the civil powers and duly constituted authorities.'

Such was the urgency of the situation, the Conference directed that the resolution 'be read and spoken to in every place of worship on the Sunday following the Conference or as soon as possible thereafter.'

Furthermore, the resolution was printed and published by our Church in an eight-page pamphlet and widely circulated throughout our congregations.

The person drafting and driving forward that resolution was Rev. Eric Gallagher, the Conference secretary and superintendent of Belfast Central Mission, to whom I have referred elsewhere in these pages.

Such words from a church conference may seem unremarkable today but at the time they broke new ground for at that time we were more outspoken than most. And it was consistent with this Methodist perspective that the same Eric Gallagher was the first person to publicly advocate the sharing of Cabinet power in Northern Ireland on the basis of party strengths after a PR election, at a conference in Edinburgh in November 1971.[15] In the same month he met leaders of the Provisional IRA at their request in Dundalk when they asked him to convey a message to then opposition leader Harold Wilson – for onward transmission to then Prime Minister Edward Heath – that they were ready to contemplate a ceasefire and were flexible about a date for British withdrawal.[16]

Fast forward to December 1974 when Eric Gallagher and fellow Methodists Stanley Worrall, lay preacher and former headmaster of Methodist College and the Rev. Harry Morton, of the British Methodist Church; together with the Clerk of the General Assembly of the Presbyterian Church in Ireland, Rev. Dr Jack Weir; Church of Ireland

Bishop of Connor, Dr Arthur Butler; Rev. Ralph Baxter, Secretary of the Irish Council of Churches; Canon William Arlow, deputy secretary of the ICC; and Rev. Arthur MacArthur, Moderator of the General Assembly of the United Reformed Church in England and Wales, met secretly with the leadership of the Provisional IRA in Smyth's Hotel, Feakle, Co. Clare.

But in the middle of serious engagement the meeting was abruptly halted when the IRA leaders were tipped off that the Irish Special Branch were about to pounce.

However, it was not without significance that PIRA did call a temporary ceasefire over the following Christmas period. Was this a respectful gesture towards those with whom they had engaged? Or was it a sign of what could be achieved in the event of further talks?

Inevitably, there were both political and church voices raised in anger and criticism of this initiative. But Eric Gallagher was greatly moved by the positive response of his Grosvenor Hall congregation following worship on the following Sunday.

THE ANGLO-IRISH AGREEMENT 1985 AND BEYOND

For those of us struggling with the things which might make for peace there was to be a new challenge in the aftermath of the November 1985 Anglo-Irish Agreement that for the first time gave the Republic an official say in the governance of Northern Ireland.

Unionists felt betrayed by Mrs Thatcher and her government and condemned it outright. There were violent protests on the streets and numerous attacks on the homes of RUC officers in the months that followed.

While in no way supportive of such protests, Methodists were also divided in their response to the Agreement. So, in our quintessentially methodical way our Church's Council on Social Responsibility, co-chaired by the Rev. Sydney Callaghan and Professor Desmond Rea, carefully critiqued the Agreement clause by clause and presented a balanced and nuanced report to our Conference. It was a report that contrasted with so much of the rancorous political commentary that dominated the media and epitomised that distinctive Methodist approach for which we had become known.

It said the Council 'has been conscious of its paramount duty to seek and to set forth the mind and will of God as revealed in Jesus Christ. The Christian's first duty must always be to Christ. All other loyalties – whether denominational or political – are relative.'

'Methodists', it said, 'pride themselves on being "the friends of all and the enemies of none". As such we owe it to ourselves and to those we call friends, and they are all the people of Ireland, to study the Agreement with the utmost care and objectivity and always in the light of what Jesus taught and died for.'

It concluded: 'The Agreement is now a fact of life and history … it is also a fact of international life and recognized as such in the world of international affairs.'

And not anticipating the chicanery of Boris Johnson it continued: 'International treaties entered into after long months of delicate diplomacy and registered at the United Nations are not changed or abrogated overnight.'

It would take more than twelve years before the Anglo-Irish Agreement would be superseded by the Good Friday Agreement.

In reporting the contribution of the Methodist Council on Social Responsibility much credit must be given to successive lay secretaries, two of whom were to play significant roles in the wider socio-political life of Northern Ireland. I refer to my classmate Sir Desmond Rea, founding chair of the Northern Ireland Policing Board, and Sir Nigel Hamilton, who was to become head of the Northern Ireland Civil Service.

It is also worth noting the key role played by Methodist laymen who participated in the small denominationally mixed and visionary Northern Consensus Group. The Methodist members of this group included Desmond Rea, Professor Bob Stout and the lawyer John Neill. Other key members included Terence Donaghy, an open-hearted

Catholic lawyer and another solicitor, David Hewitt, a Presbyterian and former Ireland and Lions rugby star. We must be grateful to all of them for their insight and wisdom.

It was this group who were responsible for the drawing up of the five crucial principles which ultimately, without recognition or acknowledgement of the source, were at the heart of the Good Friday Agreement of 1998.

Those principles were:

- No change in Northern Ireland's membership of the UK unless a majority agrees.
- The responsibility of government must be shared between the two traditions.
- The institutions of government must reflect the different traditions.
- All must give full support for the law, impartially enacted and administered.
- All must renounce violence as a means towards political ends.

Initially these principles were published in the three Belfast newspapers as early as September 1982, following which they were unanimously adopted and publicly promoted by the Methodist Conference, meeting in Belfast. They were also at the heart of our church's evidence to the New Ireland Forum in 1983 and later published in the pamphlet *Northern Ireland – Untying the Knot*.

As a worldwide community of 80 million people who identify as Methodists, 'peacemaking' has been central to the mission of Methodism. In the late 1970s the World Methodist Council instituted a World Methodist Peace Award. The intention was to acknowledge the efforts of men and women, of all faiths and of none, who had made a significant contribution to the work of peace and justice. As I read down the list of recipients I am astonished as well as humbled to find my own name amongst such iconic figures as Jimmy Carter, Mikhail Gorbachev, Kofi Annan and Nelson Mandela.

But amongst them are names of lesser known but equally heroic 'warriors' for peace and justice. The first recipient was 'our own' Saidie Patterson from Belfast's Shankill Road. As a dogged social activist it was Saidie who confronted the injustices and the exploitation of young women 'slaving' in the mills of Belfast. In 1940 she led 2,000 Protestant and Catholic women on a strike which lasted seven weeks, achieving better working conditions, a 33 per cent rise in wages, paid holidays and maternity leave. As a respected and active trade unionist, Saidie worked tirelessly to bring Protestant and Catholic workers together in the ongoing struggle for justice in the workplace and was a founder member of 'Women Together', a strident organisation demanding and working for peace. As a faithful Methodist it is entirely appropriate that Saidie and her work for peace and justice is commemorated in a coveted 'Blue Plaque' on the gable wall of Shankill Road Methodist Church.

While most of those who have been honoured have not been Methodists, amongst them was another Irish Methodist, Gordon Wilson. As someone who never sought the limelight, 'the wee draper from Enniskillen', as he described himself, Gordon was catapulted to national and international prominence in the most tragic of circumstances imaginable.

I first knew Gordon when my father was Minister of Darling Street Methodist Church in Enniskillen, where Gordon and his wife, Joan, were devoted members, and to which Joan brought her very special gift of music. I remember Gordon for his genuine warmth, his generosity to me as a young student and his rich sense of humour.

It was on Remembrance Sunday, 8 November 1987, that Gordon and his beloved 20-year-old daughter, Marie, a student nurse, gathered with fellow citizens of Enniskillen at the town's Cenotaph to remember those who died in two world wars.

In a moment of unspeakable horror an IRA bomb exploded, killing eleven Protestant civilians and injuring 63 others at the time. As Marie and Gordon lay under the rubble, Marie's hand found her dad's hand

and as she lay fatally wounded her last words to him were 'Daddy, I love you very much.' She died a few hours later in hospital.

That evening, at his home, in response to a question from Mike Gaston, a BBC radio reporter, Gordon said:

> The hospital was magnificent, truly impressive, and we shall miss her. But I bear no ill will, I bear no grudge. Dirty sort of talk is not going to bring her back to life. She was a great wee lassie. She loved her profession. She was a pet. Don't ask me, please, for a purpose. I don't have a purpose. I don't have an answer. But I know there has to be a plan. If I didn't think that, I would commit suicide. It's part of a great plan, and God is good. And we shall meet again.

As historian Jonathan Bardon correctly recounts, 'No words in more than 25 years of violence in Northern Ireland had such a powerful emotional impact.' The impact upon Her late Majesty Queen Elizabeth II was such that she made reference to them the following month in her Christmas message to the nation and to the Commonwealth. But what could not have been expected was the impact of his words in the most unlikely quarters.

In a BBC series entitled *Defining Moments*, well-known people were asked to tell of a most defining moment in their lives. One of whom was Danny Morrison, a leading republican and former director of publicity for Sinn Féin. As he spoke of the Enniskillen atrocity he recounted how, upon hearing the words of Gordon Wilson, he could no longer be an apologist for the actions of the IRA. I wondered if I had heard him correctly, did he really mean what he had said? I sought an opportunity to ask him directly and he confirmed that I had indeed heard him correctly.

As a chaplain at the City Hospital in Belfast I visited a patient in the secure room where prisoners were held. I was fascinated to note that spread out on his bed were notebooks, Bibles and study guides. Noticing my surprise he explained that he was studying for a diploma in Biblical Studies via a correspondence course. As an IRA volunteer he had been personally involved in one of the most heinous atrocities of the Troubles, causing the deaths of several people. But listening to the words of Gordon Wilson he consciously turned his back on all that had gone before, repented of what he had done, sought forgiveness and committed himself to following the way of Christ.

Having been nurtured in his faith in the small congregation of people called Methodists in County Leitrim, Gordon took his faith seriously and in the truest evangelical sense Gordon and Joan were witnesses to that faith and the amazing grace which sustained them.

Inevitably there were those who neither understood nor appreciated Gordon's words, for which he was heavily criticised by some, but both he and Joan made it very clear that they totally understood how difficult their response might be for others who had suffered grief and injury in this or other atrocities. And in no way would they suggest that those who had difficulty with their response to their tragedy were any less worthy than they.

When Gordon died suddenly of a heart attack in June 1995 at the age of 67, I made the journey to Enniskillen to attend his funeral service in Darling Street Methodist Church. It was attended by the 'great and the good' from both sides of the border, including the President of Ireland and the Secretary of State for Northern Ireland.

Following the service there was the customary invitation to share refreshments and friendship in the adjoining hall. As usual, people gathered in groups in conversation with friends and colleagues they already knew. When looking for a familiar face I noticed a lone figure in a corner whom I recognised as Mitchel McLaughlin, then chairman of Sinn Féin, obviously there to represent his party. Given the circumstances, it must have taken much thought as well as considerable courage for him to attend this service. I also understood why nobody was rushing to greet him.

In response to an inner pastoral prompt to speak with anyone on their own, I introduced myself and engaged in conversation. As we sat balancing our cups on our knees it was an uneasy conversation for both of us, given the sensitivities of the situation. I asked if he had heard that morning's 'Thought for the Day' on BBC Radio Ulster, in which the Rev. Eric Gallagher recalled Gordon's bitter disappointment that his meeting with the IRA leadership had been a wasted journey. They had not wanted to hear what he had to say.

Mitchel McLaughlin replied by assuring me that this was not the case and that if Gordon believed that he wasn't heeded it was regrettable that he had not known of the influence he had exerted before his sudden and untimely death.

I parted from Mitchel McLaughlin with the suggestion that we should continue our conversation, to which he readily agreed. This was to be the beginning of a friendship and a 'working relationship' over the years that were to follow that has resulted in many honest and fruitful conversations. Some of them in his impressive office at Stormont when he was Speaker of the Assembly, where, as I sipped tea from an ornate china cup, I thought of our first conversation in a corner of the Methodist Church Hall in Enniskillen when another door had been opened.

When I received the astonishing news that I was to receive the World Methodist Peace Award — referenced earlier — I thought of all those with whom I had walked and talked and engaged during these long and 'war weary' years. It was at the award ceremony that I had opportunity to explain that I was but the 'captain' or 'manager' of a remarkable team and that I was honoured to accept the award on their behalf.

Elsewhere in these pages I write about my invitation to lunch with Her Majesty Queen Elizabeth II where I was particularly privileged to have been seated next to her. After we left the table I found myself with other guests in conversation with the Duke of Edinburgh who confused us with his comment, 'I suppose you don't eat like that every day'. Was he suggesting that we were underprivileged and underfed or was this a more elaborate lunch than we might normally consume? I ventured to break the embarrassed silence by saying that indeed it was but that we had thoroughly enjoyed it and did not feel in any way guilty. To which His Royal Highness replied, 'You don't feel guilty, that's interesting coming from you.'

'Not in the least,' said I, and went on to say that it was those sad puritans who felt guilty about enjoying themselves. 'But are not Methodists puritans?' he replied. 'Gosh no,' said I, 'please don't confuse us with those miserable puritans, as Methodists we are the joyful people. On great state occasions I have seen you singing one of our best loved Methodist hymns, *Love divine, all loves excelling, JOY of heaven to earth come down!*' I was greatly relieved when one of my fellow guests came to my aid by voicing her approval and agreement. Wisely I left it at that as he and I raised our coffee cups to each other in an obvious 'game, set and match' agreement. Here was I, an apologist for Methodism in the Queen's drawing room, arguing my case with her husband. But I could only speak from my experience of the tradition in which I had been nurtured and privileged to serve.

9

DECOMMISSIONING: A WITNESS TO HISTORY

'There goes the last gun out of Irish politics.'

Fr Alec Reid

It was on a pleasant September morning in 2005 that I found myself standing in a totally unfamiliar rural and isolated location, out of sight and out of sound from any neighbouring properties. My family and friends would have had good reason to wonder what on earth I was doing there, dressed uncharacteristically in a boiler suit and wellington boots. But they would not have known where I was, nor did I. I only knew that I was somewhere on the island of Ireland and that I was about to witness one of the most historic events in the long running story of Irish conflict and politics.

This was the first day of decommissioning of the remaining arsenal of IRA weapons hidden in various dumps around the country and within the constraints of confidentiality I will share what I can of my role in this process.

It all began when my home phone rang on the evening of Thursday, 18 November 2004. I remember the date for it was my daughter

Sharon's birthday. The caller was Aidan McAteer, a close adviser and confidant of Martin McGuinness.

As I went to answer it, I was not to know that this phone call was to have such an impact on my life. For that call was to trigger a chain of events that saw me becoming a witness to history.

The multifarious background to my account of the final decommissioning of the weaponry of the IRA has been well documented in greater detail by others. But in summary, the decommissioning of all weapons held by both republican and loyalist paramilitaries was a key component within the Belfast Good Friday Agreement of April 1998. While there was much reluctance and procrastination on the part of some, ultimately the crucial question was not 'whether' but 'how?'

Given the bloody history of our conflict the decommissioning of IRA weapons was not an unreasonable demand by unionists, although it remained a considerable challenge for all paramilitary groups, loyalist as well as republican. But it was of republicans that most was demanded in this area if the peace process was to go forward. For, unlike Sinn Féin, none of the loyalist political parties linked to paramilitaries commanded sufficient electoral support to qualify for a seat in the Stormont Executive or Cabinet.

It was the failure to resolve this exasperating issue in the early years after the Good Friday Agreement that fatally undermined the late Ulster Unionist leader, First Minister David Trimble and led to the collapse of power-sharing in October 2002 with the re-imposition of direct rule from Westminster when John Reid, the Northern Ireland Secretary of State, suspended the institutions for a fourth and final time. And with what was seen as failure on the part of David Trimble, the Democratic Unionist Party leader Ian Paisley became the unassailable leader of Unionism.

Interestingly, it was not the issue of decommissioning by itself that led to the return of direct rule – rather a bizarre development quickly dubbed 'Stormontgate' that appeared out of the blue. This referred to a police raid on Sinn Féin's Stormont offices, allegations of a Provisional IRA intelligence gathering operation at the heart of government, and a series of arrests, including the arrest of Denis Donaldson, the head of the party's administration in Parliament Buildings, who it turned out had been a paid British agent over a period of twenty years.

Denis Donaldson, who eventually was murdered in a lonely hideaway in Donegal, was a person whom I had come to know in various conversations, or so I thought. While I was always intrigued by him, I do have to say I was more than a little wary. Somehow he smiled just a little too much.

But a particularly memorable meeting with him took place in New York where he was heading up the Friends of Sinn Féin Group in the US. As Chair of the Northern Ireland Association for the Care and Resettlement of Offenders (NIACRO) with our director, Dave Wall, I happened to be in New York for a series of meetings. On our final night we were invited to a gathering of interested Irish-Americans, hosted by Denis Donaldson in a pub in Lower Manhattan known as Mustang Sally's, a popular meeting place for Irish republicans.

We spoke openly and very directly about the way forward and the obvious need for decommissioning. I pursued the suggestion of an independent body of international standing which would facilitate and oversee the completion of decommissioning. Denis rubbished my ideas as being unrealistic. Little did I know what was coming down the road in my life and his.

The Good Friday Agreement had merely required the parties to 'reaffirm their commitment to the total disarmament of all paramilitary organisations' and to 'confirm their intention to continue to work constructively and in good faith with the Independent Commission, using any influence they might have, to achieve the decommissioning of all paramilitary arms within two years'.

This is what has been described as 'the constructive ambiguity' which miraculously helped to get the Agreement over the line on that Good Friday. While Unionists interpreted this as meaning that all IRA weapons had to be disposed of within two years of the North and South referendums of 22 May 1998, republicans believed that their political interests would be better served by stringing things out indefinitely.

This ambiguity enabled the IRA to hold off for three-and-a-half years before their first of four acts of decommissioning in October 2001. While it was a crossing of the Rubicon in physical force republican theology, it was insufficient for Ian Paisley and the DUP. Not unreasonably, they insisted that they could not engage with those who still 'had guns under the table'.

In spite of the intervention and efforts of internationally respected figures the issue of complete disarmament remained unsolved. To manage this process of decommissioning professionally, on a basis that would command the confidence of all the parties, the Independent International Commission on Decommissioning (IICD) was established in August 1997.

It had three internationally distinguished experts, General John de Chastelain, the Chairman from Canada; Brigadier Tauno Nieminen from Finland; and Ambassador Donald C. Johnson from the US, the latter being replaced in 1999 by another US diplomat, Andrew D. Sens.

Their job was clear. To oversee and carry out the effective destruction of IRA and loyalist weapons. But key to the success of the process was the devising of a methodology for the disposal of weapons that did not look like a surrender by republicans and cause a split in the republican movement.

The Rev. Ian Paisley's and his Democratic Unionist Party's (DUP) demand for photographic evidence of decommissioning was unacceptable to the IRA for many reasons, such as humiliation and the more obvious risk of identification of those involved.

So, in seeking an alternative process of verification which would command the confidence of people across the community, it was suggested that there be two independent witnesses, one a Protestant minister and another a Roman Catholic priest. While nobody is entirely sure where this idea originated, it has been suggested that it was the idea of the Rev. Ian Paisley who would have had his own idea as to who the Protestant witness might be.

Given Redemptorist priest Fr Alec Reid's significant role as an interlocutor between Gerry Adams, John Hume, and Taoiseach Albert Reynolds, it was generally assumed that he would be an obvious choice. By November 2004 there was much speculation as to who would be his Protestant counterpart

Many names were suggested in the media and elsewhere. Thankfully I was not one of them. Clearly, strict confidentiality was being maintained by the small number who needed to know about such a sensitive matter.[viii] Only that God-fearing Protestants were not supposed to place bets there would have been an interesting 'field' on which to place the odds! Who knows, perhaps some enterprising pundit did open a book.

Much later it was Ian Paisley himself who admitted to me that he had a particular minister in mind, the late Rev. David McGaughey, a former Presbyterian Moderator from Kilkeel, Co. Down. Had he had his way, Paisley told me, upon his return from the decommissioning exercise Rev. McGaughey would have publicly resigned from the Commission, relinquished his obligation to maintain a decent measure of confidentiality and would have told him all that he wanted to know, even in the absence of photographs.

Not getting the witness of his choice and not knowing until the official announcement that the final and conclusive act of decommissioning had taken place and that it was I who was 'the chosen one' does in part explain Paisley's initial reluctance to accept my role and

---

[viii] Brian Rowan, arguably the most informed journalist of the peace process, wrote in his book *Paisley and the Provos*, p.157: my name only publicly emerged when he broke the story on Sunday evening, 25 September 2005, the day before the official announcement of the IRA's final act of decommissioning.

his attempt to undermine my 'testimony'. That is until public opinion had clearly turned in my direction.

***

I recall the phone conversation with Aidan McAteer in November 2004 because it was my daughter Sharon's birthday, and I did jot down some thoughts in a personal journal that I kept intermittently, sensing that important developments were coming.

When Aidan told me in strictest confidence that Martin McGuinness would like to meet me the following day, Friday 19 November 2004, I suspected what it might be about. But genuinely I did not think that I would be the witness, rather that I was being asked for advice on who might be a suitable person. I actually had some suggestions in mind.

The following day, after that call from Aidan, I was driven to a discreet location in west Belfast for a conversation with Martin McGuinness.

My suspicions were correct, but the discussion was not about who I might suggest. As I recalled in my journal dated Friday 19th:

> Instead the request was direct. Would I agree to be the co-witness with Fr Alec Reid? DUP and SF are in intense negotiations with both [British and Irish] governments. While nothing [is] guaranteed a 'defining moment' was the phrase. Next weekend would be 'make or break' time. It appears that the two-clergy witness proposal has been accepted in principle by all concerned but the names will be suggested by Republicans. How will DUP react to my name? Would Paisley accept me as 'trustworthy'? It was assumed that since I have the trust of Jeffrey D [Donaldson] he – as a key player – will accept it as a good suggestion.

That evening in west Belfast I accepted Martin McGuinness's invitation, in principle, but made it clear that I would only be willing to be considered for this most sensitive of roles if I could be assured that I would be acceptable to all the parties involved, and especially to those who mattered in the unionist community. After all that David Trimble had been through over the decommissioning issue, the torrid criticism he had received from a large section of his own Ulster Unionist Party (UUP) and from the Democratic Unionist Party (DUP), they were the community that needed to be convinced.

I have been asked many times: why me? How come I was thought of to undertake such a sensitive and indeed important role. The likely answer is that my encounters with republicans going back 20 years gave them reason to believe I could be trusted. These encounters included informal dialogue in Corrymeela; a dialogue instigated by Pax Christi [Peace of Christ] and my more formal contact as a member of our Methodist Council on Social Responsibility. And there were the many very private conversations at my kitchen table with Martin McGuinness, Jeffrey Donaldson and others about which I speak in another chapter.[ix] Hopefully in these conversations I would have come across as someone who could be trusted, ready to listen while never flinching from asking the hard questions.

In seeking to be the 'friends of all and the enemies of none', as we are encouraged to be, that did not mean we accepted the violence which had blighted our country and caused so much hurt. But neither did we indulge in the kind of ritual condemnation that had the effect of shutting doors and obstructing dialogue, which would take us nowhere.

But whatever some sceptical Protestants might think, on paper I had all the right credentials. As well as being a senior church leader I had twice been honoured by the Queen and was a direct descendent of Dan Winter in whose cottage it was decided to form the Orange Order. If known, I was also the grandson of a signatory to the Ulster Covenant of 1912 who as a member of the original UVF drove to

---

[ix] This chapter and all references to Sir Jeffrey Donaldson were written prior to the news of 29 March 2024, about which I can make no comment.

Larne on the night of 24–25 April 1914 to collect the weapons secretly imported by Col Crawford to fight Home Rule.

I must say that I was emboldened in my decision to say 'yes' in principle to Martin by comments by two Protestant Church leaders in response to the reports about possible Church witnesses to decommissioning. Archbishop Robin Eames and Presbyterian Moderator the Rev. Ken Newell had both spoken of the moral obligation and the need for Church figures 'not to be found wanting' if called upon.

Martin McGuinness readily agreed that I would have to be acceptable to a crucial swathe of unionist opinion and we talked at length about what this might mean for me personally as well as for what it might achieve.

He indicated to me that things could start moving very quickly and much could rest on meetings in Downing Street and elsewhere in the coming days.

I explained to Martin that Clodagh and I were scheduled to depart on a trip to the US in four days. As a patron of Habitat for Humanity I was scheduled to be in Atlanta for the presentation of the World Methodist Peace Award to Millard Fuller, founder of HfH, for his remarkable contribution to the housing of the most vulnerable and needy across our world.

Not that it was my primary concern, but I was assured there would be no problem refunding my fares. Later I noted in my journal: 'Upon reflection, must be careful about from whom I receive money. Must clearly not in any way be "payment". If this exercise proceeds I must be totally independent and objective. This will be the essence of any commitment on my part.'

By the time I returned home Clodagh had very sensibly gone to bed. As I slipped in beside her she was still awake and naturally curious as to where I had been. My explanation was not quite what she had expected. Realising that it was a big 'ask' of Clodagh as well as of myself, I had already said that my answer would be dependent upon how she also might feel about it. I continue to be moved by her response. 'Given all that you have tried to do over all of these years, there would be a "completion" in what you have been asked to do.' I thought of how, as a young wife and mother from Waterford, she had found herself alongside me in the heart of the Shankill Road at the height of the Troubles and how unwavering had been her support through the darkest of those days and nights. Thank you, Clodagh, for the sharing of this journey, even when you neither understood nor agreed with what was happening around us.

The next day I confirmed my agreement to be a co-witness and within four days I had met Fr Alec Reid in the first of several 'preparatory meetings' with those who were to be involved in the 'exercise' to discuss in greater detail all that was to be expected of us.

All of this was happening amid intensive media speculation and apparently endless meetings in Downing Street with at one point Ian Paisley – the infamous 'No' man of our politics – coming out of a meeting with Tony Blair and raising hopes by saying that it had gone much better than he had expected.

On *Sunday Sequence* on BBC Radio Ulster[17] there was further speculation as to who the clergy witnesses might be. It was suggested that Ken Newell would be an excellent witness but that it was unlikely that he would be acceptable to Paisley. Thankfully, I wasn't mentioned, but I did wonder if Ken was unacceptable why should it be assumed that I would be more so?

Then I went to church and was moved by the anthem as the choir sang 'Down by the Riverside' with the refrain 'I'm going to lay down my heavy load, down by the riverside, I'm going to study war no more, down by the riverside.' Was this a sign, or was it just coincidence?

Meantime, our planned trip to America was drastically curtailed and then aborted as the odds on a resolution of decommissioning became more certain. As we were later to discover, this was not to be the only time that we had to be decisive and imaginative in explaining changes in our plans.

While the DUP and Sinn Féin were engaged in frantic proximity talks with the British and Irish governments we were holding our preparatory meetings, mainly in Clonard Monastery's Room 007

– with all the sense of conspiratorial secrecy associated with a James Bond movie. Only this was for real.

In my journal I noted the first of those preparatory meetings at Clonard on Tuesday, 23 November, just four days after my conversation with Martin. This was attended by Martin McGuinness, Gerry Adams and Fr Alec Reid.

Gerry, articulate as ever, following a meeting in Downing Street the previous day, gave an overview of where the talks were at that moment, and of the need to 'give a victory to the DUP' to bring them on board.

Martin McGuinness spoke of what he considered to be the positive influence of that morning's 'Thought for the Day' on Radio Ulster and the contributions of thoughtful clergy of all denominations.

I scribbled down some key questions that had to be addressed:

- In whose gift was the choice of clerical observers?
- Who would actually appoint us?
- Terms of reference?
- Relationship with/to General de Chastelain.
- Given failure of the last attempt by de Chastelain to convince [David] Trimble, etc. in what way – apart from Alec and me – would Unionists see this time as any different?
- Timescale?

I found myself deeply conscious of the moment and of the trust invested in us. When Gerry Adams and Martin McGuinness had left that room in Clonard to just the two of us, in a moment of uncharacteristic piety I suggested to Fr Alec that we might pray together. 'Oh dear,' said he with a mischievous smile, 'You are just like Father Gerry [Reynolds]. He always has to pray about everything!' But pray we did. And not for the last time.

Up to this time I did not know Alec Reid very well. We had met at meetings and discussions here and there but had never really talked. He was the quiet man around the place and did not readily engage in the cut and thrust of debate between those of us who had opinions on everything – particularly on how to solve the problem of Northern Ireland. I recall one evening at St Gerard's Redemptorist Retreat Centre on the Antrim Road in Belfast, when Alec appeared to be fast asleep throughout the conversation.

Perhaps he was, who knows? But quite suddenly he opened his eyes and there followed a protracted but accurate commentary on all the issues we had been discussing for the previous hour. And little did we know of the discreet contribution he was quietly making in facilitating contacts and conversations between 'significant others', including his intervention in a republican feud in 1975 and his letter to John Hume in 1986 that ultimately resulted in the seminal Hume–Adams dialogue.[18]

As late as 9.00 p.m. on the evening of Monday, 6 December 2004, I was at a meeting with Martin McGuinness and Alec Reid in a house in Belfast where all the indications were that 'the deal' was on. Paisley's talk about 'humiliation' and 'sack cloth and ashes' and the DUP demand for photographs were seen as problems that could still be 'resolved'.

Such was our hope and expectation that Alec and I stayed on by ourselves and discussed what to say if the story of a deal broke and we were approached by the media. We agreed that we would say as little as possible and keep to the following line that I drafted: 'We are very much aware of the expectations of the whole community and of the trust that has been invested in us by all concerned. We will do all we can to ensure that expectations are realised, and that trust will not be betrayed.'

But, by teatime next day it became clear that there would be no deal. I went to see Alec and, as philosophical as ever, he said: 'We leave it to the Holy Spirit, His timing.' We exchanged phone numbers and agreed to keep in touch. That night I should have been in Atlanta and events had now shown that I needn't have cancelled that commitment after all but there was no point in rueing that.

So it was that decommissioning was once more put 'on hold'. On 8 December I noted in my journal:

It all came tumbling down – like a Jenga tower! The papers have it all well documented. Who is to blame? Who knows. Whatever, a sad day for us all. Still, the two PMs are not giving up – so why should we? There will be much activity in next week or so and who knows. Florida may still have to wait. On the other hand, Alec and I may be written out of the script. We shall have to wait and see but not for too long, I hope! What Clodagh so well described as an opportunity for 'completion' is sadly still far from complete!

Any lingering hopes of a change of heart by either side and a deal to lift spirits for Christmas were well and truly dashed by the Northern Bank Robbery, less than a fortnight later, on 19 December.

The £25m plus robbery put such a huge question mark over the credibility of the IRA that no act of decommissioning, however well managed and verifiable, would have been treated with anything other than derision. While decommissioning was still expected at some future date, we were given no indication as to when.

Over the next while I often found myself in meetings with fellow clergy of both 'persuasions' and there was still much speculation and guessing as to who might have been or who might yet be asked to be the 'chosen ones'. Naturally, to divert attention from myself as well as enjoying the banter I too joined in the guessing game. Interestingly, my name was never suggested.

For me, life continued very much as usual. A busy 'retirement' punctuated by preaching, meetings, travel, and family – with no further indication as to if and when Fr Alec and I might be called upon again.

However, on 28 July 2005, the IRA made an historic announcement in which they 'formally ordered an end to the armed campaign' and ordered their units 'to dump arms'.

And towards the end of August I received the anticipated but delayed call. Could Fr Alec and I be ready in early September to 'pick up' where we had left off the previous December?

But once again, what was asked of me was to coincide with our latest travel plans! Having led 'Journeys in Understanding' to Israel and South Africa, Clodagh and I had organised our 44 faithful fellow 'pilgrims' for another such journey. Having heard us speak with enthusiasm of my sabbatical study visit, they had asked us to take them with us on a return visit to China.

So when contacted with a new date for what would be the conclusive act of decommissioning I had to explain that I just could not be available. At this late stage there was no way I could either cancel China or leave the group to find their own way.

My suggestion that there must be an alternative witness was not accepted. I was to be the 'chosen one'. So, in a spirit of mutual compromise, it was agreed that decommissioning be delayed by one week which would allow me to go to China for the start of our study tour. I would then leave the group in the capable hands of Clodagh with the support of her sister-in-law Daphne and our good friend Brenda Callaghan.

For me it was a busy but fascinating week in China. From Beijing we travelled by overnight train to Sian to see the Terracotta Warriors. Wow!

But now the time had come for me to break from my part of the journey and return to the task which awaited me in Ireland. Earlier in the day I had the difficult task of informing the group that I would be leaving them that afternoon. During the night I had rehearsed and re-rehearsed what I could say that might sound credible without 'perjuring' myself or giving any hint as to why I was abandoning them.

I mumbled something about retired ministers being expected to be available when situations with which they were particularly familiar needed to be resolved – and urgently. I must have made it sound credible as no one questioned what I had said. On the contrary, all of them were sympathetic and assured me that they understood and would look after Clodagh and help her in any way they could. So, I boarded an extremely comfortable and efficient train and sped towards Shanghai from where I was to fly home to Ireland.

After a wander around 'downtown' Shanghai I resisted the temptation to visit the high tower overlooking this city of 24 million residents, had a totally unexpected conversation with a stranger about the popularity of hurling in Shanghai and found a taxi to take me to the airport.

It was midnight when I boarded the plane and settled into the totally unfamiliar surroundings of Premier Business Class, having been told weeks previously to book the most comfortable seat available as the IICD had an adequate budget and did not 'do steerage' when it came to international travel.

So, following on the busyness and responsibilities of the previous week I wallowed in the sheer luxury of my in-flight 'accommodation', had a meal like nothing I had ever experienced on any other flight, turned my seat into a splendid bed and slept soundly for eleven hours.

Arriving back on Friday, 16 September, I was grateful that I had a free evening before I was to meet up with Fr Alec, the IRA high command, and General de Chastelain and his team at a secret location.

In the media, both North and South, there was increasing speculation as to the timing of the anticipated decommissioning as well as the identity of the clerical witnesses. Though my name had not been publicly mentioned I sensed that being spotted in Ireland would arouse suspicion in the mind of anyone who knew I should be in China. Happily, no one called at our door, and I ignored phone calls. I would not have been surprised if there had been a call from a snooping journalist whom I would have to avoid at all costs.

The next day, I travelled down to Dublin by train. As I was not to meet Fr Alec for a few hours, I had a morning to myself and after an overdue haircut I found myself in the precincts of Christ Church Cathedral. I wandered in and joined a small group of worshippers for meditation and the sharing of bread and wine in the daily Eucharist. As you can imagine, the sharing of the Peace had a special significance for me on that day.

As I left this magnificent cathedral within my inner ear I could hear myself humming verses from a hymn that I often repeat to myself ahead of challenging moments in my ministry. None more challenging than the one on which I was about to embark:

> Forth in thy name O Lord I go,
> My daily labour to fulfil
> Thee only thee desire to know
> In all I speak or think or do.
>
> The task your wisdom has assigned
> Let me cheerfully fulfil
> In all my work your presence find.
> And prove your good and perfect will.

Realising that I had not brought a book to read, I wandered into the city centre and the Veritas bookshop. While idly browsing and having no idea to what purpose I would put them, I purchased some attractive prayer cards on which was printed the timeless prayer of St Francis of Assisi: 'Make me an instrument of your peace'.

By then it was time to meet Fr Alec at 'Marianella' – the Redemptorist House in south Dublin where we were to meet with a select group from the most senior level of leadership within the republican movement.

It must be respected that this 'exercise' was to be conducted within an understanding of complete confidentiality and we were very conscious of the trust which had been invested in us. Therefore, disappointing as this may be to some of my readers, not least historians and journalists, I will not name any of those with whom we met prior to or during this week of decommissioning. Nor will I disclose any detail which might identify locations or individuals. In this I ask for understanding as well as acceptance.

During the first of several 'briefing' sessions, the necessity for absolute secrecy was emphasised and impressed upon us. No one but no one was to know either the timing or the detail of what collectively we were to undertake. Within me there was a mixture of thoughts and feelings. Amongst them was a sense of apprehension as I began to realise the huge historical significance of what we had let ourselves in for.

In particular I was conscious of the responsibility on my shoulders of persuading those in the Protestant, U/unionist and loyalist side of our community that the IRA 'war' was over. In Ken Newell's perceptive words, rather than 'silent photographs'[19] Alec and I were to be the 'talking eyes'.

As planned and on time, Fr Alec and I were met by our 'handlers' at a pre-arranged location for a further briefing' and were introduced to those who were to have the 'hands on' responsibility for the management of the actual process of decommissioning.

Not quite knowing what to expect, but with the sincerity of the welcome and appreciation for our willingness to be a part of what was to follow my first impressions were entirely positive. I had no reason to doubt that for those with whom we met and were to travel this was a genuine, unambiguous, and unequivocal ending of the conflict.

We were given some very practical instructions. For example, appropriate clothing and footwear would be provided and we were not to bring our mobile phones or watches or any electronic devices of any kind. Apparently, with sophisticated intelligence and surveillance equipment our whereabouts and activities could be monitored by security forces on either side of the border.

Following this detailed briefing we set off in what was a specially adapted vehicle. Contrary to some later speculation, we were not blindfolded. Blindfolds would have indicated an absence of trust and I appreciated the trust invested in me. While I felt comfortable in the vehicle, there were no windows, so we had no idea where we were going, nor did we know the identity of those to whom we had been entrusted. By dusk we had arrived in a remote area where we were to spend the first night of our journey. While we could not see any neighbouring properties, we were asked not to go outside the house nor to appear at windows. Awaiting our arrival was the unassuming but nobody's fool, General John de Chastelain, who with his colleagues,

Brigadier Tauno Nieminen and Andrew Sens, and interlocutors from the IRA, had so meticulously planned this operation in very great detail.

I had met the General briefly on two previous occasions. Once at a meeting with representatives of the Methodist Council on Social Responsibility and once at a British-Irish Secretariat reception in Belfast during which he quietly said, outside of the hearing of others, 'Thank you for what you are doing'. At the time I was unsure as to what he was referring but imagined that he had been well briefed regarding the discreet conversations which some of us had been facilitating.

Overall, I found the General to be a respectful, slightly distant person who eschewed small talk and pursued his decommissioning mission with single-mindedness, diligence, uncompromising commitment and the military precision you would expect of one who had risen to such heights in his chosen profession.

This house, which was to be our 'home' for the coming days, had been well prepared for our arrival and for our comfort. Our physical care had been entrusted to a most pleasant lady whose splendid home cooking left nothing to be desired. Many weeks later, I was very touched by her thoughtful and very personal Christmas card.

Awaiting us in our shared bedroom Fr Alec and I found a boiler suit, wellington boots, a wash-bag complete with razors, shampoos and toothbrushes, plus a more than ample supply of spare clothing, socks, and underwear – all perfectly sized. Again evidence, if needed, of the detailed preparation for the whole operation.

Having been divested of our watches, we were intrigued to find an old-fashioned wind-up alarm clock between our beds. Given our early morning starts it was a very necessary addition to complete our 'kit'.

On our first night I found myself unusually early to bed. Before 'lights out' Alec brought out his breviary for his evening devotions and I my daily Bible notes. I confess that it was I who broke the silence with my exclamation:

'Alec – guess what is my passage for this evening?'

From Paul's letter to the Ephesians [Ephesians 6:10–18] I read to him that fascinating passage about the 'whole armour of God' emphasising that the weapons we need are not the predictable weapons of this world but a spiritual armoury including 'the shield of faith', 'the sword of the Spirit' and 'being shod with the good news of peace.'

'Good old Paul,' I said, 'He has a word for every eventuality, but how did he know about this decommissioning?'

Within five years my 'fellow traveller' had died, and I was privileged to be invited to choose a reading and share a thought at each of the three services held in the Redemptorist churches in Dublin and in Belfast. This passage and this story were my obvious choice for the ecumenical service at Clonard Monastery.

Early to bed and early to rise. And following a more than adequate breakfast we set off on the first day of our 'mission'.

As we were driven off on the first day of that historic adventure I thought, 'What would Grandfather Isaac make of this?' He of the Ulster Volunteers (UVF) who drove to Larne on that night in April 1914 with his neighbours from Co. Armagh to meet with Colonel Fred Crawford and return with their share of the consignment of the 20,000 guns which had been smuggled from Germany. Deadly weapons to store in their lofts and thatch in preparation for war with Britain to stay British. Could he ever have imagined that one day his grandson would be setting off with the quartermasters of the IRA to witness the decommissioning and destruction of their arms and explosives?

And what about my father, who at the height of the 1956–1962 IRA Border Campaign, as President of the Methodist Church in Ireland, had gone directly to the republican leadership in Dublin to argue face to face against the use of force. Could he have imagined it?

The specially adapted vehicle was comfortable, but not being able to see out it was somewhat claustrophobic. On some days, the journey felt long, on others less so. But there is no doubt that over many days we covered many miles, even though we had no idea where we were at any moment of time. Occasionally, when we were halted at a road junction or when our driver stopped to buy us our daily papers, we were told to be totally silent until we had driven off.

There was always the possibility that we might encounter a security check, on either side of the border. However, serious though it would have been in terms of compromising the confidentiality of our exercise, we did carry authorised papers of indemnity in the event that we might have to answer for ourselves and our activities.

The Decommissioning Acts of 1997, by both the Irish and the British governments and passed by both parliaments in Dublin and London, defines 'decommissioning' as putting weapons and weaponry 'beyond use' and 'beyond reach'.

While journalists and authors would have rejoiced in obtaining a detailed account of what this meant, and I'm sure some newspapers may have been prepared to 'purchase' more detailed information, I have to say that then and since I sensed nothing but respect from journalists in response to my position and the responsibilities that I had to discharge. So, whatever else accompanies me to my grave, this information will travel with me. When asked what did we see I welcome the opportunity to say that what I saw was hugely significant, but what I heard was even more so.

Obviously, hands-on responsibility for the modalities of the exercise were the responsibility of General de Chastelain and his colleagues, as agreed with senior members of the IRA who accompanied us or who met us at pre-arranged locations. For an organisation whose historic constitution stated that the surrendering of one's weapon was a 'capital' offence, it was important that this act of decommissioning was not to be seen as 'surrender'. This was the genius of this process.

I can fully understand the curiosity of those who want to know the details of the 'how'. However, for me to describe this in detail would be a breach of the coveted trust which I will forever seek to protect. But having said that, for me the 'how' was all important. For me to expect sceptical politicians and at times a doubting public to have confidence in what I would report, it was essential that I personally should have total confidence in the veracity of what I had been asked to witness. So without disclosing the detail, on the very first day I confided in John de Chastelain my unease about the way in which an important aspect of the process was being implemented. It was not that I doubted either the integrity or intention of those involved, but I had to be absolutely certain that those weapons of war and destruction could never ever be accessed and or used again. I had to be convinced of the indisputable veracity of every detail of the process.

My concerns were fully understood and accepted, not only by the General and his colleagues but by the representatives of the IRA who were responsible for the practicalities involved. So despite a well-planned and tight timetable for each of the days that were to follow, my concerns and my suggestions were taken very seriously and time was taken to ensure my approval. This confirmed for me that my role was fully understood and respected, and that I was not to be seen as a 'token' presence.

For those who still ask how could we be sure that ALL the weaponry and the munitions of the IRA had been collected and brought together it is important to say that prior to our setting out on this mission, the intelligence services of both the Irish and the British governments had agreed estimates of what was in the possession of the IRA. At the end of each day, what had been decommissioned on that day was very carefully logged and set against these estimates.

Having said that, somewhere in the middle of our 'mission' there was some anxiety about the gap between what had so far been decommissioned and the estimated totality of what was known to be available. However, by the end of the exercise, the gap had been so significantly narrowed to enable the General to make his announcement as to what had been achieved with complete confidence, as witnessed and verified by Father Alec and myself.

He did also explain it was likely that some weapons may well have been secreted by IRA activists who had since died and that others may have been retained by dissidents who, in spite of the orders of the leadership, were opposed to the decommissioning of their weapons.

While I thanked God that those weapons would never be used to kill or maim in the future, I was very mindful of those who would have been killed or maimed by those same weapons. I was also aware that in the destruction of weapons forensic evidence would also be destroyed. We live in a messy world.

It had been a long week and I was wondering to myself where next and how much longer this exercise was going to take. Throughout our travels and at each of the sites the single-minded John de Chastelain had been totally focused on the task in hand. He was a man of few words, but as if he had read my mind he turned towards us, relaxed and wiped his hands as if to say it's all 'done and dusted'.

At that same moment a young man with a weapon slung over his shoulder stepped forward from the shadows. It was not the first time we had noticed him for he was hovering in the background wherever we went and as part of 'the scenery' we had become indifferent to his presence.

But now, as he stepped forward his role in this drama became clear. In best military tradition with his rifle over his shoulder he walked up to the General, stood smartly to attention, saluted, and handed him his weapon. The silence of this moment which descended upon us was broken when Father Alec whispered into my ear, 'there goes the last gun out of Irish politics.' What a moment!

To me, this was a very visible confirmation of the desire of the IRA personnel present to be liberated of those weapons of death and destruction. During that week, particularly in the evenings over a meal or in quiet conversation with some of our 'fellow travellers' I found myself in something of a 'pastoral role'. For republican activists this 'exercise' had brought back memories of friends and comrades who were now no more. While I was not there in the role of a 'confessor' I had no doubt that their regret was for all who had died in this bloody and senseless conflict and that they who had survived wanted to make sure that no one else will ever have to die in that way. The sorrow was not in the loss of weapons but in the loss of life. For them their war was over. They did not want their children and their children's children or anybody's children to live through what they had lived through. Again, as I have said many times when asked what did I see, I have emphasised that what I heard was no less important than what I saw.

It was when we gathered to say our farewells that I remembered the prayer cards/bookmarks with the Prayer of St Francis of Assisi that were still in my pocket. I explained that I was not one of those 'Prodie preachers' who went around distributing tracts but that I had something I would like to give each of them before we parted. On seeing the cards in my hand one of the men called out with a good-natured, 'Are those tickets for the All-Ireland final?' (which was to be played shortly).

I responded by saying that I was sorry I did not have what he would have wished for but said that when this year's 'All-Ireland' would be long forgotten people would still be praying the words on this card. A prayer that I needed to pray regularly and perhaps one that we all might pray in our own time. Each one accepted my gift with obvious respect and appreciation.

So, our momentous week or so that would help change the course of Irish history for ever had come to an end and in the All-Ireland Football Final Tyrone beat Kerry by 1–16 to 2–10 to win the Sam Maguire Cup. I have no way of knowing whether our travels that week took us to Kerry or to Tyrone.

Four years later, when I was taking part in an event in a border region, one of those attending shared with me a message he had been asked to bring. One of his friends, who had seen my name on a poster advertising the event, asked him to tell me that he still carried 'that card' in his pocket and prayed that prayer every day. I share this in response to those who ask me what was I as a pastor and preacher doing in that situation. As well as with others who have been sceptical about decommissioning amid the sincerity of those with whom I shared that 'journey'.

But we were all very conscious of the challenge that now awaited us. Press speculation was rife and we knew that there would be a waiting world anxious to hear what we had to say. It was agreed that, as well as the formal statement from General John, Fr Alec and I would have to face the cameras and give media interviews. So between us, Alec and I carefully crafted and agreed the statement we would make the following day.

This I knew would be a challenge, and particularly so for Alec. For he was the one who had kept his head down and operated most effectively in the shadows. He was uncomfortable and potentially 'accident-prone' under the media glare.

On the evening of Sunday, 25 September, after what for me had been a remarkable week, as it was in modern Irish history, I travelled home to Holywood in the company of Aaro Suonio from Finland. Aaro was the lesser known but incredibly competent 'in-house manager' of the IICD whose wise and warm friendship I came to value. To ensure confidentiality and the secrecy surrounding what we had been doing, there had been no prior announcement and no arrangements for what was to be a momentous press conference. So as we travelled, on his mobile phone, Aaro shared our good news with all of the leading international and local media outlets.

Nor had there been any venue booked. Being unsuccessful in his first call to a city centre hotel, I suggested the Culloden, with slight self-interest as it was just five minutes from my home. Happily they confirmed that they could accommodate the press conference.

Having completed our journey home and our preparations for the next day, I was happily re-united with Clodagh, who had just flown home from China and enjoyed a well-earned night's sleep in our own bed.

Given such short notice, I wondered who beyond the predictable local papers and channels might be there. To my astonishment, when we arrived for a 2.00 p.m. live news broadcast the large hall was packed with journalists and cameras from every known local and international outlet. Many had flown in at such short notice. All of which emphasised more than we had realised the international as well as local significance of what we had witnessed.

As it was significant elements in the Protestant, Unionist and Loyalist (PUL) community that had to be persuaded, it was agreed that following General de Chastelain's report I would read our prepared statement.

First, though, the Independent International Commission on Decommissioning (IICD) headed by General de Chastelain delivered a report to the British and Irish governments.

This historic announcement by the IICD contained in paragraphs 3 and 8 of the report to the governments dated Monday, 26 September 2005, stated in part: '… we believe that the arms decommissioned represent the totality of the IRA's arsenal' and 'In summary, we have determined that the IRA has met its commitment to put all its arms beyond use in a manner called for by the legislation.'[20]

As joint independent witnesses Alec and I stated in part:

> The experience of seeing this with our own eyes, on a minute-to-minute basis, provided us with evidence so clear and of its nature so incontrovertible that, at the end of the process, it demonstrated to us, and would have demonstrated to anyone who might have been with us, that beyond any shadow of doubt, the arms of the IRA have now been decommissioned.[21]

Following a 'flurry' of hastily arranged interviews I returned home, content with what we had said and done. While in the following days there were some predictable critical and dismissive letters, phone calls and radio callers – there was overwhelming endorsement from a wide spectrum including heads of state, church leaders, progressive politicians and a cross-section of society.

However, I was under no illusion that one person above all had been watching and listening to every word and making the ultimate call on whether I could be believed. That person was the Rev. Ian Paisley, MP MLA, leader of the DUP and First Minister-in-waiting of Northern Ireland.

My grandfather Peter Good from Skibbereen.   My formidable grandmother Minnie Good.

The landlord's house at The Argory where my maternal grandfather, Isaac, stored UVF guns. From a painting by his 'decommissioning grandson' Harold G.

With my parents and brothers strapped in my trolley in the garden of our home in 'Derry.

My parents, Bob and Doris, on their wedding day in 1932.

With my brothers, Peter and Robin, c. 1940, shortly before I was grounded for years by bovine tuberculosis.

My maternal grandfather, Isaac Allen.

Ordination day, Wesley Chapel, Cork, 18 June 1962. I'm in the front row, first on the left.

Wedding day, 11 August 1964.

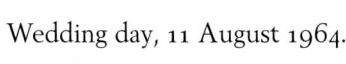

My uncle's billhead to the IRA during the Irish Civil War.

With Peter and Robin and their wives, Jean and Jennifer.

Searching for my roots in Goodville, Pennsylvania in 1966.

Sailing home from the USA – with our two additions, Carolyn and Sharon, in 1968.

Arriving at Corrymeela with Jonathan, baby Richard, Sharon, Carolyn and Sparky, our Border Terrier, July 1973.

With Judi, my present much-loved Border Terrier and fellow walker. © Bobbie Hanvey Photographic Archives, John J. Burns Library, Boston College. Used with kind permission.

Messing about in my boat at Ballycastle.

E ANTRIM TIME

81st Year FRIDAY, JANUARY 26, 1973 5p

Greenisland minister's suggest

MOVE TO LEAD EXTREMISTS 'TO THE TABLE

Candles,

Urging peace talks in my local paper to reporter David McKittrick. (Upon my return from the World Council of Churches meeting in Bangkok, January 1973.)

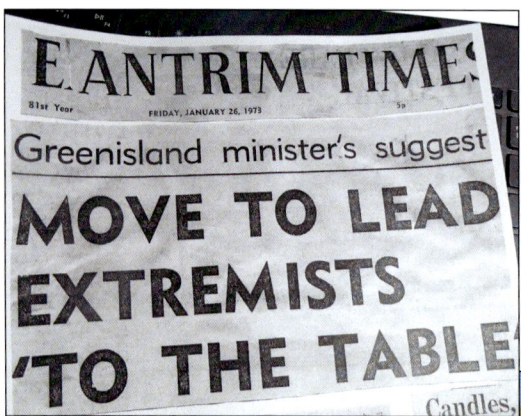

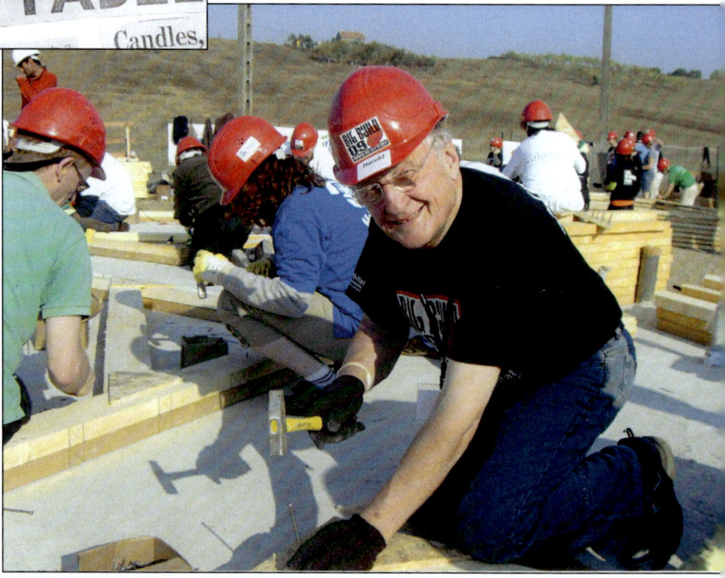

Lending a hand to Habitat for Humanity in Romania.

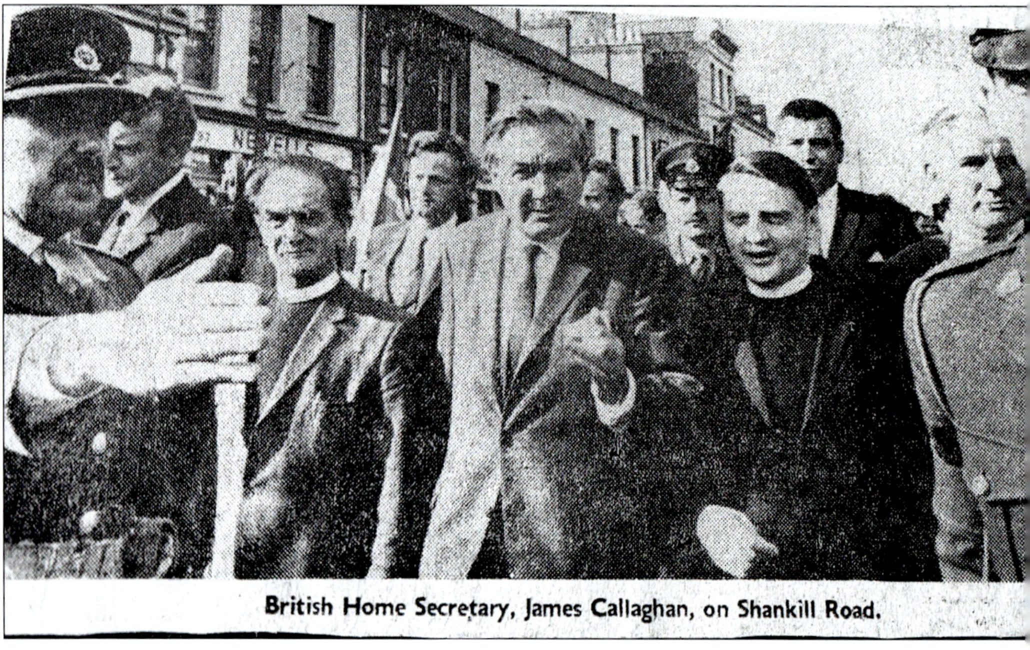

Touring the Shankill with British Home Secretary James Callaghan, 27 August 1969.

Installation as President of the Methodist Church in Ireland with Rev. Dr Edmund Mawhinney and Rev. Dr Inderjit Bhogal, in 2001.

At Number 10 with Prime Minister Tony Blair, Presbyterian Moderator Alastair Dunlop and Archbishops Robin Eames and Seán Brady, in 2002. © 10 Downing Street, used with kind permission.

Fr Alec and I with Professor Richard English, historian and political scientist, receiving honorary doctorates from Queen's University Belfast. See Appendix III for the speech I made on that occasion.

Two presidents and their partners, with Mary and Martin McAleese.

Greeting Queen Elizabeth II at Saint Anne's Cathedral, on her Diamond Jubilee visit to Belfast in 2012. © NIO, used with kind permission.

Receiving the René Cassin Human Rights Award from the Lehendakari (President) of the Basque Country, December 2005.

Receiving the 2007 World Methodist Peace Award.

Fr Alec Reid and I facing the world's press at the decommissioning announcement in the Culloden Hotel, 26 September 2005. See Appendix I for the statement we made.

A cartoonist's impression of Ian Paisley's dismissal of IRA decommissioning. I am flanked by General John de Chastelain and Fr Alec Reid. © Ian Knox. Used by kind permission of Ian Knox.

Devolution Day 8 May 2007. Watching the swearing in of Ian Paisley and Martin McGuinness from the VIP gallery in Stormont. © EIS, used with kind permission.

A very personal memento from the key players on Devolution Day. © EIS, used with kind permission.

With Senator George Mitchell celebrating the 25th anniversary of the Good Friday Agreement in April 2023.

With Tony Blair at his seminar in Yale University, November 2008. (Photo: Screenshot from YouTube.)

With Archbishop Desmond Tutu on a visit to Belfast.

With Bertie Ahern in Bilbao.

With Archbishop Matteo Zuppi handing over an inventory and locations of ETA weapons to Ram Manikkalingam, chairman of the International Verification Commission, 8 April 2017.

Addressing the peace rally in Bayonne, Basque Country, to celebrate the decommissioning of weapons by ETA, 8 April 2017.

With MPs Paul Maskey, Mark Durkan and Jeffrey Donaldson in discussion with FARC leaders in Havana, Cuba in October 2015.

Remembering our conversation about women at the Cross, I took this photograph in Colombia for Baroness Eileen Paisley.

With Clodagh at the Taj Mahal, while on a presidential visit to the Church of North India. One of many shared and privileged journeys.

60th wedding anniversary celebration with four generations of our family in August 2024.

10

Ian Paisley:
As I Came to Know Him

'There is a time for everything and a season for every activity under the heavens.'

Ecclesiastes 3

I have to confess to some hesitancy and reluctance when I come to share my thoughts about as consequential and divisive a figure as Ian Paisley. For it was a bewildering journey for both of us, from when our paths first crossed before taking us to places where neither of us could ever have foreseen.

So let me begin where the story will end. The scene is his small 'grace and favour' room in Parliament Buildings where he invited me to meet him shortly after his 'involuntary' retirement from the office of First Minister and Moderator of the Free Presbyterian Church. Adorning the walls were impressive pictures of himself with admiring world leaders and I was welcomed with the statutory china cup of tea.

My reason for being there was to thank him for his part in taking us to where we never thought he would go and letting him know of my personal appreciation as well as that of others from whom he might not have expected to hear. Before I close this chapter I will share more of that conversation, our exchange of gifts and our parting with a prayer.

It is neither my wish nor my role in the telling of my story to either demonise or canonise Ian Paisley, rather to relate as candidly as I can my memories of our encounters and of the Ian Paisley with whom I sat in the intimacy of that small room.

This is not to say that I am unmindful of the much more 'controversial' side of the Paisley story. This has been well rehearsed by others and I will leave it to them to record and remind us of that.

While ultimately he and I had a mutually respectful relationship, that was not always so. As I was growing up his name was synonymous with sectarian bigotry, rabble-rousing and division. Understandably, in my home it was his railing against 'Romanism' and his vitriolic attacks on mainstream denominations for their 'apostasy' that disturbed my father and his generation of ministers. While there were many Paisley jokes, there was the underlying fear of what he was stirring and that 'Paisleyism' was not going to go away. I say 'Paisleyism' advisedly, for what he was articulating was alive and well long before he was born. His particular skill was in his vehement articulation and promotion of the fears and prejudices which he and so many of his time had inherited.

My first actual sighting of Ian Paisley was on an autumn evening in 1953 when with my friends I was at a 'Youth for Christ' rally in a marquee on what was known as Blitz Square on High Street – an area so named after it was devastated in the Belfast Blitz of 1941 and which was known as Belfast's 'Speaker's Corner', where, as well as tent missions, ardent socialists and others would hold protests and political rallies.

Like many young people at that time I found the 'Youth for Christ' events enjoyable. The preachers and song-leaders were trendy young Americans in gabardine suits and D.A. haircuts. And in place of traditional hymns they crooned gospel songs, such as 'I was drifting along on life's pitiless sea'. I confess that at sixteen going on seventeen I had no sense of 'drifting' and to me life was entirely enjoyable, and I had no sense of the world as a 'pitiless sea'. As young people in those halcyon post-war days, life was very enjoyable and Belfast was a safe city where we felt we could walk where and when we wished.

It was during lively singing that I was aware of the competing strains of a flute band approaching from the Albert Clock. It was a foggy evening but from where I was seated I could see marching out of the mist a straggling group of men and women bearing a Union Jack, led by a tall figure in a long coat and black hat. To me it was reminiscent of my *Boys' Own* image of Custer's Last Stand. Curiosity got the better of me and I slipped out to get a better view.

After a doleful singing of 'Shall we gather at the river?', the tall man who had headed the parade stood on a platform with a large book in his hand. From newspaper pictures with which we were familiar there was no doubting that it was the Rev. Ian Paisley, who, following a bitter dispute with the long-established Presbyterian Church of Ireland, had founded his own Free Presbyterian Church of Ulster: a story which has been extensively documented elsewhere.[22]

The author of the book that Paisley held in his hand on that evening was the Rev. Professor James Ernest Davey, Moderator of the Presbyterian Church (1953–54) and principal of the former Assembly's College (now Union Theological College), the college of the Presbyterian Church where generations of Irish Presbyterian ministers had been trained. In Paisley's eyes, Davey was an unrepentant apostate.

A quarter of a century earlier, in 1927, when Paisley was an infant, Prof. Davey was accused of heresy by some from within the Presbyterian Church, which led to a formal trial that exonerated him. This decision was upheld by the General Assembly of the Presbyterian Church in Ireland by 707 votes to 82.

However, the fundamentalist Ian Paisley was not convinced of his innocence and was incensed by Davey's recent election as Moderator in 1953 and the purpose of this gathering was to indulge in a very public burning of Prof. Davey's writings. Whatever was going on within the mission tent behind me, this scene was more than a curious schoolboy could resist, albeit at a safe distance.

From his elevated position, which added to his aura of authority, Paisley read extracts from Davey's book, which he considered to be heretical, in defiance of the decision of the General Assembly. Having denounced one 'heresy' after another, he tore out the offending pages, consigned them to the flames of a brazier one by one and after each led his assembled followers in an enthusiastic rendering of yet another verse of 'We have heard a joyful sound, Jesus saves'.

In one extract, Prof. Davey was apparently daring to speculate on the circumstances of the birth of Christ. As a relatively innocent teenager in the 1950s, I had not yet fully understood the process of human reproduction let alone the theological mysteries of the 'immaculate conception'. But Ian Paisley clearly did and was not impressed by the 'speculative theology' of Prof. Davey. Like most of the onlookers, I did not understand the niceties of his argument and I had an instant reaction to what I was witnessing. As a young lad of sixteen I saw it as reminiscent of the stories I had read of the burning of crosses in the Southern states of America and of the burning of books in 1930s Germany.

I clearly remember returning to the Youth for Christ tent and contrasting Paisley's message of hatred with the story of love and grace that was unfolding within the tent behind me and with the understanding of the Gospel in which I had been nurtured in my home and church family.

It was to be another defining moment in my life. I could take you to the spot where I stood and said: 'Lord, I am thinking of ministry and if you want me to be a minister or preacher help me to preach against that kind of hatred.'

In a strange way I should be grateful to Ian Paisley for that night as it was to define my understanding of faith and ministry in the years that were to follow.

Fast forward five years to 1960. I am now 23 and a student studying in Edgehill, the Methodist Theological College in Belfast, and I can recall my second sighting of Ian Paisley.

As students we were encouraged to go to hear different preachers to learn from their respective styles and approaches. Notwithstanding my previous experience, I chose to visit Ian Paisley's Free Presbyterian Church on the Ravenhill Road to observe what was happening. This was the old church that preceded the mega Martyrs' Memorial Church that he opened further up the road in October 1969.

The church was full, and I just managed to squeeze into what appeared to be the only remaining seat in the narrow gallery. Then came the large and imposing figure of Paisley, filling his galleon-style pulpit from which he quoted copiously from numerous books and pamphlets, comparing his pulpit to a 'nosebag' containing his sources of spiritual wisdom and insight.

I recall that much of his sermon was devoted to a passionate and very personal attack on the then Archbishop of Canterbury, Geoffrey Fisher, with whose 'apostasy' he had obvious disagreement. From one of the pamphlets, it was revealed that His Grace was given to bowing numerous times to the East, which contrasted unfavourably with the number of times he had prayed in other directions.

Whatever about Paisley's fundamentalist separatist anti-ecumenical stance, with which I strongly disagreed, he was a master at holding his audience. From my vantage point in the gallery, I could see a woman in the front row who could contain herself no longer.

'Mr Paisley', she called out, 'thon man's head's cut!' She had interrupted the great man in full flight, but after a pregnant pause and the laughter had receded, the man himself responded, 'the servant of the Lord hath spoken, need I say more?'

After further laughter he waited for his moment. To his 'And all the people said …', his enthusiastic and adoring audience responded with a resounding 'Amen', following which the sermon came to an abrupt but well-timed conclusion.

It was a master class in holding an audience. But all so contradictory within the context of Christian worship, particularly a service of Holy Communion.

In the years that followed, especially in the period after his first spell of imprisonment in 1966, the Free Presbyterian Church expanded and Paisley's congregation grew so rapidly that it necessitated the building of the new and imposing Martyr's Memorial Church.

Clearly, many disaffected Presbyterians and others were attracted by Paisley's uncompromising fundamentalism, believing him to be the saviour and protector of evangelical Protestantism. They came by the busload – with scores from the more rural and theologically conservative rural areas.

It has to be said as Ian Paisley's popularity and congregation grew, so did the antagonism and distance between him and mainline Protestantism, although on reflection the main Protestant denominations, including my own, could have done more to call out his malign influence over the religious and political life of Northern Ireland.

* * *

Eleven years were to pass before my next 'in-person' sighting of 'the Big Man'. It was mid-October 1969 and Northern Ireland, and Belfast and 'Derry in particular, had been convulsed by the worst violence in the memory of everyone too young to remember the horrors of the early 1920s.

As I have recalled earlier, following a four-year period of wider experience and study in the United States, I found myself serving as the minister of Agnes Street Methodist Church on Belfast's 'Protestant' Shankill Road.

On the night of Saturday, 11 October 1969, against the background of Protestant and unionist anger at the Hunt Report that recommended the disbandment of the B-Specials and the disarming of the RUC, serious violence erupted on the Shankill Road, during which soldiers and police were shot at by loyalists.

Three young lives were lost that night in separate incidents. Constable Victor Arbuckle, the first RUC officer to die in the Troubles, was shot dead by the UVF, and two local Shankill men, George Dickie and Herbert Hawe, were killed by the Army. Their bodies were carried into our church hall and volunteers had to mop up the blood in preparation for the Sunday school class which was to meet in that room the next morning.

Before going home in the early hours of next morning I visited the young widow of Constable Arbuckle. What was I to say? What could I say? And though not of my congregation, I decided to attend the funerals of the two local lads who had been shot. The first funeral was to leave the family home in one of the neighbouring small streets behind our church – now long demolished due to redevelopment. As a local pastor I wished to show solidarity with the bereaved family and to be seen to empathise with the local community, who were naturally angry at the killing of their neighbours by the British Army.

Surprisingly, the Shankill community's restrained reaction to those deaths contrasted with more forceful responses in nationalist areas after similar killings by the security forces.

On the previous day I had visited the family but on the day of the funeral I stood outside with the neighbours when suddenly the crowd fell silent as the announcement 'He's coming' was passed through the crowd. It was rather like our biblical images of the events of Palm Sunday with the expectation of the arrival of a Messiah. We did not have long to wait until down the narrow street came the tall, imposing figure of Ian Paisley in a long black coat. While there were no 'hosannas' some excited onlookers did applaud his arrival. But in response, the Big Man (as he was affectionately called by his admirers) gestured that he did not want such acknowledgment in circumstances such as this.

When he came to the low doorway of the modest house, he had to stoop as he entered. After some minutes one of the family came out to inform me that it was the wish of the family that Paisley and I should act as pallbearers at the front of the coffin. It was one of those occasions which called for a swift and imaginative response. Often in life I have thought that the good Lord has given me answers that I wasn't quick or smart enough to have thought of myself. This was such a moment. I explained that I was aware of 'an obvious imbalance' between Mr Paisley and myself and I did not think it a good idea.

He glanced at my relatively diminutive stature, looked in the direction of the house where my fellow pallbearer was waiting and said that he understood and would explain this to the family. I'm not sure that he understood what I meant when I spoke of 'imbalance'! Whatever, I got away with it, and when the coffin was carried from the home Ian Paisley was not a pallbearer. A potentially awkward encounter between us had been avoided.

But sometime later, it was some ill-judged words from his pulpit which were to potentially damage my credibility and put me at risk of physical attack.

When I was posted to the Shankill I adapted a programme for young persons in my church confirmation class that had worked well in Ohio. To help young people understand the history of the Church and the relationship between the Old Testament and the New this involved a visit to the synagogue to learn about our roots in Judaism as well as churches of other traditions, including our local Roman Catholic church.

So, in our first visit to the Jewish Synagogue on Somerton Road we were warmly received, and the young people were fascinated by the scrolls and other symbols of the faith with which Jesus would have been familiar in his boyhood. Our second 'field trip' was to the Holy Cross Church on the Crumlin Road. Once more, the young people were intrigued by what was different, particularly when the very jovial young priest introduced them to the mysteries of the confession box. Our next visit was around the corner to our neighbouring St Michael's Church of Ireland.

After each of these visits we would discuss what was different and learned how these visits helped us to understand what we would now call the timeline of our faith, bringing us to where we now were within the history of Christendom. Of course, as I had hoped, it also gave opportunity for a healthy discussion on differences and the need for mutual respect as well as an understanding of what we shared in common.

Realising that this was innovative for a Protestant church, on the Sunday before going to Holy Cross I had asked the young people to tell their parents of our planned visit. The only 'abstentionist' was a teenage girl whose mother said she could go to the door or stay outside in the car and wait for the class to return.

Within the context of our class, the young folk found it all very enjoyable as well as constructive. But there was at least one person who was not happy. It was reported to me the Rev. Ian Paisley had publicly denounced our visit to Holy Cross by informing his congregation that 'instead of taking the children for a Sunday school outing to Ballywalter the Rev. Harold Good took them to Holy Cross Chapel.'

Shortly after this I was called to a tense situation at the 'peace line' on Dover Street, where police were trying to restrain an angry crowd who had been fuelled by a rumour that IRA gunmen were about to launch an attack from the Divis Tower. Handing me a megaphone, I was asked to warn the crowd of the danger and appeal to them to disperse. However, before I could deliver my message I was interrupted by a very angry woman who screamed at me and told the crowd to ignore me as I was the minister who took children to the Holy Cross Chapel. Already fearful, it did not take much for the crowd to turn their anger towards me.

Not to be too dramatic, I sensed a verbal if not physical lynching when out of the crowd stepped a man I recognised as the father of one of the young people in my class. He was a hard-line loyalist with whom I had engaged in several honest conversations, including my insistence that he must attend his daughter's confirmation, which he reluctantly did. When he asked me for the megaphone I did not know what to expect. However, he told the crowd that because he trusted me, he allowed his daughter to go on that visit. 'Rev. Good was only wanting them to see for themselves how wrong and how stupid them people are,' he said. Given the situation I was not about to contradict him and the crowd quietened down.

When I met with the stewards and leaders of my congregation to explain the visit and the context in which it had taken place, they unanimously expressed their support for what I was doing. One woman memorably said, 'I wish I had that opportunity when I was young, instead of being brought up in fear of that church every time I passed it.'

There is a sequel to this story. Years later I was doing my rounds as part-time chaplain in the City Hospital in Belfast when a patient with his wife at his bedside looked up at me.

'Hello', he said, 'how are you doing? Do you remember me?'

'Help me,' I said.

When he replied, 'Dover Street', I had to think for a moment.

'I've got you,' said I, 'and I will always be grateful to you for you saved my skin that night.'

Jocularly, he replied, 'Bad and all as you are, I wouldn't have allowed them to harm you.'

Mention of my work as a hospital chaplain reminds of when my ministry extended to part-time prison chaplaincy in Crumlin Road prison. One day in the 1980s I met a loyalist prisoner who had been convicted of a sectarian murder and I asked him how he had ended up there. He traced his descent into extremism to when as an eighteen-year-old he heard Paisley speak at a rally in Larne in 1968 in support of the restoration of the *Clyde Valley*, the UVF's gun-running steamship during the Home Rule crisis in 1914.

I will never forget that prisoner's words: 'Paisley lit something inside me that night that brought me to this place.' Still, this did not absolve the prisoner from personal responsibility for his crime.

* * *

The first indication that Ian Paisley might be open to listening to any of us who might have a different view of how we might 'fix' Northern

Ireland came by way of a letter addressed to me personally in response to an 'Open Letter' which he, along with all other party leaders, had received from 'Members of the Methodist Church in Ireland', authorised by our President, Rev. Chris Walpole.

This 'Open Letter' to all of the Northern Ireland political party leaders was written in response to the ending of the IRA ceasefire with the Docklands bomb in London on 9 February 1996. I had placed a copy on the porch tables of our churches on the Lisburn Road and University Road congregations asking that those who felt this represented their views to sign it. Which most did.

After assuring all of our political leaders of our prayers for each of them as well as for the victims of the bomb and their families it stated:

> While we are fully aware of the enormous difficulties, we would ask you to urgently seek a mutually acceptable way of working together to secure the peace for which we all yearn. Like others, we also must come to terms with our own fears and feelings but, in obedience to the demands of the Christian Gospel, we re-affirm our own commitment to work and pray for a lasting peace.

Having drafted and signed several such letters over the years, I was not overly optimistic in receiving meaningful replies. Particularly from Ian Paisley, to whom in his capacity as our local MP in North Antrim I had posted several invitations to events whilst at Corrymeela without ever having received a reply. So it was most encouraging to receive a personally addressed letter in which he noted our request to urgently seek a meaningful way of working together to secure the peace.

He wrote:

> I should be grateful if you could give some explanation and clarification of this statement. Do you suggest that democratic constitutional politicians should work together with Sinn Féin/IRA and if so how would you suggest this should be done?

Best Wishes,
Yours sincerely

Unfortunately, I do not have any record of our response to Ian Paisley's encouraging reply, other than a copy of a very detailed and comprehensive paper entitled 'Taking Stock' which detailed options and formed the basis of ongoing conversations with his and other party representatives which sought to address the 'How' question in his letter to me.

Building on this paper, and in preparation for a further meeting with Michael Ancram, then Minister of State for Northern Ireland, another document in our files contains further and very carefully considered suggestions for government in its desire for a way forward. While it would be presumptuous to suggest that this was the template for the process that resulted in the Good Friday Agreement, it did clearly emphasise the principles which ultimately were accepted. In this, as in many other initiatives, we were greatly indebted to Sir George Quigley for his wisdom and guidance.

The years roll on and on Thursday, 29 September 2005, within a few days of my participation in the de-commissioning of the weaponry of the IRA, I had my first in-person meeting with Ian Paisley. Not securing the photographic evidence he had demanded, nor the person he had suggested to be the independent verifier from the unionist/Protestant community, Paisley's immediate response to the statement of the IICD and the joint statement by Fr Alec Reid and myself of Monday, 26 September was one of scepticism. He attacked the two governments for their 'duplicity', adding that 'instead of openness there was the cunning tactics of cover-up' and that the two witnesses (Fr Alec and I) could not be independent as they were 'approved by the IRA'. While not appointed by the IRA, it was important that we were acceptable to the IRA.

However, the pickle in which Ian Paisley now found himself was captured nicely by cartoonist Ian Knox in *The Irish News*, whose cartoon depicted General de Chastelain, Fr Alec Reid and myself at our press conference with Ian Paisley making a dismissive gesture in our direction with one hand and shooting himself in the foot with a pistol in the other.

And he soon found himself out of step with world opinion as well as significant sections of Protestant and unionist opinion closer to home.

Messages of unequivocal acceptance and commendation for what had been accomplished were widely published in local media. From the White House to the Vatican; from the Secretary General of the United Nations; from Premiers Tony Blair and Bertie Ahern; from the President of Ireland, Mary McAleese; from the Catholic Bishops of Northern Ireland, the Church of Ireland Primate, Presbyterian Moderator and the Methodist President.

All of which confirmed that in the eyes of the world as well as in the well-informed responses from Church leaders across the denominations and progressive politicians, what had been accomplished was authentic and, in the words of Kofi Annan, secretary-general of the United Nations, 'a major obstacle to the search for a lasting and sustainable political settlement in Northern Ireland has been removed.'

At a personal level, I was touched by the endorsement of Danny Kennedy, deputy leader of the Ulster Unionist Party, who said it was wrong to question the honesty and integrity of the church witnesses and stressed that I was regarded as a person of integrity by people in Bessbrook who recalled my ministry there.

And from my local MP, Lady Sylvia Hermon of the Ulster Unionist Party: 'I have known Rev. Good for almost 20 years ... so when he says he is utterly certain beyond any shadow of doubt, the arms of the IRA have now been decommissioned, his word is good enough for me.'

So with such international as well as local endorsement there was a growing tide of opinion against which it would be difficult to swim. Even for Ian Paisley.

Having responded positively to the request of other party leaders for an in-person meeting, we readily agreed to a meeting with Paisley and his top team from the DUP, in spite of his initial scathing dismissal of our role and our statement.

While all of the other parties agreed to meet us in my home, the DUP asked to meet with us in Parliament Buildings. So it was that, feeling like two Daniels, we entered the DUP den. We were greeted cordially and respectfully by the party leader, accompanied by Ian Junior and several other well-known DUP personalities including David Simpson MP, a beneficiary of the IRA's tardiness in decommissioning, who had defeated David Trimble in Upper Bann in the general election nearly five months earlier.

As an icebreaker and very amicably, Paisley spoke to Alec about the Basque Country, where he had been on holiday and which he had found a very nice place. After a little more pleasant small talk Paisley got down to business and spoke of his personal difficulty in being asked to believe something that he had not seen with his own eyes.

As he spoke I was reminded of the conversation between Thomas the doubter and Jesus, as recorded in the Gospel according to John.

'Ian,' I said, 'as a preacher of the Word you will be familiar with the conversation between Jesus and Thomas who was finding it difficult to accept that which he had not seen for himself. You will remember how Jesus said, "how blessed are those who have seen and believed – but how much more blessed are those who have NOT seen and yet believe."'

'Ian,' said I, 'surely you would not wish to be excluded from those who are MORE blessed.'

He quickly responded by telling me that this was not what this story is about. David Simpson chipped in light-heartedly to say, 'Harold, don't argue with him over scripture for he will beat you every time.'

But I wasn't having that and in turn I reminded him that he was the person who more than anybody had made it clear that every word, dot and comma of the biblical text was to be respected as the inspired and authoritative word of God.

As he spoke, Father Alec, who could be endearingly naive in his unscripted remarks, was going beyond the parameters we had agreed. As a caution I touched his adjacent knee.

Quick as a flash, Ian Junior, who had observed this, turned to me: 'See, Fr Reid is prepared to tell us more than you are prepared to go.' Even at the risk of discomfiting my friend I had to point out that there were limits to what we could reveal. Limits which had been agreed between the IRA and General de Chastelain and his colleagues which we could not ignore.

However, this conversation in itself was not sufficient to convince Ian Paisley that circumstances were such that he and his party could enter a power-sharing Assembly as ordained in the Good Friday Agreement. There was more to be sorted, such as issues to do with policing and justice which was primarily for Sinn Féin to negotiate and resolve. And I will be relating my part in facilitating those negotiations in Chapter 12.

But having waited so long for my first meeting with Ian Paisley I was to have my next in a matter of months. It was in the spring of 2006, during a period of time when I was hosting entirely discreet and sensitive conversations that I felt 'led' to visit Dr Paisley. To be honest, I doubted whether or not I would be granted an audience!

My Filofax from the time tells me that on Monday morning 3 April, I phoned Paisley's daughter, Rhonda, who kept his diary, to request a meeting.

To my surprise, Rhonda replied very promptly to my request with an apology. Her father would be in London until late morning on the following Wednesday, 5 April – but if I could give him time for his lunch he would see me in his home in east Belfast at 2.00 p.m. I was amazed that he was making time for me in his diary, and so speedily – the man who had never replied to my several invitations to come to visit Corrymeela.

Upon my arrival at his Cyprus Avenue home I was very graciously received by Mrs Eileen Paisley, who asked very kindly about my disabled niece Emma, with whose story and book of childhood prayers she was familiar. Leaving me in their spacious and well-appointed drawing room, her husband greeted me warmly, 'Well, young man, what is on your mind?' or words to that effect. It would be inappropriate for me to record all that passed between us – but what I anticipated would be a brief encounter of 20 minutes became an honest conversation which lasted well over an hour.

My objective was to build some trust, initially between the two of us, so that in turn that might be channelled into facilitating a private encounter between Ian Paisley and Martin McGuinness and the building of trust between those two political leaders, who more than any other politicians held the future of our region in their hands.

So, within our conversation I suggested that should he be open to it I could arrange for a discreet meeting between him and Martin McGuinness, who I already knew would very much welcome such an opportunity, and my home was available if he wished to take this further. I suggested that if and when he might agree to such a meeting he would be pleasantly surprised at how well they might get on with each other for I said, 'You might well find that you are two of a kind!'

By this I meant that they were both men of personal warmth and charm who could get on well both publicly and in private. They were exceptional leaders in their own right, who did not go in for what we in Ulster call 'palaver'.

Before leaving I reminded him of what I had said to him privately six months earlier as we left that post-decommissioning meeting in Stormont. As we parted back then I said that I realised he must be wondering why I would get myself involved in all of this. Not surprisingly, he looked puzzled when I explained that I did so because I wanted to see him become First Minister of Northern Ireland. 'Because', I said, 'until you claim your rightful position as voted for by the people of Northern Ireland, democracy cannot be restored to the people of Northern Ireland.'

About a year was to pass until our paths crossed again, a year that would see the removal of the remaining obstacles to the formation of an historic Paisley–McGuinness DUP–Sinn Féin-led power-sharing government at Stormont under the provisions of the Good Friday and St Andrew's Agreements.

But before this could happen, a major obstacle had yet to be resolved. This was the requirement of Sinn Féin to support policing and the courts. Elsewhere I say something about how I helped things along behind the scenes, essentially through facilitating private engagement between Jeffrey Donaldson and Martin McGuinness.

On 26 March 2007, Ian Paisley and Gerry Adams surprised the country and much of the world with their joint appearance around a diamond-shaped table at Stormont at which they agreed that the institutions of the Good Friday Agreement would be restored and that a power-sharing devolved government would be formed on 8 May 2007, Devolution Day, as it became known.

This spectacle was for so many of us a wonder as well as a joy to behold, which helped to restore some of the buoyancy that had been present at the time of the 1994 ceasefires and the Good Friday Agreement.

That communal buoyancy was evident when I next met Paisley at a British-Irish Association event at Ulster Bank HQ in Donegall Square, a splendid building once known as the 'mother church' of Methodism.

The BIA is an organisation that works quietly behind the scenes fostering friendship and understanding and debate around the big issues of the day, culminating in its annual conference that alternates between Oxford and Cambridge and is attended by politicians, civil servants, academics, Church figures and journalists.

In anticipation of the formation of an Executive, the BIA had invited many of us who would have attended their annual conferences to celebrate the progress that had been made. The guest list included First Minister-Designate Ian Paisley.

There was a wonderful spirit at that BIA meeting and Paisley was in his element. As 'man of the moment', he went round the room and discovered that he had friends he thought he would never have. People who previously wouldn't have a good word to say about him were being extraordinarily gracious. The positive atmosphere was enhanced further when Archbishop Seán Brady, the Catholic Primate of All-Ireland, and Paisley greeted one another warmly and struck up a lively conversation.

He greeted me with a cheery 'Well young fella, are you behaving yourself?' As I wished him well in the onerous responsibility that he would shortly assume, I knew by the twinkle in his eye that he remembered what I had said more than once about my wish to see him take his rightful place as First Minister.

So it was, that on Devolution Day, 8 May 2007, Fr Alec and I sat with Prime Minister Tony Blair, Taoiseach Bertie Ahern and a host of other contributors to the peace process in the public gallery of the Northern Ireland Assembly to witness Ian Paisley and Martin McGuinness take their oaths of office as First Minister and deputy First Minister of the newly constituted government of Northern Ireland. An historic moment indeed, and entirely moving as I looked around and thought of the separate and shared journeys we had all taken which had brought us to this time and place.

Amongst the photographs of that day was the striking image of Martin McGuinness and Ian Paisley entering Parliament Buildings, with the hand of the younger 'warrior' on the arm of the older 'warrior', gently and respectfully guiding him through the revolving door. I remembered what Tony Blair had once said in relation to his own role, but for me this truly was 'the hand of history'!

Sitting with us were Martin McGuinness's wife, Bernie, and his mother, Peggy. She who had told him as a young lad that he must never put his foot inside that Stormont place! Now here she was, as proud as any mother would be in such a moment. What I remember most was the genuinely warm chat between Peggy and Tony Blair. She thanked him for his very personal handwritten note of good wishes when she had been in hospital for a heart procedure. In his note he had told her of his own 'op' and trusted that her recovery would be as good as his. As we made our way from the gallery, I watched the British Home Secretary and former Northern Ireland Secretary of State, John Reid, take Peggy's arm and gently lead her down the steep steps to the Great Hall, as gently as a caring son would guide an elderly mother. As

I thought of what this moment represented I knew this was another 'hand of history' moment. A handwritten letter and a helping hand. Simply being human to one another. Simple gestures, yet profound in what they represented in that context.

To anyone unfamiliar with hymns it may sound strange that as I watched proceedings from my vantage point of privilege, I heard from within myself some lines from one of Charles Wesley's great Advent hymns. In attempting to help us understand the great mystery of the Incarnation he wrote of 'widest extremes to join … that we the life of God might know …'. Good old C.W. – writing a hymn for such a moment as this 200 years before his time!

The events of the next thirteen months, when Ian Paisley served as First Minister are well recorded elsewhere, with good-natured stories of the 'Chuckle Brothers' as Ian and Martin became known. They appeared to always be smiling and, despite their deep political and constitutional differences, treated each other with respect.

It was a strong political partnership between the two most unlikely party leaders. On their joint visits to New York and the White House to meet President George W. Bush in December 2007, they had a remarkable personal relationship, one that was not just 'put on' for the cameras.

Sadly, as Ian Paisley was to discover, this was to lead to something of a bloodless coup within both the DUP and the Free Presbyterian Church, with Paisley being dumped both as party leader and Moderator of his Church.

Such was the price of positive, progressive leadership. Ironically, what he had vehemently and at times viciously opposed in others was now to tumble him. But as he accepted the rulings of Party and Church, both of which he had personally brought into being, it was not so much a fall from grace as a fall with grace.

Having been a lifelong and consistent critic of Ian Paisley, I could not but be impressed by the change within himself which had undoubtedly led to a change in our political landscape. Only he could have taken us across the Rubicon to a new place in Irish as well as Ulster politics. I do not subscribe to the cynical view that his entire motivation was personal gain of power and prestige. The man who said 'Never, never, never' was savvy enough to anticipate the potential cost of a change of heart and political style.

So it was that sometime after his ousting I felt I wanted to personally acknowledge what he had achieved and the place to which he and Martin McGuinness had brought us. Once again, my request for a private meeting was readily granted and we met in that small 'grace and favour' room that had been granted to him within Parliament Buildings upon his 'retirement'.

I will be circumspect about what I record of that conversation, for to me it was much more pastoral than political. I asked him if he remembered what I had said on more than one occasion. About wanting to see him take his rightful place as First Minister of Northern Ireland. And how I had suggested a meeting with Martin McGuinness with whom I said he would be pleasantly surprised at how well they would get on together and discover that were indeed two of a kind.

In response he told me of their first morning in the office when he said:

> Deputy, there are two ways that we can play this. We can spend all day arguing about the things on which we are not agreed. Or we can focus on the things on which we are agreed. I suggest that will keep us fully occupied all day and every day. And this is what people put us here to do. And he replied that he fully agreed and that is how we did it.

Later in the conversation he told me of another morning that they arrived at the office.

> 'Deputy', I said, 'we have a hard day's business ahead of us. It will take us a lot of prayer to get through it.' And he said to me, 'well why don't we pray about it.' And we did!

Imagine, '... widest extremes to join'. As a personal gift I had brought a book – in which I had inscribed a few words expressing my gratitude and appreciation of the courageous journey he had made personally in the interests of the wider community. It was entitled *Exclusion and Embrace* by the Croatian theologian Miroslav Volf. I said, 'Ian, I think you will enjoy this, as it is entirely biblically based.'

From a nearby shelf, he took down a copy of his own splendidly illustrated *History of the '59 Revival* – signing it with his 'trademark' verse from Ephesians Chapter 6: 'And for me, that utterance may be given unto me, that I may open my mouth boldly, to make known the mystery of the gospel, For which I am an ambassador in bonds: that therein I may speak boldly, as I ought to speak.'

Before leaving, we prayed with each other, for each other, for our 'beloved province' and for our troubled world. I can be forgiven for revealing that in the quiet moments within that time of prayer I travelled down the years, from the teenage boy watching the book burning on Blitz Square to where we now were. For me it was a moment of 'Amazing Grace'!

It was nearing the end of his earthly life that we met at the joint British/Irish Secretariat's pre-St Patrick's Day reception on 15 March 2012.

The 'Big Man' was seated and greeting numerous well-wishers with hearty laughter and good humour and with a very personal and friendly word for myself. Noticing that the Baroness, Eileen Paisley, was standing on her own, I approached her, shook hands and after some small talk I heard myself saying, 'Eileen, if rumour is to be believed you played a much more significant part in our peace process than is generally recognised.'

Even as I spoke I heard myself asking was this appropriate, might this embarrass her, soliciting a response which she might not wish to give? And why did I say what I said about her role in the process – other than I had heard it said that it was she who conducted family prayers each morning at the breakfast table, where she shared her interpretation of the scriptures.

There was a thoughtful pause, before she replied: 'Well Harold, I often think of the women who stood at the foot of the Cross. Women can so often see things that men don't see.' She had answered my question, confirming what we had often heard.

Sometime later I was in Colombia, meeting, among others, leaders of FARC, the guerrilla group that had now been dissolved. On a free afternoon with Fr Michael Kelleher, a Redemptorist confrère of Fr Alec Reid, I took a cable car trip to the top of Monserrate outside of Bogota. From a particular viewing point, we looked down upon a beautiful garden at the centre of which there was a large life-size crucifix, at the base of which stood two women, the two Marys from the Gospel story. I immediately remembered my conversation with Eileen Paisley and paused in a moment of prayerful respect and understanding. Having my camera, I took what I immodestly suggest was one of my better efforts, had it enlarged and framed and as a Christmas gift I brought it to Eileen Paisley at her home, where she very graciously received it. Over afternoon tea from one of her exquisite china teacups we shared a happy conversation about children and grandchildren, her appreciation of Martin McGuinness's friendship and visits at the time of Ian's illness and his passing, and our shared concern for Northern Ireland. And, as with every pastoral visit, we shared our prayers before I left. For me it is a special memory of a gracious lady who in her own unobtrusive way has had a gentle but largely unrecognised hand in our history.

On Sunday, 19 October 2014, I was one of 850 invited guests, including First Minister Peter Robinson, deputy First Minister Martin McGuinness, Scotland's First Minister Alex Salmond and former Taoiseach Bertie Ahern, at a memorial service for our late First Minister, Lord Bannside. As I sat in that congregation I could not but reflect on my very personal experiences and encounters with this man, remarkable in so many different ways for so many different reasons.

My abiding thought that day was, without denying it, let us not dwell on the former part of Ian Paisley's life but rather on who he became and the journey he made. Without making direct comparisons, there are other stories we tell. Such as that of a man called Saul of Tarsus and, in more recent history, a transformed slave trader called John Newton who now has the entire world singing of 'Amazing Grace'.

11

Martin McGuinness: As I Knew Him

'The best way to find out if you can trust somebody is to trust them.'
Ernest Hemmingway

Despite the forecast of a 'barbecue summer' by the British Met Office in April, the summer of 2009 was disappointingly wet. However, I do recall one exceptionally beautiful sunny summer morning that year.

That was Monday, 3 August 2009, when Martin McGuinness, two years into his ten-year spell as deputy First Minister, or joint head of government in Northern Ireland, visited Clodagh and me in our mobile home on the north coast just outside Ballycastle, Co. Antrim.

It is an idyllic part of the country, full of the sound of sea birds with seals on the rocks and dramatic displays by the increasing presence of dolphins. From our window we look across the straits of Moyle to Rathlin Island in view of where I love to fish for mackerel in my modest open boat. Beyond Fair Head on a clear day, we can see the Mull of Kintyre and to the west beyond Lough Foyle is the vast expanse of the Atlantic, next stop Newfoundland.

We have holidayed there for over 40 years, ever since we and our now grown-up family fell in love with the place in the 1970s during my time as director of the close-by Corrymeela Centre.

I had forged a close friendship with Martin McGuinness over the thirteen or so years that I had known him up to that point and he had visited us on numerous occasions in our home in Belfast and in our 'retirement' home near Holywood, Co. Down. This was the first visit that he was to make to us during our time in Ballycastle. He had come seeking counsel on an issue related to the peace process that weighed on his mind.

Martin was an early riser, leaving his Bogside home with his driver well before 7.00 a.m. to arrive with me around 8.00 a.m., taking a 50-mile detour on his way to his office at Stormont.

That August morning in 2009 is memorable (and indeed poignant) not just because it was his first visit but because of something he said right after his arrival as well as what he was to write in our visitors' book before he left.

When he came in the door he paused and, looking out at the stunning view over the beach and across the Straits of Moyle to Rathlin Island, he exclaimed, 'Harold, is this where you go when you die?'

'Martin', I said, 'I will find out long before you and if there is a way of letting you know I will!'

Little did I know which way it was going to be.

And before he left Martin wrote in our visitors' book:

Harold & Clodagh, Liked the photo with the five pollock but what about the five mackerel that you promised me, at least Clodagh came up trumps with the scones and the strawberry cream cake. Delicious. Your friend always, Martin McGuinness

3.8.2009.

I should add that Martin, as a 'proper' fisherman, would tease me about my mackerel fishing, which true anglers would not consider real fishing. But knowing how much he relished a fresh mackerel, when there was an opportunity to deliver I would often surprise him with an unexpected treat.

Without fail, next day he would text to thank me and pronounce on the delicious mackerel breakfast he had enjoyed before heading back to Stormont for another long day's work. We never ceased to be amazed at his ability to cope with such a hectic schedule. But as a devoted family man, getting home to 'Derry, to Bernie and the family, even for a few hours, was a priority.

Martin McGuinness and I were both 'sons of 'Derry', albeit mine was a much shorter stay as I was 'snatched' from it when only eight years of age. Nevertheless, I too am a proud son of this remarkable city and after all these years I still feel very much at home when I visit.

We were born within thirteen years of each other on different sides of the river Foyle. He in the Bogside and I on the Waterside. I have been heard to say that if through the 'accident of birth' it had been the other way round, he might well have become the 'Rev' Martin McGuinness and I … well, who knows?

There have been many books and biographies written about the life of Martin McGuinness. Several of them adorn my shelves. They vary in their assessment of Martin the man, and that is not surprising. Many regard the former commander of the 'Derry IRA as a terrorist responsible for the killing and maiming of an unknown number of people and contributing directly to a large part of our legacy of suffering and loss. To others he is not just one of the finest politicians of our age but a statesman and a peacemaker who changed the course of our history for the better. Saint or sinner or both, opinion on him will aways be divided. I can only write of the Martin McGuinness who I came to know as a trusted friend, of whom I will speak primarily from a very personal and pastoral perspective.

The first time that Martin visited my home – then our manse in south Belfast – was in August 1998 when he responded with alacrity to join me for an evening meal with Brian Currin, the South African lawyer who was very much involved in that country's Truth and

Reconciliation Commission (TRC) and who was later to co-chair the Northern Ireland Sentence Review Commission. I had come to know Currin through my work as Chair of the Northern Ireland Association for the Care and Resettlement of Offenders (NIACRO) and, having heard me speak of Martin McGuinness, asked if it would be possible for me to arrange to meet him discreetly.

Following this visit, Clodagh and I have lost count of the number times Martin McGuinness was to visit our home in south Belfast and, more frequently, in our retirement home in Holywood where over a period of time he was to have discreet but hugely important conversations with 'significant others', including Jeffrey Donaldson, which I recount in some detail in the next chapter.

So it was that we formed a friendship that went far beyond the 'formal' facilitation of meetings related to our troubled times. Like others, I came to value his genuine and personal warmth. When both Clodagh and I were facing health challenges, including hospitalisation and surgeries, Martin would call us regularly to hear how we were and to wish us well.

In my tribute at his funeral, I said that his journey and mine began at our fireside. In our home in Holywood he admired the inglenook fireplace which I had designed and built with rustic red brick. He asked if I would mind if he took a picture to pass on to someone who was building one for him. So it was that we shared not one fireside, but two. I suggested that instead of the porcelain bust of John Wesley on our mantle shelf he might prefer one of the Pope. 'No', he said, 'I would be very at home with John Wesley'. Later, from the Wesley museum in London, I procured and gave him a porcelain plate with Wesley's image and one of his oft-quoted sayings, 'The best of all is, God is with us.'

Prior to my account of my first meeting with Martin McGuinness, which took place two weeks after the breakdown of the IRA ceasefire, or 'cessation' as they called it, in February 1996, I will share stories from the early noughties which give an insight into the Martin McGuinness

I came to know and a side of the man whom many would not have opportunity to see.

These stories relate to past atrocities by the IRA, including on the day that became known as Bloody Friday. They illustrate his openness to requests from people such as myself and his sensitivity to the hurt experienced by others.

A fellow member of the Human Rights Commission was Tom Donnelly, a retired businessman and former SDLP councillor in north Belfast. Tom had lost his much-loved sister, Margaret O'Hare, a mother of seven children, in the carnage of Bloody Friday on 21 July 1972. She had been shopping on the Cavehill Road and was one of nine killed and 130 injured in numerous explosions in Belfast. As we were approaching the thirtieth anniversary of this outrage Tom suggested that it would provide an opportunity for the IRA/republican movement to 'apologise'/express deep regret for what they had inflicted upon his family and others on that day. He believed such a gesture could help towards the healing of the deep hurt felt by his family and others. Knowing of my contacts with republicans, he asked if I might put this to them.

I suggested that such a request would be much more likely to be heard if it were to be conveyed by him personally. So it was that together we went to see Martin McGuinness in his Minister of Education office at Rathgael, Bangor, Co. Down. He listened intently to Tom and his request and assured us that he would take it forward. As time passed, I received two messages assuring me that what had been asked had not been forgotten and that we were not to interpret 'silence' as a negative. Then on Tuesday, 16 July 2002, I received a message asking Tom and me to watch out for the news the following morning. While for the families of police and security personnel it was a qualified regret, Tom Donnelly stated very publicly that he was overwhelmed by the IRA's apology and acceptance of responsibility.

In March 2002 I received a distressed call from a young woman called Marina Hassard from Co. Fermanagh. I had met Marina some time before when as Methodist President I had visited her local church in Churchill and Marina was the soloist.

Hers was a plea for help. On 4 August 1988, her father William Hassard and his friend and work colleague Fred Lowe were savagely murdered by the Provisional IRA. As a joiner, William and his builder friend Fred had been doing maintenance work on the local police station in Belleek, Co. Fermanagh. This was their 'crime' in the eyes of PIRA, whose twisted logic made them 'legitimate targets'. So it was that these two hard-working family men were mercilessly gunned down on their way home after their day's work. It is not difficult to imagine the grief of these families and the fear it put in the minds and hearts of a small Protestant community.

This was compounded by the erection of a memorial to three IRA volunteers on the very spot where William and Fred had been murdered, although the IRA members had died in other locations.

The families and their representatives had sought the removal of this memorial through various channels, including a legal challenge relating to the violation of planning rules, but without success. Hearing that I was a member of the Human Rights Commission, Marina contacted me to ask if there was anything we could do from a human rights perspective.

So it was that my fellow Commission members, Brice Dickson, Tom Donnelly, Christine Eames, and I drove down to Fermanagh to meet with Unionist councillors and to visit the site.

Before the day was out, we were publicly criticised by the local Sinn Féin MP Michelle Gildernew, who asserted that it was none of the business of our Commission. In one sense she was right, in that we had no powers to intervene under our terms of reference, but we considered it was important that we be seen to share concern for what was clearly a denial of human hurt and of the right for both the living and the dead to be treated with respect.

Once again I requested a meeting with Martin McGuinness, who met me in a Sinn Féin office in Belfast, accompanied by Gerry Adams.

When I outlined the problem and spoke of the deep personal hurt suffered by these two families and the damage to trust and relationships in the community, I was clearly heard. They were totally agreed that this should never have happened and that the siting of this memorial was totally inappropriate. They asked me to trust them to do what they could and assured me of their best efforts. Once again, I was given advance notice and was greatly relieved when it was publicly announced that the memorial to the three volunteers had been moved to an alternative site across the border, close to where at least one of them had died. Once more, the man who I was coming to know gave me every good reason to believe that he himself was on a new journey. A journey that was going to have huge significance for all of our futures as well as for him, personally and politically.

* * *

It is said that there is no greater honour than that bestowed by one's own people. So it was that I was astonished and humbled to receive the 2007 World Methodist Peace Award. The ceremony was scheduled to take place in my home church at Knock. I was most anxious that in addition to family and friends my guest list would include those from within the Church and the wider political community with whom I had shared the long and challenging journey in our search for peace. For reasons which you will understand when you read further, I was particularly disappointed to receive a genuine apology from Jeffrey Donaldson, who was in China, and to hear that deputy First Minister Martin McGuinness was tied up in Washington DC. You can imagine how moved I was when, having managed to reschedule his morning meeting with President George W. Bush, there he was, smiling broadly at me from the front pew.

* * *

Several years later, on 26 December 2010, I had been asked to conduct morning worship in our Dundonald Church on the Ballybeen estate on the outskirts of mainly Protestant east Belfast. As was my custom when invited to preach on the Sunday following Christmas, my sermon was based on the wonderful story of Simeon and Anna. How they rejoiced in the sight of the Christ child who had been brought to the Temple by Mary and Joseph, 'to do for him what the custom of the law required …' [Luke 2: 22–40]. In setting the scene I explained how at that time there were those who believed they could only be liberated from the rule of their oppressors by an 'armed struggle'. But there were others, like the faithful Simeon, who believed that one day God would send a Saviour in a very different and unexpected way to deliver His people Israel.

I drew the obvious parallels between then and now. How there were those in our world of today who believe that what they desire can only be achieved through physical force and violence. Not just where we live – but in other places of conflict around our world. I emphasised that there is an alternative and we must seek the way of peace rather than the way of physical force and conflict. I sensed (as preachers do) that I had been heard and understood.

But as it happened, I had unwittingly committed what some would consider to be an unpardonable sin. I had not switched off my mobile phone and as we were singing our closing hymn it rang in my cassock pocket. Anxious to stop it without delay I pulled it from my pocket, assuming it might be Clodagh asking me to bring home a litre of milk. Instead, I noticed it was a Christmas greeting and text from Martin McGuinness, our deputy First Minister, who never failed to remember us at Christmas. As the congregation sang on, oblivious to what was happening, I glanced surreptitiously at the message. As well as a very personal Christmas greeting to myself and love to Clodagh, it was his wish that in the coming year all of us would share peace and hope.

'Will I or won't I', I thought as the hymn was concluding. Should I share this before I pronounce the benediction? How would it be received in a Protestant church in the heart of loyalist Ballybeen? But in response to one of those mysterious inner 'prompts' that preachers get, I did. Having confessed to not having switched off my phone, I wished to share a message which was directly related to the sermon I had just preached.

It was a message, not from Simeon, but from someone who himself had discovered that there was a much better alternative to the way of violence. After I read the message, revealing from whom it had come, I pronounced a final blessing and went to the door. Almost without exception, the congregation clasped my hand and thanked me for sharing what several of them said they had found to be profoundly moving.

* * *

As related earlier, in Chapter 8, the Feakle Talks in late 1974 between Protestant clergy and the IRA had collapsed before they had properly started due to the arrival of the Irish Special Branch.

Such setbacks could not be allowed to deflect Christian leaders, clerics and lay, from continuing against the odds to initiate possible paths to peace even if the prospects looked bleak.

My first encounter with suspected and/or former militant republicans and loyalists had been during my period in Corrymeela in the seventies. This had reinforced my view that non-judgemental engagement and honest dialogue is always better than a sterile condemnatory approach.

From the earliest period of our troubled years our Methodist Council on Social Responsibility sought to be open and courageous in our response to the deepening crisis within and across our community. In our regular meetings we sought to update ourselves on an ever-changing situation with compassionate responses to tragic events as well as statements of critical analysis that challenged government and our political representatives. Given the circumstances of the time, some of these statements and pronouncements were relatively radical. For example, our response to the Anglo-Irish Agreement of 1985 did not conform to what was expected of us as representatives of a section of the Protestant and largely unionist community. But there came a time when it was realised that statements in themselves, including robustly worded statements condemning violence, however good, were not enough. Neither could we go on talking *about* people. The time had come to talk *with* people.

So it was that we began to meet with people of political influence from across our community, initially with political representatives and 'influencers' from within unionism and moderate nationalism. However, not before time we realised the need to reach out beyond the relative comfort of these valuable but relatively unchallenging conversations with comparatively like-minded people and seek engagement with militant protagonists from republicanism as well as loyalism.

I cannot be precise about dates as I did not keep records at the time. Meetings were often arranged at short notice and fitted in with my myriad other duties as a pastor.

It is important to note that Methodists did not have a monopoly on pushing boundaries in terms of dialogue and public debate. Reverend Ken Newell, of Fitzroy Presbyterian Church, close to Queen's University, Fr Gerry Reynolds CSsR of Clonard Monastery, David Porter, the leader of ECONI (Evangelical Contribution on Northern Ireland), Sir George Quigley, a distinguished retired civil servant, and the members of the Northern Consensus Group were among those we knew to be involved in similar conversations.

Also in the early 1990s, in response to an invitation from Pax Christi (Peace of Christ), the international Catholic peace movement, the Rev. Lesley Carroll from the Presbyterian Church and I were engaged in challenging meetings with significant republicans in Connolly House, Sinn Féin's west Belfast headquarters.

I remain grateful that I and fellow Methodists involved in such conversations were doing so with the unconditional blessing of our Methodist Council on Social Responsibility. What was vitally important to those of us engaged in these contacts was that we did not have to seek permission or report back on the details. This enabled us to engage and develop relationships naturally at a pace that was mutually comfortable.

This early engagement with Sinn Féin came at a time when such dialogue was considered in many political and other Church circles to be disloyal as well as potentially dangerous. At best it was considered 'not to be the right time' to talk with the perceived enemy. Tragically, while people waited for 'the right time' more lives were being lost.

To those who opposed our 'talking to the enemy' I also tried to explain that talking does not mean condoning their violence nor being unmindful of the pain and suffering of victims. Nothing could be further from the truth. The ultimate goal had to be an end to violence and no more killing.

However, within our discreet conversations I increasingly heard it said, 'we need to talk to this man, Martin McGuinness'. But this was not to happen until shortly after the breakdown of the IRA cessation of violence on 9 February 1996.

At the end of January 1996, very senior Sinn Féin representatives, including Mitchel McLaughlin, Tom Hartley, Alex Maskey and Jim Gibney, with whom we had regular meetings over the preceding years, asked for an urgent meeting. They were deeply concerned. They were saying: 'We need to be taken seriously, at the very least we need a picture of our leaders going into Downing Street.'

Because there had been no positive response from Downing Street to Sinn Féin's request for a personal meeting with the Prime Minister they were finding it very difficult to 'hold back' the elements within republicanism who had been given to believe that there would have been a swift and positive response to the 1994 ceasefire.

The situation was critical, we were told. Unless there was visible/concrete evidence of the government being serious there would be those who would wish to send another kind of message which could destroy all of the progress that had been made in our search for peace, putting the peace process back years. Could we get this message across to the government – and urgently? We were assured that this was not to be seen as 'blackmailing' but as stating a reality, a genuine effort on their part to avoid what they believed would be a disaster. All they were asking for was a meeting between the Prime Minister and the Sinn Féin leadership. All it would take was a photograph on the steps of Number 10 as evidence that the ceasefire was recognised for what it was. A genuine gesture towards a political resolution and an end of conflict.

In response, on 2 February 1996, with Rev. Henry Keys, Methodist chaplain at Queen's University and a member of our CSR group, I secured a meeting with Sir David Fell, head of the Northern Ireland Civil Service, having reason to believe that he would be sympathetic to our representations.

We reported our conversations and our belief that what we had been told must be taken with the utmost seriousness and we urged him to convey this directly to Downing Street. Perhaps we should not have been surprised, but we were deeply disappointed at the response. The government would not give in to threats nor do deals with terrorists. We sought to persuade him that we did not see this as a threat but a plea from those we knew to be committed to the search for peace and an alternative to violence who were facing the reality that without evidence of 'good faith' from the government there would be those who would take matters into their own hands. There would, we believed, be consequences over which our confidantes would have no control. We left that meeting with no reason to believe that our message would be delivered.

At that time I had a contact with a 'well-placed' friend in London, who, on their visits to Northern Ireland, had shown much interest in our situation. And being in a position of influence as far as government was concerned had suggested that if I thought they could be helpful in any way to please ask. This was such a moment. In those days we did not have email, but we did have fax, so I wrote down our request as carefully and clearly as I could and faxed it. Sadly, I can find no copy of it.

Tragically, we were quickly overtaken by events, when on Friday evening, 9 February 1996, our worst fears were realised with the tragic news of the London Docklands bombing, devastating one of the United Kingdom's biggest financial and economic centres. While even more tragic for the families of the two men who died and for the 100 plus who were injured, it was also devastating for confidence and progress in our peace process.

While there may well have been others who were privy to Sinn Féin's concerns and may well have conveyed them, to this day I personally regret that I did not get on a plane, make my own journey to London and sit on his doorstep at Number 10 until John Major agreed to hear me.

Coincidentally, at the same time there was another high-profile plea to our Methodist Church at presidential level from John Hume and Gerry Adams, with a request for an urgent meeting. This took place in Clonard Monastery and was attended by our President, Rev. Chris Walpole, the Rev. David Cooper and Dr David Gallagher, as Convenor and Secretary of our Council on Social Responsibility, and the Rev. Henry Keys, with Fr Alec Reid looking in from time to time.

The import of what Hume and Adams said was what we had already been given to understand: that the ceasefire was in imminent danger due to intransigence on the British side. Their plea was that Major be sent an urgent message that the situation could only be retrieved by the Prime Minister convening a meeting between himself and Adams and Martin McGuinness in Downing Street. In response, my Methodist confrères considered that the best person to convey that message was Archbishop Robin Eames, who had recently been elevated to the House of Lords by Major in recognition of his contribution to the peace process. And that I was the person best placed to contact Robin, which I did. He subsequently confirmed that the message had been delivered. The word back was similar to the answer we had received from David Fell. Although John Major personally was not unsympathetic, he felt he could not proceed with such a meeting owing to pressure from his backbenchers.

Mention of John Major prompts me to digress briefly and recall how before the year was out I, with others, was invited to meet Major on his last pre-Christmas visit as Prime Minister as the year that had already being remembered for the collapse of the ceasefire neared its end. The venue was the fascinating Folk and Transport Museum at Cultra, just outside Belfast. We were 'herded' into small groups of five and instructed that when the Prime Minister would come to our group each of us would have an uninterrupted personal one-minute opportunity to say what we felt we wanted the Prime Minister of the United Kingdom to hear. Quite a challenge for a Methodist preacher who is accustomed to having all the time he chooses to address a captive 'audience'.

So, I had to think quickly. As we were standing in the shadow of an historic locomotive, I chose this as my 'object lesson' and spoke of the need to bring everybody on board if we were going to embark on a new journey. Interestingly he listened and, in agreeing, said emphatically that this is what he hoped to do. But he emphasised that this required a willingness on all sides to come aboard – or words to that effect.

The ceasefire or 'complete cessation of military operations' as the IRA called it, had been a momentous, deeply consequential development and its breakdown filled us all with sadness. But I knew that it also underlined the fragility of the peace that many had come to take for granted. It also meant that we had to work all the harder to help rebuild the peace and the confidence and this would call for yet more dialogue and respectful, honest engagement.

This meant that we must now seek to engage directly for the first time with 'this man, Martin McGuinness' – perhaps something we should have done earlier. Certainly, now was the time for our Methodist Council to step up a gear and go to the top and build on our earlier conversations with less senior Sinn Féin figures during which trust was sown and nurtured.

First Meeting

So, within days of the breakdown of the ceasefire, as members of our Council of Social Responsibility, we invited ourselves to a private meeting with Martin McGuinness in his Bogside office in 'Derry. Joining me were the Rev. Jim Rea of East Belfast Mission, the Rev. Dr Wesley Blair, and Dr David Gallagher, who acted as secretary. We found that we were pushing an open door. My Filofax confirms that what was to be my first and probably most memorable meeting with McGuinness took place precisely a fortnight after the Docklands bomb, on the evening of Friday, 23 February 1996.

We met in a small back bedroom of a modest house overlooking the Bogside. Our Secretary, Dr David Gallagher, son of the Rev. Eric Gallagher, who was one of those who had met with the IRA at Feakle, Co. Clare in 1974, had prepared a list of ten very direct key questions/opinions that we wanted to ask/share.

My abiding memory of that meeting was Martin's intense and focused attention to what we were saying, and in particular to David's list of points, which were as penetrating as they were comprehensive, capturing as they did the potential drastic implications of the IRA decision to resume violence.

We had not come to 'Derry to give Sinn Féin's chief negotiator (and probable lynchpin of the IRA leadership) an easy ride. He knew that and respected us for that, just as we treated him with respect, listened to him and took care to avoid the self-defeating 'preachiness' he may have experienced in meetings with others.

Those points drawn up by David are worth reproducing in full:

1. Morality: is method more important than cause? Is republican unity/purity more important than peace? Who does the IRA speak for?
2. Risking abyss – including loyalist violence – explosives, death squads. Bosnia-type situation. Who will suffer most?

3. Effect on attitudes – [first] ceasefire not seen as 'generous' because violence shouldn't have occurred in first place – consider how slow the pace of movement/degree of trust there was after 25 years of violence so how much more difficult will it be now.
4. Effect on children – fear/bigotry.
5. No win/No Lose – what's the point of continuing/stalemate? Doesn't the IRA not understand British/Unionist reaction to violence/threat … i.e. very stubborn. Have lessons of Feakle/G. Wilson not been learnt?
6. Fledgling reconciliation (which was spontaneous and adventurous) now jeopardized. The unimaginable was beginning to occur but now risked, for what? A tragedy!
7. Tempting people to return to the political process but not the peace process – will lead to further alienation, exclusion, 'pariah status'. Is this what the IRA wants for the republican community?
8. PR disaster – pan nationalist front strained/American support now questionable/enhanced. Paisley 'I told you so' position/ made things more difficult for those of us arguing for inclusion and accepting the reality of no decommissioning 'gesture'.
9. Personal reaction – stunned, angry. Is this the thanks for going out on a limb? If the MCI [Methodist Church in Ireland] a position was supportive of power sharing/N[orth]S[outh] dimension/ Parity of esteem then now more difficult to convince others of that.
10. Legitimacy – who does the IRA speak for?
11. Republican community must address unionism. Stop blaming the Brits and looking to them to 'persuade'. Let's say that violence encourages Britain to 'persuade' or withdraw, is this the best way to reach 'lasting peace'? Widespread accommodation? Do you become generous to the other when pressurized/feeling isolated/let down or more committed/determined/maybe more irrational?

Upon reflection, there was a similarity in what we were saying with the message my father had delivered to the then republican leadership in 1959 when he sought to impress upon them that, even if through violence they were to succeed in their mission to re-unite Ireland, there would be 'serious moral as well as political consequences to answer'.

As we talked through those points, McGuinness carefully wrote down all our questions and concerns, to which he responded in considered and thoughtful detail, assuring us that he had heard us and would give very careful consideration to what we had shared with him. 'This guy is serious', was what we confided to each other as we drove home.

Martin's very warm handshake, his welcoming personable attitude and positive body language throughout the greater part of two hours, his completely unpatronising approach, his careful listening and considered replies, his overworked pen and extensive notetaking had all pointed to a very serious engagement.

On reflection, I suspect that it may well have been the first time he had encountered people like us from a Protestant/unionist perspective in a considered and non-confrontational conversation. For me it was to prove to be the basis and the beginning of a very personal friendship based on trust and mutual respect.

***

It was with the encouragement of Martin McGuinness amongst others that the respected and skilled 'Derry City Centre Manager Jim Roddy and I were asked to help broker an agreement to bring an end to the difficulties surrounding parades and protests in the Twaddell/Crumlin Road areas of Belfast. Having been refused permission for their traditional 2013 Twelfth of July return parade, the local Orange lodges set up a protest camp, declaring that it would not be removed until they were permitted to complete their return 'home'. This resulted in a three-year standoff between the lodges and nationalist residents, costing the Police Service of Northern Ireland more than £20 million to provide 24/7 cover of the camp and the community.

A key turning point in this dispute occurred in April 2016, following the murder of Michael McGibbon, a Roman Catholic taxi driver who was the innocent victim of a dissident republican so-called 'punishment shooting'. The entire community was outraged. None more than loyalist leader Winston Irvine, who, being deeply moved by the bravery of Michael McGibbon's wife and in sympathy with the wider Ardoyne community, successfully convinced the camp to put their protest 'on hold' as a tangible mark of respect for the vigil being held just yards away. Irvine vividly remembers the call he made to Fr Gary Donegan to inform him of the decision, which was to be a watershed moment in the longstanding dispute. The significance of this gesture resonated across this divided community and set the stage for the pivotal negotiations which were to follow.

For Jim and for me it was a privilege to be trusted by both 'sides' and we were greatly impressed by the spirit in which each sought to understand the position of the other, while defending their own with mutual respect and acceptance of constructive compromise. So it was that following many months of honest and respectful engagement an agreement was signed in September 2016 and, to the credit of all concerned, the protest camp was dismantled and the Ligoniel lodges completed their return parade on 1 October 2016.

To build on what had been achieved and to look to the future there was the establishment of a Community Forum, committed to the terms of the agreement and to the building of trust and good relationships.

At the table were an equal number of residents and members of the loyal orders, together with a seat for an elected MLA from each of the parties which held Assembly seats in the area. Sadly, for reasons of their own, the only party not to participate was the DUP, which puzzled representatives of the lodges as well as us. A dismissive meeting with Nigel Dodds, MP for the area, did nothing to reassure us of his party's support for our positive efforts.

The agreement we reached between the local Orange lodges and nationalist residents that ended the Twaddell protest was widely welcomed and Jim and I went to Stormont to personally brief First Minister Arlene Foster and deputy First Minister Martin McGuinness. Given the significance of this breakthrough, it was beyond our understanding when we were informed that the First Minister did not have time to meet us. However, we were warmly welcomed and encouraged by the deputy First Minister to continue with what at the time of writing as yet 'unfinished business'.

Given his personal interest in how the Twaddell agreement was progressing, Jim Roddy and I arranged to review things with Martin McGuinness over an early breakfast in a Belfast hotel in late 2016. It was unusual for him to have stayed overnight in Belfast, but he had been at a late meeting in Dublin the night before. As we left him, Jim and I shared our unease at how Martin had looked, as well as what appeared to us to be a lack of his usual energy.

A matter of weeks later, on 9 January 2017, I and everyone else was shocked at how poorly he looked on television while announcing his resignation as deputy First Minister in light of the Renewable Heat Incentive (RHI) scandal.

What a sad moment that was and devastating for our political process. And even more traumatic for him, his wife, Bernie, and his family when they were told of the nature of his illness and the prognosis. I felt humbled and privileged to be taken into the family's confidence.

Respecting his need for privacy but remembering his concern for any of us in our times of illness, my phone calls were spaced and brief. But knowing it would be a last opportunity, I arranged with Bernie that I would call and see him at his home. We both knew it would be a final but fond farewell. And before I left the three of us knelt, held each other's hands and prayed. Giving thanks for what we had shared and praying for strength and grace and peace. As I left, I felt this prayer had already been answered.

When his mother had died, Martin said he would have so much wanted me to have taken part in her funeral service, but somehow assumed that this might not have been possible. So it was that I was grateful for the opportunity to take part in his funeral service on 23 March 2017.

And what a remarkable service it was, a de facto State funeral bringing together figures as diverse as the President of Ireland, Michael D. Higgins; former US President Bill Clinton, who delivered a powerful eulogy; the Taoiseach, Enda Kenny; First Minister Arlene Foster, who had suffered at the hands of the IRA as a child, and her predecessor, Peter Robinson; the Secretary of State for Northern Ireland, James Brokenshire; PSNI Chief Constable George Hamilton, who had lost so many colleagues down the decades to the IRA; old enemies and as yet unreconciled adversaries; comrades and former combatants from the days of conflict. All of these figures gathered along with his family and as many of his neighbours and friends from his beloved city as could be accommodated in the historic Tower Church, not far from his home in the Bogside.

I had been invited to choose a scripture reading and was privileged to be asked to preface it with a personal tribute. But first I quipped that the chief celebrant, Fr Michael Canny, had in his homily referred to Martin's love of good fish, including salmon, but had omitted to say how much he had enjoyed my mackerel in Ballycastle, for which he had always taken the trouble to text thanks next day, provoking laughter and loud applause.

'How often during this past week', I said, 'has the life of Martin McGuinness been likened to a remarkable journey, and rightly so.'

I continued:

Would that more of us were open to new journeys in our lives. As with so many of you, on Martin's personal journey and mine our paths crossed many, many times. Often on the path to our home and to our fireside where friendship was forged. But, in particular, I am mindful of the road that took us to the decommissioning of the arms of the IRA.

The night before Father Alec Reid and I set off on that remarkable journey on which we were to witness the last gun removed from Irish politics, we shared a room. As stumbling pilgrims, followers of Jesus on our journey of Christian discipleship, we went quiet as we attended to our personal evening devotions, he with his prayer book and I with my daily Bible reading.

You can only imagine my astonishment when I was guided to the reading for that day which was from the ever familiar and powerful passage contained in Paul's Letter to the Ephesians, where he speaks of 'The Whole Armour of God'. Reminding us that for those of us who seek to be obedient to Christ, there is always another and a better way.

The last time I read this passage in public was at Father Alec Reid's funeral service in Clonard Monastery. As I read it, I glanced down at my friend Martin McGuinness and I saw him nodding in agreement.

I then proceeded to read from that passage (Ephesians 6:11–18) in which we are reminded that the real battle now as then is not against 'flesh and blood', but against the spiritual forces of evil in a very dark world. In such a conflict we need weaponry of a different kind, which will include the belt of truth, the breastplate of righteousness, the Gospel of peace, the shield of faith, the helmet of salvation and the sword of the Spirit, which is the Word of God. What to me was most gratifying was that I did not receive one letter, phone call or confrontation on the street criticising me for taking part in a funeral Mass, let alone that of Martin McGuinness – a sign of the times, but much more: confirmation of the respect the man had earned in the latter years of his life.

In thinking how I might conclude this chapter is there any tribute more eloquent than that offered so publicly, so graciously, and unexpectedly by Ian Paisley Junior when he said on the day that a gravely ill Martin McGuinness announced his retirement:

> I can say thank you honestly and humbly and recognise the remarkable journey Martin McGuinness went on has not only saved lives, but has made the lives of countless people in Northern Ireland better because of the partnership government we worked on and put together.

I can only add to these further words of the same Ian Junior that formed part of his tribute to Martin McGuinness after his death: 'As a Christian, it is not how you start your life that's important, it's how you finish your life.'

12

WHEN MARTIN MET JEFFREY

'A watershed is where two streams meet.'

Anon

I was deeply aware that my outreach and that of my Church to republicans (and to Martin McGuinness in particular when it became known) was not to everyone's taste. But I passionately believed that we could only begin to heal our divisions through honest dialogue.

Indeed, as Convenor of our Council on Social Responsibility, my colleague the Rev. David Cooper came under much criticism from some individual Methodists as well as others when he formally reported at our Conference in 'Derry in 1997 that our Council was actively engaged in meetings with Sinn Féin at a time when the IRA had still not restored their ceasefire. On reflection, it was unfair that David had to carry that responsibility although the Conference as a whole was supportive.

As I have recounted earlier, my dialogue with prominent figures in Sinn Féin had begun in the early 1990s as part of an initiative by Pax Christi, by which time I had moved from Knock and become minister of University Road and Lisburn Road congregations.

However, I should stress that I and others from our Church were not just talking to republicans. We knew that to make meaningful progress we had to move away from talking only with those who agreed with us and develop honest respectful engagement with any and all of those whose suspected involvement in or support for violence we deplored, but with whom we and others must have honest engagement if we were ever to break the cycle of violence and make peace, however 'messy' the process.

Not all of these conversations were 'secret' or behind the curtains. For example, there was an initiative by our Methodist District Superintendent, the Rev. David Kerr, who invited every circuit to send a minister and two lay persons to an event in our University Road church. We began the evening with an honest conversation with those whom we knew to be loyalist paramilitaries, which was followed by a separate engagement with prominent republicans.

This was not seen as an opportunity to lecture captive audiences. Rather, it was essentially a listening exercise, giving time to those with whom we were meeting to inform us as to their thinking and their aspirations. But at the same time leaving them in no doubt as to where we were coming from. At the close of each of our separate conversations one of our ministers had been asked to lead us in a quiet moment of reflection and a prayer before we parted. Following our conversation with republicans the Rev. David Clements, whose RUC father had been murdered by the IRA, read from his father's Bible the passage which his father had read on the morning of his death. Leading republicans who were present spoke of how they had been moved by David's very personal reflection. It was to prove to be an important and useful exercise. Particularly as it was not reported in any of the newspapers.

Several years before the ceasefires of 1994 and long before our respectful and constructive engagement with Martin McGuinness in 'Derry, I went on something of a 'solo run'. Believing that such conversations need to be widened, I invited myself into private conversations with those who I viewed as 'significant others' on the Protestant or unionist side. This was at a time when there was still too little engagement, even between supposed moderate unionists and nationalists.

To the unionist mind even quiet 'below the radar' conversations with republicans would have been seen to ignore the brutality of the 'armed struggle' and concede the possibility of a radically different future for Northern Ireland. It was a conversation for which people were not yet ready.

I felt it was now time to encourage unionists, large 'U' politicians and small 'u' people of influence from the then 'majority' community, to engage in private conversations with republicans, those with whom they were diametrically opposed, politically and ideologically, and had never met with face to face.

Those I sounded out included politicians in the Ulster Unionist Party and the Loyal Orders but, sadly, without success. I was politely told that there was no interest at all in pursuing this, at least not until republicans gave up their armed struggle and repented of their actions.

However, in the longer term it was to be proven that my previous efforts were by no means in vain. For one of those I approached was the young and articulate Ulster Unionist politician Jeffrey Donaldson. I invited him to lunch à deux in a city centre restaurant known as The Beaten Docket in Great Victoria Street. There was only one other table occupied that day so there was little background noise to aid privacy. To make matters worse, the young waitress kept coming to see if there was anything else we needed. I sensed my guest felt uncomfortable in the setting and perhaps wondered had he been set up in some way!

I have to say that in the context of that time, while disappointed, I could understand his negative reaction and that of the others to my suggestion of very discreet conversations between them as individuals and individual republicans.

But that initial engagement with the future Ulster Unionist MP and MLA, and DUP MLA, junior minister, MP, and party leader was to prove invaluable as it laid the foundations for a relationship of mutual respect and trust which years later resulted in an extremely fruitful contact. For he too was to become a frequent visitor to our home.

With my election as President of the Methodist Church in Ireland in 2001 I was to become one of 'the four Church leaders' and enjoy the access that goes with that honour and privilege. That access can be to the great as well as to the good. For me and my fellow Church leaders, Archbishops Seán Brady, Robin Eames and Presbyterian Moderator Alastair Dunlop, that meant an invitation to a breakfast meeting hosted by Prime Minister Tony Blair in his official residence at 10 Downing Street on 24 January 2002. The Prime Minister was accompanied by his Northern Ireland Secretary of State, John Reid. This was at a time when the Executive at Stormont was still functioning under the co-leadership of David Trimble and Mark Durkan. Once we got over the 'awe' and at whose table we were sitting, we enjoyed a splendid breakfast and shared an entirely serious conversation as to how we might advance the peace process against the continuing logjam over decommissioning.

Also in attendance was Francis Campbell, the Prime Minister's Co. Down-born private secretary and foreign policy adviser, who had arranged the meeting.

Later, Francis – a future UK ambassador to the Holy See – surprised me by saying that the PM was particularly interested in my contribution and asked to see my biographical details. These included playing a role on such bodies as the Northern Ireland Association for the Care and Resettlement of Offenders (NIACRO), the NI Human Rights Commission, and the UK Social Security Advisory Committee.

Apparently, Tony Blair had noted my experience of the wider world outside the comfort zone of 'churchy people', which, in his view, had enabled me to make a distinctive contribution to the conversation.

Sometime later I received a visit from a senior NIO official who was conveying a request from what I was told to be 'the highest level', asking if I could facilitate some person-to-person discussions that might contribute to building trust between political adversaries or words to that effect.

So, building on the respective engagements years earlier in The Beaten Docket and in 'Derry, I invited Jeffrey Donaldson and Martin

McGuinness to our home and to our table, assuring them of complete confidentiality. I knew that of all the politicians these two would be crucial to any future restoration of power-sharing and any hope of the revival of the institutions of the Good Friday Agreement. Having no idea as to whether or how my invitation would be received, I was very pleased at the ready acceptance of both.

At first, I would characterise the mood between the two men as cautious. Understandably so given the respective journeys both had made to that point: McGuinness a self-confessed IRA leader, whose organisation had murdered numerous people, and who had lost numerous comrades in the conflict. Donaldson, a former Ulster Defence Regiment soldier who lost two first cousins, both RUC officers and brothers, to the IRA, as well as many comrades in the UDR, and friends, including Edgar Graham, the young UUP Assembly member and barrister.

Having first met as strangers to one another, over a period of time the atmosphere lightened. While obviously they had no grounds to be best friends, they showed mutual respect for each other, progressed to trust one another and engaged with honesty and with resolve, in the hope of an outcome which they could live with and, even more importantly, sell to their respective parties. Which in time they finally did achieve when Martin McGuinness and Ian Paisley finally came to power in 2007.

In my view and in my experience, Martin and Jeffrey were senior politicians of skill and nuance who were sensitive to the needs of the other and were determined to do business on behalf of their respective constituencies. But also on behalf of our wider community which they knew only too well had endured and suffered so much together.

I have lost count of the number of times they met in my home. For most of these visits Martin was accompanied by his special adviser, Aidan McAteer. While Jeffrey was on his own for most of these meetings, I sensed that Peter Robinson was the 'unseen presence' in the room.

While anxious not to betray the trust that they invested in me during these conversations, elsewhere in these pages I describe something of the process that resulted in my witnessing the final and conclusive act of IRA decommissioning in September 2005. And my emotions at being present at Stormont to witness the swearing in of Martin and Ian Paisley as our joint heads of government on Devolution Day, 8 May 2007.

But before that could happen, decommissioning had to be completed and the issue of Sinn Féin's support for policing and the administration of justice had to be resolved to the satisfaction of all who had signed up to the Good Friday Agreement, as well as to the Democratic Unionist Party.

Following the final act of decommissioning, which I had witnessed in September 2005, Tony Blair and Bertie Ahern had worked tirelessly with the Northern Ireland parties, and especially the DUP and Sinn Féin, to coax them towards a restoration of the Good Friday institutions.

In spite of the radical reform of policing following the publication of the Patten Report in 1999 and its subsequent implementation, often in the teeth of unionist opposition, Sinn Féin had not yet agreed to support the newly formed Police Service of Northern Ireland (PSNI).

But a fresh opportunity came with the St Andrews Agreement of October 2006, when the DUP effectively agreed to share power with Sinn Féin if the latter supported the police. Understandably, this had to be resolved before the DUP would feel able to join a mandatory coalition with republicans who had been so inextricably linked to the IRA – an organisation that had been responsible for the deaths and maiming of so many people, including the killing of 300 police officers. And from a republican perspective, given the history of their relationship with the RUC, this was to be no less of a challenge for them.

This then was to be the next and crucial challenge. There would be many months of behind-the-scenes discussions and negotiations before Sinn Féin were to make their landmark decision to support the PSNI and the administration of justice.

Recently I have recovered my sporadically updated journal for the period between November 2004 and January 2007, along with a cache of text messages from May 2006 to March 2007, evidencing the commitment of both Martin and Jeffrey, who, from entirely different backgrounds and conflicting ideologies, worked tirelessly and respectfully to anchor the peace and give us the opportunity of a brighter future.

My journal recalls that when I first contacted Jeffrey Donaldson in March 2006 he had anticipated my request. And 'yes, he would be willing' to meet Martin again. 'The timing is right', he said and suggested my place. Martin immediately gave an equally positive response, via Aidan McAteer as my journal notes, 'M cannot use his phone to call me ... nor I to him ... lines regularly tapped.'

So, building on the relationships that had been nurtured in previous approaches and engagements, this was to be the catalyst for the commencement of a long series of further private conversations in our discreetly located home on the outskirts of Belfast. Conversations which were fortified by Clodagh's tea and scones, the only witnesses being myself and our elderly cuckoo clock whose interruptions lightened the mood during particularly tense moments – of which there were surprisingly few.

Significantly, around the same time I also noted a conversation with Jeffrey Donaldson when I asked if he thought 'it would be a good idea for me to see his leader', Dr Paisley. According to my journal, 'he felt it would and encouraged me to do so, in a one to one.' So it was that on 5 April 2006 I met Ian Paisley, as I have related in Chapter 10.

As we approached Christmas 2006, the outstanding issues between the DUP and Sinn Féin remained policing and justice. Very importantly, and entirely reasonably, the DUP required of Sinn Féin unequivocal support for the PSNI and the courts.

As a next step, Sinn Féin was to organise an Ard Chomhairle (National Executive Committee) followed by a special Ard Fheis (conference) at which they would decide whether or not the conditions were right for them to cross the Rubicon once more to endorse policing and justice. For this to happen there could be no doubt that the DUP would keep their word and share power.

On Christmas Eve Jeffrey texted me: 'Thanks, Harold. Hope you and your family have a blessed Christmas. Thank you for your willingness to share the journey into uncharted territory!'

On Christmas Day Martin texted: 'Thank u H, in my eyes u are one of the brightest stars of the PP [peace process] God bless Clodagh, U and all ur family on this special day for all of us. C u soon my friend.'

A text from Aidan McAteer also on Christmas Day read: 'Many thanks. Happy Christmas to you and all your family. The break will be short. We need to come to see you on Wed [27 December] if that is OK.'

In my journal I wrote: 'A bit surprised by this as I thought that by and large everything was "done and dusted."' Obviously there had been a hitch and Sinn Féin needed urgent reassurances.

So, on the morning of Wednesday, 27 December my mobile bleeped out a message from Aidan: 'Can we see you at 11?' I texted him back, 'Certainly – but have you confirmed this with your other guest?' Quickly he replied, 'That's done, Thanks.'

This time Jeffrey was, unusually, accompanied by Timothy Johnston, a DUP staffer, and his DUP colleague Sammy Wilson. As usual, Martin McGuinness was accompanied by Aidan McAteer.

In my journal I wrote: 'Over Clodagh's mince pies and Christmas cake we began with good natured chat about Christmas, sport, etc. M [Martin] revealed that he loved to watch cricket, a fascinating game, though confessed that he had never been to an actual match. As usual A [Aidan] was anxious to get on with the business.'

I continued, in what amounted to be a private minute of the meeting for my own use which I believe it is now appropriate to share here (as with Cabinet papers that come out after Christmas each year). It sheds light on the dynamics of high-stake negotiations and the pressures involved and evokes appreciation of the skills that make good politics work in the interests of the common good.

From my journal:

> SF explained that they need unambiguous clarity in terms of the DUP response in the event of an endorsement of the motion which they (SF) were bringing to the Ard Chomhairle due to meet on Thursday [the following day] evening. [It actually met the following Friday, December 29.] There was discussion as to the actual wording of the statement which IRKP [Paisley] would make. Assurance was given that this had been agreed with Downing Street and would therefore not be different. This was obviously vital for SF as they would need to assure their AC [Ard Chomhairle] that acceptance of their position would be forthcoming from DUP as well as Government/s.
>
> Clarification was sought on detail as to what and when. It was explained that IRKP would make the expected statement soon after the AC result was announced. This would be as Party Leader. Over the w/end he would make a further statement as Leader of his church which would be more in the form of a New Year message. Upon further request for assurance/s Tim [Johnston] left for our guest room to 'phone 'The Doc'.
>
> T returned with assurance that IRKP would be responding as indicated ... would keep to the script ... would not go beyond it and would not elaborate upon it. A positive feel all round.
>
> Much being made of the diffs each would have to face – for SF following the AC which would be seen as a sell out and for the DUP which would be seen as giving in ... being fooled ... Etc, etc.
>
> One a mirror image of the other. Throughout these meetings I have been acutely conscious of the effort of one side to convey to the other their understanding of their partic[ular] difficulties as well as their own.

DJ [Jeffrey Donaldson] made it very clear – whatever the reaction of [Nigel] Dodds, [Jim] Allister [DUP MEP, now leader of Traditional Unionist Voice and an MP] etc … The party line was very clear and this was the one to be believed. The Doc has made his leadership role and that of his party very clear on more than one recent occasion. If he says it – that's it. DJ also went on to say that should there be any deficit in the statement of the party leader he (DJ), R [Peter Robinson] and S [Sammy Wilson] would issue a further statement making the position totally clear. It was also agreed that it was best for the two parties to say as little as possible – and certainly not to undermine the position of the other. There would be enough to contend with from within each. I counselled that they be not drawn by the media who would want to create confusion and confrontation.

It all seemed to be very clear and acceptable all round. While we must not underestimate the difficulties which lie ahead I said that I would like to say 3 things before they left.

1. Our times together have been all about trust. What takes place in this room must stay in this room … except for what it was necessary for either party to take back/take forward as appropriate …
2. I shared with them that I found their manner of doing business with each other to be hugely encouraging – at times moving. Wished I had some way of sharing it with the world which is so cynical of how we do politics. This must be the template for how they will move forward and do the business. There followed some discussion about the need to begin to be more open re engagement and communication. As soon as time is right. Also need to be seen to be working together towards positive outcomes on issues which matter to the people. The most obvious being constructive and joint pressure on a realistic economic package.

3. Most important word was HOPE. I told them what I had said from the pulpit on Christmas Eve morning … the alternative was to preach on despair. DJ followed this by telling of his Maiden Speech in Commons and how he took the motto of [his] daughter's school Wallace [High in Lisburn] Esperance [which comes from] the Latin word for Hope. Very clear and visible expressions of agreement and of shared responsibility to bring HOPE to all our people.

Again handshakes were exchanged before one party followed at a 'safe space' by the other. Every reason to believe a good day's work after a hard week's work – interrupted by Christmas! Though subsequently heard that a lot of work had been done over Christmas Day!

It was after guests left that Clodagh noticed the game we had received from one of the family lying on the nearby stool … 'Deal or No Deal'! Sorry I had not noticed it before they left … would have distributed the chocs from the game.

Soon afterwards it was announced that the AC was to take place next day, Thursday 28th @ 1 pm. Great Expectations.

The Ard Chomhairle did eventually take place as planned (on Friday, 29 December) and more than the required two-thirds majority gave the green light for an historic Ard Fheis at the end of January that would for the first time see Sinn Féin endorse policing and criminal justice.

But there was a serious wobble when Paisley's subsequent statement fell short of what had been agreed in advance in my home. Amid jangled nerves within both the DUP and Sinn Féin, a second Ard Chomhairle meeting had to be called for 13 January to keep the show on the road. Such was the frantic pace of it all I found it difficult to keep up with developments.

I recall anxiously listening to the news bulletins on the afternoon of the first Ard Chomhairle.

My journal records:

> Just after 6 pm received a call from Martina Anderson (SF liaison person with Prods and Unionists). Told me of the AC result and of GA's [Gerry Adams'] impending statement. I sounded surprised as if I knew nothing but said it was encouraging etc. She asked if I could encourage Methodist Church and if influence other church leaders to respond positively.

Shortly afterwards the news bulletins reported the successful outcome of the Ard Chomhairle meeting.

From my journal: 'Desired result! Excellent presentation from GA. [Gerry Adams] Espec. "We are doing this because it is the right thing to do!"'

I arranged for our President, Rev. Ivan McElhinney, to issue 'a strong but short statement' in support, which was immediately reported on the news bulletins. A few days later I confided to my journal:

> Anticipated/predictable reactions from public and from politicians. Especially from Jim Allister and Maurice (Lord) Morrow [chairman of the DUP] followed at w/end by David Simpson [MP for Upper Bann] naturally very nervous as the person who defeated David Trimble on basis that he was too soft and too trusting of Republicans!

Naturally, I was very concerned that Paisley had not followed through and used the wording that he had apparently agreed to in the phone call with Timothy Johnston during the 27 December meeting between Martin McGuinness and Jeffrey Donaldson in my home.

My journal entry dated New Year's Day 2007 is explicit.

On listening to news on radio etc and on reading papers became uneasy by [lack of] positive progress. Was unsettled as we were settling to watch last episode of *Vicar of Dilby* [sic]. About to call one or other [Martin or Jeffrey] trying to decide which when Maraid [Aidan McAteer] called me! Told me of alarm ... Had seen statement to go from IRKP [Paisley] tomorrow. Fell far short of what had been shown to them as agreed between IRKP and Blair. Wanted a meeting first thing in morning. We agreed 9 am but there followed a series of calls between me and DJ ... M[artin] & M[araid] ... M [Martin] and DJ [Jeffrey] ... HG [me] and M etc.

I asked [Jeffrey] very specifically was the statement dismissive, rubbishing or damaging. I was assured by DJ that overall its tone was positive – but agreed that it had not gone as far as we had been led to believe it would and which SF had given the AC to understand would be the position. On which they had based their judgement that it was safe to proceed with the AC and the AD [Ard Fheis] to follow on Jan 27. [Actually on Jan 28.]

SF fear (as well as feeling once more a betrayal of trust) that without the anticipated strong and positive statement from DUP leadership in particular there might well be those who would demand the leadership of SF to pull back ... how could they go to the Ard Dheiss [sic] without strong reason to believe that they would not be left out to dry by refusal of DUP to acknowledge, trust and failure to keep their word as agreed with Downing Street etc.

I counselled them [SF] to focus on the positive tone and reminded them that DJ had committed himself and 2 very senior party colleagues [Peter Robinson and Sammy Wilson] if necess to come out with a much stronger statement to make up the deficit. This he had (in presence of S [Sammy Wilson] and later in presence of T [Timothy Johnston]) promised to do in the event that it would be needed. There was concern that if it did not come from 'the Doc' it would carry little weight. I tried to persuade them [SF] that added to what doc [Paisley] would say it would send out a very strong signal/message about party line and collective leadership position. DJ said rather than come to meeting at 9 am with nothing to put on the table he would prefer to do some hard work on the issue and we would communicate and if necess meet later in day.

Pleased to hear that there was some direct 1-1 telephone engagement on the matter and this approach has been agreed. So we will await the outcome of 2 meetings tomorrow.

1. DUP intra-party discussions
2. SF Meetings 'out of town' [an apparent reference to republican grassroots consultations] ... Will keep close to the mobile! May be a need for another meeting tomorrow – we will see.

While a nervy Sinn Féin continued to prepare its base for a landmark decision and a fraught DUP leadership wrestled with tensions in its ranks, the sudden death of David Ervine, the Progressive Unionist Party leader, on 8 January united the political spectrum in mourning, even if there was no let-up in the behind-the-scenes efforts to restore devolution.

David, a former UVF prisoner, had made an immense contribution to the peace process. On the day of his funeral, 12 January, there was a hastily called 9 a.m. meeting that included Martin McGuinness and Jeffrey Donaldson at our home, before some of us left for the funeral. I sensed that Martin and Aidan were not as confident as we had hoped and were nervous as to how the proposition would be received at the second Ard Chomhairle meeting that was to take place the following day, Saturday, 13 January 2007.

Later in the day I phoned Jeffrey and asked if it would be helpful for me to have a meeting with Peter Robinson – to which he agreed. Peter, who had been at David's funeral, arrived early evening on his way to another event. But he took time to reassure me of the sincerity of the leadership of the DUP and went as far as explaining disciplinary proceedings against any of the party who would go against the leadership.

I took notes and asked his permission to forward a letter to Martin McGuinness to use as he chose in his presentation to the Ard Chomhairle – to which he agreed without hesitation. I then composed the following letter addressing Martin and Gerry Adams directly, which I emailed to Martin and Aidan and which they received on the road to Dublin. The wonders and blessings of technology. The letter was as follows.

Friday evening, January 12th, 2007

Dear Gerry and Martin, As we have trusted each other in the past I ask you to trust me again, at what I believe is a no less important moment of time.

In asking for that, I want you to know that I do very much appreciate and understand the difficulties which you must address at tomorrow's meeting of the Ard Chomhairle, none of which I would wish to minimise in any way.

While I am also aware of the considerable difficulties of others, almost entirely to do with serious internal party differences, I do not wish to pass judgement on how well or otherwise these difficulties have been handled by them. However, it is abundantly clear that there now exists considerable misunderstanding, suspicion and uncertainty as a result of what has been said and/or what has not been said.

In saying this, I also wish you to know that I have taken time to engage very personally at leadership level within the DUP. It is therefore from a first-hand conversation that I am in a position to share the following assurances which were given to me and which I undertook to pass on to you.

While little can ever be guaranteed in this life I must add that, given the certainty and the manner in which these assurances were given, I personally have no reason to doubt the sincerity of intention.

In summary:

1. The Leadership of the DUP is committed to the restoration of a devolved power-sharing Assembly.
2. It is determined to make it happen.
3. It will do what it can to make it happen.

The next step will be dependent upon what it is hoped will be a clear and positive resolution from the ardfheis. At some point following this there would be a meeting of the Party Executive – at which it is expected there would be a positive response from the Party Leader.

While such a response may well incorporate the phrase 'subject to credible delivery', I am given to understand that this relates to the implementation of the very clear terms of the motion relating to policing on the ground, and not as defined by the un-constructive voices from within that party.

For your party not to proceed to an ardfheis at this moment of time would, I believe, be in danger of doing one or both of two things ...

1. Give credence and 'victory' to the strident but negative voices from within the DUP ... even though we are given to believe they constitute a minority within the party.
2. Give opportunity to those who would very readily wish this to be interpreted as default on the part of Sinn Féin.

It would not be in any of our interests for either of these possibilities to happen.

I want you to know that I, and others, have been greatly heartened by your insistence, in spite of all that has happened, that you 'must do the right thing.' This in the longer term is where we must focus. It is this which will take us forward and hasten the realisation of the vision of which we heard much this afternoon. [A reference to the uplifting messages from David's funeral, at which Gerry Adams had poignantly conveyed his condolences to Jeanette, David's widow.]

I hope you sensed how much your [Gerry's and Alex Maskey's] presence at that event was noted and appreciated.

While this is a personal letter to yourselves, and not for publication, feel free to refer to it in any way that may be helpful within your internal debate.

Very sincerely,
Harold Good

The strong leadership of Adams and McGuinness again carried the day at the Ard Chomhairle. They had argued that support for policing and the courts was the right thing to do whether the DUP kept their word or not, in which case both governments would have to proceed on the basis of some form of joint stewardship. I immediately conveyed my congratulations to Martin and I know he texted straight back because his text is dated '13th Jan':

Wasn't easy, H, Gerry [Adams] and I got your message, many thanks for that and the many great works that u do. Really pleased David's funeral sent all the right messages. God bless you and C. M.

In the end, fifteen days later, on 28 January 2007, Gerry Adams and Martin McGuinness again secured a huge victory at the Ard Fheis. They were kind enough to tell me that it was my letter that did it.

The remaining obstacles to a big Paisley–Adams moment included tying down the arrangements for the devolution of policing and justice powers and my journal noted my understanding that both Sinn Féin and the DUP had 'already agreed to a voluntary arrangement' that neither party would take the Justice portfolio in a first Assembly term, which I considered to be 'magnanimous'.

Reading the text messages and my journal, and reflecting back, I now realise that my role as diary-keeper and back-channel facilitator was consuming my life at this time, but it was something I felt deeply privileged to be involved in.

I was struck by how determined both negotiators were to remain committed and sort out diary clashes so that not a moment was wasted. No one was saying 'I am too busy' or 'I can't be bothered.' They were both standing on their heads to try to make progress.

This is vividly illustrated in texts I received from Donaldson and McGuinness on 13 March 2007, as I facilitated another meeting in which they endeavoured to remove remaining obstacles to the Paisley–Adams meeting now less than two weeks away.

Jeffrey: 'I hope to get clear from PfG [Programme for Government] Committee at about 3.45. I have to catch a flight at 5.30. Cud we do the meeting at 4 pm? This wud give me time before flight. Let me know if this works.'
Martin: 'More like 4. thanks H.'
Martin: 'B with u in 10 mins.'
Jeffrey: 'OK.'

On Saturday, 24 March 2007, Clodagh and I were on an errand to the Donaghadee Garden Centre. Unusually for me, my mobile phone was switched to 'silent' and when I reopened it there was a message, 'H, can u ring me urgently. M.' It was just under 48 hours before the historic Paisley–Adams moment. When I did reply to Martin McGuinness's text he phoned me back to say that he had needed my home once again so that he could meet the DUP delegation including Peter Robinson, Nigel Dodds and Jeffrey Donaldson to resolve the remaining points of contention but given the pressure of time they had decided instead to go to Stormont Castle, a less discreet location.

I remember his words to me: 'We will be at it all night, Harold.'

So at least I got some sleep. And that night they did resolve those remaining issues standing in the way of a Paisley–McGuinness DUP–Sinn Féin-led government, and the rest is history.

At 11.32 a.m. on Monday, 26 March 2007, Aidan McAteer texted me: 'Meeting DUP now. Agreement reached.'

At 12.45 p.m. Jeffrey Donaldson texted: 'Thanks Harold. An answer to prayer! Let's have lunch sometime soon.'

At 2.09 p.m. Martin McGuinness texted: 'Many thanks for everything my true friends. Momentous day for all of us. God Bless u both. M.'

Looking back on that engagement between McGuinness and Donaldson, I am deeply humbled as I reflect on those many meetings and conversations and the trust that grew between us. Most memorable was the day of the Paisley–Adams agreement on the way forward. Afterwards we were joined in our home by politicians and officials from both sides who had been aware of the process but not privy to all those meetings around our kitchen table.

When the question of who might be nominated for the vital role of Speaker the name of the DUP's William Hay was mentioned, 'Good choice' was the response. And coincidentally, Speaker Hay 'inherited' from his predecessor, John Alderdice, our son Richard as his special adviser. Northern Ireland is a small world.

Being aware of the significance of this moment, Clodagh provided something special for our additional guests. It was later that I heard Conor Murphy [a Sinn Féin MLA and soon to be Minister for Regional Development] say that it was Clodagh Good's apple and blackberry pie that had sealed the deal.

As always, Clodagh was there for me, playing a quiet but hugely supportive role in whatever was going on in Church or in wider society.

Once again I was aware of the importance of the three 'Ts': TALK, TRUTH and TRUST. Not forgetting the symmetry between tea-making and peace-making. It was something that both Martin McGuinness and Jeffrey Donaldson had come to understand so well.

13

Father Alec: My Fellow Traveller

'In every conflict there is a no man's land into which few will dare to go.'

Olivia O'Leary

For me, one of the less likely yet significant friendships in my life was the one that that I forged with the late and sadly missed Fr Alec Reid, a member of the Redemptorist Order, affectionately known as 'The Reds'.

As is well documented and, as discussed in an earlier chapter, Alec was my fellow independent witness to the historic destruction of the IRA's huge remaining stock of weaponry over many days at multiple arms dumps across Ireland in September 2005.

Ours was a very genuine and special friendship. Working on this book has meant reliving that relationship with Alec, who became my friend and brother in Christ, and that has been an unexpected gift in itself.

An indefatigable peacemaker, but for good reason a little known one for most of his ministry, his singular and courageous contribution to the Irish peace process was incalculable.

That contribution, rooted firmly in his Christian faith, in Gospel values, in his unshakeable trust in the support and power of the Holy Spirit, was captured with acuity by Olivia O'Leary, the distinguished Irish broadcaster and journalist, in a BBC Radio 4 profile: 'In every conflict there is a no man's land into which few will dare to go. Fr Alec was one who did.'

He was a sincere and private person who told few, if any, what he was up to. Single-minded and passionate about everything he did, he was a deeply modest man who never promoted himself and, therefore, earned and won the trust that enabled him to significantly alter the course of our recent history. Alec's manner could be misleading. In one situation he would appear to be 'as wise as a serpent' yet in another 'as innocent as a dove'. His charm lay in his belief in the innate goodness of everyone he met, and in an otherworldliness encapsulated in his mantra, *'leave it to the Holy Spirit'*. However, I confess that there were times when I would caution him against pushing the Spirit too hard.

When asked who he represented in the context of his peace-making, Alec would reply that he represented the next person to be killed in the conflict. His aim was to help create a situation where no one else would be killed, where peace and justice would reign in Ireland, in so far as that is possible in this imperfect world.

Alec once elaborated on his role in a 3,000-word lecture at St Clement's Retreat House, Belfast, two months before the Downing Street Declaration of December 1993. He entitled the lecture 'The Role of the Servant of Christ in a Situation of Conflict'. That is how he saw his role. His introduction read:

> As I see it, the role of the servant of Christ in a situation of conflict is to be the pastoral agent of the Holy Spirit in the midst of the conflict. I say, 'in the midst of the conflict' because there and there only can he come to grips with all its human and,

consequently, all its moral and spiritual dimensions, and it is the moral and spiritual dimensions of the conflict that are the business of the serving Christian.[23]

Above all, Alec was a priest and pastor who loved everyone he met. He had a pastor's heart. This was captured beautifully by Mary McAleese, former President of Ireland and close friend of Alec, in her reflection at his funeral Mass in Clonard:

> Alec, known to some as Al, Alex, Alexander or just plain Fr Reid, may at times have seemed like an enigma, a puzzling or inexplicable occurrence – but he was far from it. He was a priest. Not a liturgy-and-lace man but a humble and ever-faithful servant of Jesus; a man who really bought deeply into the idea of the healing power of love, who saw all human beings as sons and daughters of the one Father, and members of the one human family.[24]

For those who would wish to study further the mind and spirit of Alec Reid I commend the remarkable book published by his Irish Redemptorist Congregation within four years of his death. That book is *One Man, One God: The Peace Ministry of Fr Alec Reid CSsR* by Martin McKeever CSsR (Redemptorist Communications).

As I said at its southern launch in Nenagh, Co. Tipperary – where Alec was brought up – if it were within my power to do so, I would make this book mandatory reading for all seminarians and students for ministry, from whatever tradition. Simply because, as distinct from anything abstract or purely academic, what Fr Alec articulates so passionately and out of his own experience should be front and centre of ministry in any contested community.

From the example of Jesus he speaks of a 'ministry of connection' and 'compassionate companionship' as distinctive alternatives to be offered by those of us who would seek to be servants of Christ in any situation of conflict.

It is a remarkable book. Not least because it is rooted in the experience of a prophetic ministry, a prison ministry, intervention in a republican feud and the 1981 hunger strike. As well as his outreach to individual unionists and loyalists and his ministry to the families of those 'disappeared' by the IRA.

As well as a unique and detailed record of the many conversations initiated and facilitated by Fr Alec which were to provide the basis for wider dialogue which culminated in the Good Friday Agreement, it also introduces us to the many diverse personalities with whom he formed remarkable relationships. And no less important than prelates, presidents, and politicians was Liz, she from 'the other side' who 'threw him kisses' across the physical wall that divided her community from his.

The wider world only became aware of Alec Reid in March 1988 when a photograph of him administering the last rites to Corporal David Howes, a British Army soldier, murdered by the IRA in particularly grisly circumstances, appeared on front pages of newspapers around the globe, joining the grim gallery of enduring images of the Troubles.

The picture showed an anguished and distraught Alec kneeling with hands joined, praying over the bloodied almost naked body of the young Corporal Howes on waste ground in Andersonstown, west Belfast. He had also anointed a second corporal, Derek Wood, who had been murdered by the IRA at the same location.

These soldiers, in plainclothes and armed, had driven in an unmarked car into the cortege of an IRA funeral as it made its way to Milltown cemetery and were mistaken for loyalist killers.

The funeral was of Caoimhín MacBrádaigh, an IRA member, one of three people killed by loyalist Michael Stone in Milltown cemetery at the earlier funerals of three IRA volunteers who had been killed by the SAS in Gibraltar.

While one can understand the initial fear in the crowd when two corporals appeared armed and in plainclothes in an unmarked car, this could not justify them being dragged from their car and cruelly beaten without a modicum of mercy before being taken away and shot. But before they were taken away, Fr Alec intervened to try to save them, and he pleaded for an ambulance to be called. He recalled, 'Somebody came behind me, picked me up by the shoulders and said "Get up or I'll fucking well shoot you as well."'[25]

After the shootings Alec tried to give one of the soldiers the kiss of life, resulting in some of the soldier's blood transferring to his face – something that made that iconic picture all the more shocking and poignant. As he ministered to the soldiers, an envelope he was carrying, which contained a Sinn Féin position paper that he was to deliver to John Hume in 'Derry later in the day, became stained with the blood of one of the soldiers.

As Alec recalled, he had gone to the church by arrangement to receive this letter from a Sinn Féin official and had been at the head of the cortege to sympathise with Caoimhín MacBrádaigh's mother.

But prior to this, his lonely mission for peace, conducted from his base at Clonard Monastery, beside a so-called peace wall in west Belfast, had gone on in secret for several decades with 'at least the tacit approval' of his religious superiors.[26]

It was Alec who initiated and nurtured the seminal Hume–Adams dialogue in the late 1980s. He had already opened up and sustained lines of communication between republicans and the Irish government, with developments that led ultimately to the Downing Street Declaration in 1993, the IRA and loyalist ceasefires of 1994 and the Good Friday Agreement of 1998.

To be more personal, Alec and I came from very different backgrounds: he a Catholic from a republican-inclined family in Tipperary and I a Protestant son of the manse from 'Derry, with one grandfather in the RIC and the other a staunch unionist.

Despite those different backgrounds, we had much in common: our faith, our commitment to pastoral ministry and our shared understanding of the relevance of the Gospel which transcends secondary denominational or doctrinal differences. And what it means for us as preachers and pastors to move beyond the comfort of our 'cloisters' to be involved in the messy realities of a sadly fractured world.

We also shared a conviction that the resolution of conflict lay in building relationships and dialogue rather than fruitless finger-pointing and ritual condemnation. This common approach to conflict resolution made for an easy partnership in which friendship could and did flourish.

Alec was barely six years my senior. We enjoyed the same humour and banter. To lighten things in the middle of a shared presentation, one of Alec's favourite interventions was 'Harold Good would make a great Pope.' My riposte: 'Do you not think I am in enough trouble already?'

Father Alec's very special gift was of uncomplicated, unconditional and non-judgemental friendship which opened doors as well as conversations with total strangers, amongst whom there would be perceived doubters as well as believers.

'You are so very kind', was his standard comment to the waitress who brought him a cup of tea or to a conductor who demanded to see his ticket. His seemingly innocent 'And what is your name?' was the reassuring key with which he unlocked the hesitancy on the part of someone he had never previously met. Surely it was more than coincidence that he always had a favourite aunt or sister or cousin who shared the same name. But it worked! It was Alec's way of reassuring them that they were very special people.

And it was with this gift that Alec could disarm a potential enemy. On one occasion there was an issue with his fingerprints at the immigration desk in LaGuardia Airport and Alec was unceremoniously diverted to a room set aside for suspected illegal immigrants and others awaiting clearance to enter the US. In spite of my aggressive protests on his behalf, he was detained for well over two hours before his name was called by a formidable six-and-a-half-foot tall official who I guessed to be close on eighteen stone in weight. Of all those on the high platform, he was the one I hoped would not be dealing with Alec.

'I think he's Irish,' said Alec, 'I'll ask him.'

'Don't get into that,' I counselled, 'Whatever he asks, just say "yes Sir" or "no Sir."' I watched anxiously and was greatly relieved when I saw the scowling official countenance relax into a smile as he stamped the 'magic' document permitting Alec entry to the New World.

'I was right,' said a beaming Alec. 'He is Irish; his name is O'Sullivan, his granny came from Monaghan and he has a son going into seminary in September!' Another lesson in how to disarm your perceived antagonist.

For Alec, whoever he would meet on his journey was to be respected for who they were. Neither they nor their opinions were to be dismissed, however they differed from his own. Whatever 'baggage' they were assumed to carry, Alec always saw the best in everyone. When the patience of others was exhausted, he refused to give up on his vision or his mission – or on those he knew to be critical players in the process of peace.

Up to the time of our approval as independent witnesses, I did not know Alec Reid very well. Our paths would have crossed at gatherings, but he was the quiet man who did not readily engage in the cut and thrust of debate between those of us who had opinions on everything – particularly on how to solve the problem of Northern Ireland.

In a previous chapter I have described how we came to be appointed as co-witnesses to decommissioning, our post-decommissioning news conference at the Culloden Hotel and our public comments, following which I describe our subsequent meeting with a DUP delegation led by the Rev. Ian Paisley, whose reaction would ultimately determine whether a power-sharing government would be restored in Northern Ireland.

So, following this, Alec and I had agreed that we would keep our heads down and refrain from any further media exposure. Apart from everything else, we needed a rest.

It was then that we received a request from our mutual, much respected and supportive friend, the Rev. Ken Newell, of Belfast's Fitzroy Presbyterian Church, inviting us to a meeting of the Clonard-Fitzroy Fellowship, to be hosted by himself and Alec's confrère and dedicated companion in the cause of peace and reconciliation, Fr Gerry Reynolds.

The link between Clonard and Fitzroy goes back to the dark days of the IRA hunger strike in 1981 and was something we all cherished, so we could hardly say 'no'. We reasonably assumed that the meeting would comprise a quiet, unpublicised conversation with the prayerful, peace-loving members of the Clonard-Fitzroy Fellowship, with no 'outsiders' present.

So, imagine my consternation when BBC's *Talkback* phoned me on the day of the meeting inviting me to preview it. When I declined, explaining that it was a private meeting, I was informed that Ken Newell had already been 'on air' inviting all and sundry to the event, which he had publicised as: 'Decommissioning: What did you see? What does it mean? Where do we go from here?'

While knowing Ken as we did and accepting that he was acting in good faith and with the best of intentions, you can imagine our dilemma when, on turning up at Fitzroy, we were 'set upon' by a barrage of reporters and cameras. And upon entering the room, in addition to the media and the gentle folk of the Fitzroy-Clonard Fellowship, the room was crammed with a cross-section of loyalist and Protestant opinion.

While I was aware of the potential for this event going 'all wrong', I also realised the damage that could be caused by walking out in front of the cameras. So, with nothing to hide and with confidence in what we had to say, we proceeded with the business of the evening.

It was agreed that each of us would speak in turn, prior to answering prepared and agreed questions from Ken Newell. I was at pains to make clear that while we had not been required to sign an Official (or unofficial) Secrets Act, our involvement was entirely on the basis of mutual trust – a trust we would not betray. So I repeated what I had said at the Culloden Hotel news conference and many times since.

What I saw was important, very important, but what I heard was no less and perhaps even more important than what we saw. By this I referred to our informal evening conversations with senior members of the IRA who made it very clear that for them this was a welcome end to the armed struggle in which they had lost many friends and many of them had lost their freedom. Above all, we were assured that they were doing this for the sake of their children and grandchildren. Initially this was well-received and our earlier fears of hijacking by the media were allayed.

However, in the open Q&A which followed all of this was to change. There were hard questions and robustly expressed doubts from a group of concerned women from a unionist/loyalist perspective. While it was very different from what we had anticipated to be a conversation with sympathetic and supportive folk from Clonard and Fitzroy, much of what was expressed was predictable and in the circumstances not unreasonable. But when the late Willie Frazer – a victims' campaigner whose father and several members of his family circle with security forces connections were murdered by the IRA – gave vent to his feelings, the mood of the meeting dramatically changed.

When Willie made accusations of complicity between the Redemptorists at Clonard and the IRA regarding the safekeeping of their weapons, my otherwise measured friend 'erupted'. In return for the wild accusations against his beloved congregation, Alec accused unionists of treating Catholics in the same way as Nazis had treated the Jews.

There followed a tirade of abusive exchanges which brought credit upon no one. Being totally unprepared for such a situation, I took some moments to think of what I might say. I was about to suggest that if this is how some people felt, then we needed to hear that and discuss it. But before I could say anything, Ken Newell declared the meeting over.

When the crowd had dispersed, we sought damage limitation. I did a brief radio interview and spoke with a newspaper reporter; Alec was anxious to issue an unreserved apology for his outburst, withdraw his Nazi statement and speak as he had often done of his respect and admiration of people from the Protestant/unionist tradition.

With assistance from a sympathetic journalist, we ensured that Alec's apology was reported as widely as possible on radio, TV and in print. Along with Alec's apology, I made my own statement making clear that I did not agree with his 'Nazi' comment but also condemned the scurrilous comments which had provoked his unfortunate reaction. Not surprisingly, Willie Frazer's rather ironic demand that Fr Alec be charged with a 'hate crime' came to nothing.

Understandably, I was very unhappy with the whole saga. However, following an honest conversation with Ken Newell and his expression of sincere regret, his relationship and mine was fully restored.

An entirely unpublished follow-up to this event was the acceptance of our offer to meet with anyone at the meeting. So it was that Alec and I met with representatives of the unionist women who had been so angry at the Fitzroy meeting and, away from the hysteria surrounding the event, we had a most reasonable conversation during which mutual respect and understanding was established.

When I was reunited with my family the day following the completion of IRA decommissioning, it was our son Richard who said: 'Dad, life will not be the same for you after this.' I dismissed it. I was in good health, heading towards 70 and retired, looking forward to a quiet, inconspicuous 'wind-down'.

I did not know what he meant, but now I do.

After considerable national and international news interest in the disposal of the IRA's arsenal, Alec and I were not to know that our role in witnessing this turning point in contemporary Irish history would put us under the international spotlight and turn us into an ecumenical double act, resulting in considerable travel together and a deepening of our friendship.

Fortunately, both Alec and I enjoyed travel, for there were to be many shared journeys and it was important that we enjoyed each other's company.

We quickly discovered that there was a wider world anxious to hear our story. We were anxious to oblige if it meant that others in conflict situations, or scholars in conflict resolution, might benefit in some way from our experiences of the Irish peace process.

The first of many such invitations came within weeks of our witnessing IRA decommissioning. It was a very personal invitation from Juan José Ibarretxe, the Lehendakari (President) of the Basque government, to come to Vitoria-Gasteiz, the administrative capital of the Basque Autonomous Community in northern Spain, on 27 December 2005, to receive the René Cassin Human Rights Award. As a former Human Rights Commissioner I should have known, but I had to Google 'René Cassin' to discover that he was co-author of the Universal Declaration of Human Rights and a Nobel Peace Prize winner. While I did know of Fr Alec's visits to the Basque Country and something of his contacts with the leadership of ETA (Euskadi Ta Askatasuna), the Basque separatist movement, I was surprised and curious about this invitation and its relevance for us. I had no idea that this was to be but the first of many similar invitations and awards both at home and abroad.

While happily this invitation included Clodagh, it involved flying on Boxing Day 2005, which meant abandoning our family and our traditional Christmas family reunion. We had not realised until later that for the people of the Basque region, Epiphany is the more important festival within the Christmas period.

Upon our arrival in Bilbao we met with Alec, his sister Margaret O'Meara and his niece Máiréad, and we were driven in regal style to Vitoria-Gasteiz where in the magnificent setting of the Basque equivalent of the White House or Downing Street we received the René Cassin award at a red-letter event. It seemed like a scaled-down version of a Nobel Prize ceremony. We were surrounded by a battalion of reporters and camerapersons from all of the main Spanish papers and television outlets, an experience that was to prepare us for close-up encounters with the paparazzi on many Basque visits that were to follow. As I listened to the speeches and accepted the award two thoughts went through my head. One was, 'What would my mother make of this?' The other, 'What are we doing here, and what has all this to do with two relatively unknown clergy from Norn Ireland?'

Before the night was out, and in the intensive round of media interviews that were to follow, we realised that all of this was to highlight the huge significance of decommissioning within our peace process and its relevance for the resolution of conflict in situations similar to ours. This was to be the first of many public and private visits that Alec and I were to make to the Basque Region, during which we met with political leaders, peace activists and others with 'undisclosed identities'. Sadly, Alec did not live to share with me that incredible moment in 2017 when with Archbishop (now Cardinal) Zuppi of Bologna,[x] I shared in the historic and final act of decommissioning of the weaponry of ETA, bringing closure to their more than 50-year-long violent and bloody struggle for independence for the Basque Region. All of which I describe more fully in Chapter 15.

In the years that followed that first 'outing' to the Basque Country, Alec and I made several trips to America. The first of these was to Texas at the invitation of what is now the William J. Flynn Center for Irish Studies at the University of St Thomas in Houston. The Center's director is the indefatigable Lori Gallagher, a lawyer with Irish roots who, as well as inviting us to take classes and make public presentations, developed close links with Ireland, bringing study groups to both North and South every second summer, which it has been my privilege to facilitate and mentor.

Another invitation came from Congressman Richie Neal, until recently Chairman of the powerful Ways and Means Committee, and long-time Democratic leader of the Friends of Ireland Caucus. We spoke to a packed house in the campus of a university in Springfield, Massachusetts. It was a memorable visit for many reasons. Not least because before we left the event I received an email to tell us of the

---

[x]   Now Cardinal Archbishop Matteo Zuppi, Pope Francis' Ukraine peace envoy who has been mentioned as a possible successor to the Pope.

signing of the St Andrews Agreement. A significant breakthrough in our peace process about which we had just spoken so positively.

As well as our shared journeys, Alec and I shared some very privileged moments closer to home, such as jointly receiving honorary doctorates from Queen's University Belfast, Ulster University and The Open University, and the Gandhi Foundation's International Peace Award in the grandeur of the House of Lords. On such occasions you have to 'sing for your supper', but we saw each of these events as an opportunity to share what inspired and motivated us in the hope that others might be challenged to be peacemakers in their own right.

In my Gandhi Foundation lecture I underlined the necessity of dialogue in resolving conflict, referring in particular to Alec's backstage initiatives which led to the ground-breaking Hume–Adams talks, resulting in the IRA ceasefire of 1994. At Queen's in 2008 I addressed those graduating in both the Faculty of Law and the Institute of Theology, emphasising the vital and complementary responsibilities of both 'The Law and the Prophets'.[27]

Five days later, Alec and I were in one of the world's most prestigious universities on what turned out to be the last of our shared journeys to America. This time at the invitation of former Prime Minister Tony Blair. Just sixteen months after he completed his momentous ten-year stint as British Prime Minister, we were honoured with an invitation to Yale to contribute to the university's Faith and Globalisation Initiative, held in collaboration with the Tony Blair Faith Foundation. I had previously met Sir Tony on one of his many visits to Northern Ireland and when, as Prime Minister, he invited me and other Church leaders to 10 Downing Street. And also of course on that memorable Devolution Day at Stormont.

We had been asked to lead a seminar, chaired by the distinguished Croatian theologian Miroslav Volf. This was attended by students from all over the world to explore the role religion plays in various conflicts, particularly in the two areas where Mr Blair had a special interest, the Middle East and Northern Ireland. It is easy to remember the date,

4 November 2008: the day of Barack Obama's historic election as America's first Black President.

At LaGuardia Airport we were met by Fr Michael Kelleher, Alec's superior from the Redemptorist Order, who was also his wonderfully caring 'minder'. After a seven-hour flight from Dublin, an extended security issue at the airport and a two-hour drive to Yale, Alec went to bed while Michael and I sat up into the 'wee small hours' to witness the newly elected President make his acceptance speech. The atmosphere on the Yale campus was 'electric', with a non-stop cavalcade of cars blowing loud horns through what remained of the night into the dawn of the next day.

A particular highlight of our visit was a private dinner hosted by the President of Yale, Professor Rick Levin. Along with Tony Blair, there were just three of us, Fr Alec, Fr Michael Kelleher and myself. We totally relaxed as Sir Tony regaled us with tales of his Presbyterian grandmother, who warned him not to marry a Catholic, and of his unexpected relationship with Ian Paisley.

Our commitments in Yale revolved around discerning what lessons we felt could be shared from the Irish peace process. In addition to the main seminar, we were interviewed by Professor Harold Attridge, Dean of Yale's Divinity School.[28]

This seminar centred on the theme of faith and reconciliation with a follow-up Q&A session, which included penetrating questions and observations from Blair himself, who at that time was a visiting teacher at Yale, leading a course on faith and globalisation.

Tony Blair was generous in his praise of Alec and me, and played down his central role in the peace process, remarking in his introduction that 'I just came in as a political leader and tried to do my best to sort it, they [pointing to Alec and me] lived it.'

In return, both Alec and I made a point, individually and on each other's behalf, of recognising Blair's incredibly unique and courageous role in bringing peace to our country. His truly historic achievement in Northern Ireland must never be diminished or overlooked.

I took the opportunity to state 'very publicly' how much we are indebted to him and to his Irish counterpart, Taoiseach Bertie Ahern, for their intensely personal commitment to our peace process that went far beyond the call of duty of any premier. I took particular pleasure in brandishing a copy of the Good Friday Agreement, emphasising that neither of them would let the politicians of Northern Ireland go to bed until it was agreed.

In Fr Alec's warm and carefully worded tribute to Tony Blair he recalled how he had '... played a crucial role in his openness and his willingness to try to understand Republicans, the people who were trying to negotiate with him.'

He went on to explain how in his own efforts to get the IRA to reinstate their ceasefire he was able to argue that 'now is the time to make an agreement' because there was now in power a British Prime Minister called Tony Blair – someone who was 'willing to be flexible and willing to understand everyone's point of view', and who by virtue of having an Irish grandmother from Donegal had a better understanding of the problems. 'Now that he has got the power, let's move.'

Then, turning to Tony Blair, seated immediately to his left, Alec added: 'I would like to pay tribute to him. He introduced a whole new dimension to the whole Irish–English relationship which was not there. I am sure that Irish historians when they come to write the history will give him a special place that he deserves through the contribution he made to the peace that we now have.'

Alec then promised to enumerate seven brief lessons from the Irish peace process that he had learnt not from books but from direct experience on the streets. But as often happened, he went into so much detail that he just had time to give us three. These were:

1. You need the help of the Grace of God; human resources are not enough.
2. You must respect the dignity of the human person at all times.
3. If you want to resolve a problem you must secure a male–female consensus on how to do that and implement it. Alec added ruefully

that his Church should be giving a lead in this area and had failed to do so.

He went on to say that for him 'the golden rule of peace-making' was 'you do what you reasonably can and then leave it to the Lord. You shouldn't lose sleep or put strain on your health.' Somehow, I don't think poor Alec kept to that rule. He gave his all in the cause of peace.

It was obvious to those who were close to him that Alec had been in failing health for many years. Clearly, his unrelenting and lonely work for peace took its toll. As far back as 1981, ill and worn out by his efforts to dissuade the IRA hunger strikers, his superiors had ordered him to take an extended rest in Rome.

Although he was now becoming increasingly frail, Alec's mind remained active and sharp right up to his death on 22 November 2013, at the age of 82. We spoke often on the phone right up to his final days, ever deepening our excellent relationship and special friendship born of the unique 'mission' which had brought us together.

It was a friendship for which I will always be grateful and one of the special privileges of my ministry was to be asked to take an important part in each of the three services that followed his death.

To complete this chapter, and in tribute to Fr Alec, I reproduce below the reflection that I offered at his funeral Mass in Clonard on 27 November 2013.

My Fellow Traveller

It is often said of someone who has made a unique contribution that when history is written that person will be given his or her rightful place. Happily, in the case of Fr Alec Reid, neither he nor we had to wait until after his death for a rightful acknowledgement of his contribution to the process which has brought us to where we now are.

For me it *is* a very special privilege to be asked to share a personal tribute to my very good friend and brother in Christ.

In doing so I know I will speak for all of us who have valued his friendship and have gathered in this place to give thanks for his companionship as well as his legacy of peace.

Fr Alec and I may have appeared to come from very different directions, as indeed we did. Geographically, he was a 'Tipp' man while I a "Derry' man. Church-wise we came from two different denominations. But we soon discovered, and took delight in, what we had in common. We were not too far apart in age; we enjoyed the same sort of humour and banter. And we shared a love of travel. Travelling with Alec was always an adventure! Ironically, the best known of our shared journeys was a highly secret one. Like a couple of Old Testament Patriarchs, we set out not knowing where we were going or more correctly where we were being taken. But for Alec, that journey was to be a culmination of all that he had longed for, prayed for and worked for. I shall not forget that moment when he whispered in my ear 'There goes the last gun out of Irish politics'. What a moment for him, and for all of us!

That journey was one of many we were to share across these islands and across the seas. And on those journeys I soon discovered that Fr Alec possessed two essential gifts for good travelling.

The first was the gift of instant friendship. When welcomed aboard by a flight attendant, for example a typical conversation would go like this. 'And what is your name, dear?'

'Marie Therese.'

'Marie Therese! What a beautiful name. I've always loved that name', and/or 'I have a sister (or an aunt or a cousin) by that name.' I was always fascinated by the number of relatives with the appropriate name. But whatever we had paid for, from then on we would be treated as 'business class'. It was a wonderful gift which he used to such good effect on his journeys into unknown political territory and to build trust with and between strangers.

The second was his ability to fall asleep and wake up upon arrival! In a way this was how he coped with situations and conversations which he felt to be irrelevant or pointless.

But Alec and I were fellow travellers on what for us was the most important journey of all – our journey of faith, two fellow pilgrims often stumbling, seeking to follow in the footsteps of Jesus; the same Jesus who had called each of us to follow him and who, when we were not much more than schoolboys, had called us into ministry, a ministry of reconciliation, in which each of us rejoiced.

This is not to say that Fr Alec and I were not aware of the historic doctrinal differences between the two traditions from which we came. Of course we were. One could not grow up in any part of this island without being aware of those differences. But for Fr Alec and for me difference was not about division, fear, bitterness, hatred or bigotry. We had simply been born into and lovingly nurtured in two traditions within the Christian family, two traditions from which each of us brought something which enriched the faith of the other. We were like two fellow travellers with their packed lunches, each of whom had brought food to share with the other. Interestingly, as a study of Christian history reminds us, this should not be so surprising, for historically Redemptorists and Methodists have much in common.

Both of our movements were founded in the mid-eighteenth century, one founded by Alphonsus Liguori, the other by John Wesley, both of whom shared a passion for social justice and the practical application of the Gospel. So, in the tradition of the founders of our respective orders, Fr Alec and I discovered that we brought this same passion to our shared journey. For us, a passion for peace with justice; for an end to bigotry and bitterness that invades and destroys the human soul; for the sanctity of each and every human life; for an end to violence; for the healing of our land; and a passion for a Christ-centred solution to our conflict wherever it existed.

So, I have to confess, on our shared journey of faith, Fr Alec and I did not spend precious time and energy debating academic theological issues. Neither of us was particularly interested in the number of angels one could dance on the head of a pin! For us, the pivotal question has been: 'In the harsh reality of our broken, divided world, what does it mean for us to live in obedience to the mind and will and purpose of the Christ who has called us to follow him?'

Of course, as so many of us discovered, these journeys were not always easy. There were many twists and turns, diversions, obstacles and roadblocks. Inevitably, there were those who did their best to discourage and divert us. At times it was a lonely journey, at others a weary one. But for Fr Alec in such moments, his standard response was 'Leave it to the Holy Spirit.' To which I would often respond 'Be careful Alec, don't push Him.' But how right he was, for he knew we had to wait on God's timing.

Now, this earthly part of Alec's journey has come to an end, but, for him, an even greater journey has just begun. And so on behalf of all of us who have been his fellow travellers, I bid him an ancient blessing:

'Go forth good friend upon your journey from this world;
In the name of the Father who created you;
In the name of the Son who has redeemed you;
In the name of the Spirit who has sanctified you;
And all the people of God,
Aided by angels and archangels,
And the whole company of heaven.'

And may your journey from us bring you to a place of real and lasting peace, a peace you so richly deserve. Amen.

14

THE WORLD AS A PARISH

'Round the corner of the world I turn, more and more about the world I learn'.

Sydney Carter, poet and songwriter

Whatever the undoubted attractions of foreign travel, it may be down to John Wesley's joyous proclamation 'I look upon all the world as my parish' that, from my earliest days, as one of his preachers, I have been drawn to the wider world and have welcomed opportunities to travel and inform as well as extend my ministry. As related earlier, that wanderlust brought me to the United States for four years early on and to a memorable conference in Bangkok, both of which left indelible impressions and helped equip me for the challenges of pastoring in troubled times at home.

Some years later, in 1997, my experience of the wider world was greatly enhanced by a three-month sabbatical in South Africa, China and Nepal.

And in my presidential year of 2001–2002 I was provided with further opportunities for foreign engagement when I represented Irish churches at the Synod of the Church of North India as well as a return visit to South Africa where I was to hear prophetic words from

Nelson Mandela to the Triennial Conference of the Methodist Church of South Africa. Mandela was then not just the world's best-known Methodist but arguably our planet's greatest moral voice.

With retirement from full-time ministry I could have expected a quieter life, with foreign travel confined to tranquil vacations with Clodagh and catching up with friends.

But that was not to be. I had not reckoned with all the attendant national and international publicity which followed my role in the verification of the decommissioning of arms of the IRA, with invitations to all manner of overseas conferences and conclaves, academic seminars and seminaries, and enough awards and honours to make me blush.

But equally unforeseen and even more amazing was another unforeseen 'spin-off' from that week observing the disabling of the IRA's deadly hardware in September 2005: a not dissimilar role in the decommissioning of the separatist group ETA's weapons in the Basque Country of northern Spain and southwest France and to assist, however tangentially, the peace process in Colombia where FARC, a revolutionary guerrilla organisation, had also waged an armed campaign for several decades. All this resulted in visits to places I could never have envisaged, from Bilbao to Bogota, Bayonne to Havana, and a secret farmhouse in the Basque Country where I narrowly escaped detection by security forces.

I will share recollections of my times with ETA and FARC in the next chapter but first let me recall some more of my earlier foreign adventures.

Our Church is generous with sabbaticals and every seven years offer ministers a three-month opportunity for study and refreshment. My opportunity – assisted by a travel bursary from the largely Quaker New Routes fund – came in October 1997. My chosen theme was 'The Church in a changing world', during which I explored the role of the Christian community in South Africa, China/Hong Kong and Nepal, all of which were going through radical change and challenge at that time.

South Africa was an obvious choice given its particular recent history with the collapse of apartheid, the establishment of the Truth and Reconciliation Commission under the chairmanship of Archbishop Desmond Tutu, and certain parallels with our own situation in Northern Ireland.

Hong Kong and mainland China also posed an intriguing attraction, not least in the light of the recent end of British rule in the former colony and the possible impact of this on the Churches.

Nepal similarly fascinated me: the world's only Hindu kingdom where the practice and promotion of the Christian religion was illegal until the mid-fifties but where a welcome gradual relaxation of the law had resulted in a dramatic growth in the membership of the Christian community. On route to Nepal, Clodagh and I visited some former parishioners in Singapore and I was especially pleased to revisit Bangkok for three days and introduce to her a place that I had mentioned so often down the years which had a profound influence on me during my visit there with Mairead Corrigan a quarter of a century earlier.

SOUTH AFRICA

While acknowledging that no two socio-political systems are the same and that similarities in any comparative consideration should be neither overplayed nor underestimated, in visiting South Africa one is acutely aware of the parallels between the lived experiences there and here in Northern Ireland. But, in a nutshell, racism in South Africa mirrors sectarianism here. And both countries are struggling to cope with the impact of the horrors of the past.

While there can be no doubting the extraordinary courageous Church leadership in South Africa, particularly from within Methodism, Catholicism and Anglicanism, there was, alas, the intransigence and systemic racism emanating from the Dutch Reformed Church which had justified and supported apartheid on the basis of what to us was a clearly perverse interpretation and application of Scripture.

All of this has been well-documented elsewhere. But as here, while many within what were perceived to be the more moderate/progressive churches would not have wished to be identified with the evident extremism of the Dutch Reformed Church, they too would have inherited a conscious or at times unconscious belief in their superior position in South African society.

As here, much of this was 'unspoken' until challenged by change and circumstance manifesting attitudes which were nurtured in homes, among families and within communities – never far below the surface and unseen until 'scratched'.

I share a story which is an illustration of what is common to here and South Africa. I was asked to preach at a large suburban Methodist Church in Durban which had been an all-white middle class and largely professional congregation. Since the ending of apartheid a few years earlier a number of Black families had joined and taken an increasingly active role in the life of the church. The Associate Minister was Carol Walshe, who as a child was in our church in Agnes Street on the Shankill Road, and, prior to her ordination into the ministry of the MCI, on the staff of Corrymeela. I chose to preach on 'The things that make for peace' [Luke 19:42]. I explained to the congregation that I had not come to tell them how to solve or sort the challenges that were before them in South Africa, as that would be as impertinent as it would be improper. Rather I sought to share my story about the turns and twists in our peace process up to that time and my eagerness to learn from their experiences. For it was in the sharing of our stories that we would learn from one another, and most importantly discern what was the mind and will of Christ in and for our separate but similar situations. I then focused on what I saw to be the 'things that make for peace', referring to the anguished words of Jesus as He wept over Jerusalem and yet weeps over Northern Ireland and South Africa.

This was the first of two services on that morning in which I essentially preached the same sermon. During the coffee break I was in the vestry when I heard raised voices in the adjoining choir room. When the senior pastor joined me prior to the second service I asked him was everything alright. He explained – with some embarrassment – that the organist had not taken kindly to something I had said during my sermon and was refusing to play for the second service. He assured me that while he personally was happy with what I had said he had done a 'deal' with the organist. If he played for the hymns he could leave for the sermon and return for the last hymn. So it was that when he did get up and leave before the sermon I noticed another man from the choir leave with him. Following the service, there was yet more tea and coffee on the lawn when I was approached by the man who had left with the organist. He greeted me in what was still a very distinct 'Norn Ireland' accent.

He had come from Belfast many years ago, where he had been a member of a Methodist church with which I was familiar. We did not go into what I had said in any detail, but he was clearly on a different path to mine. After all of the intervening years he had simply transferred his instinctive Northern Irish sectarianism into a not-so-subtle white South African apartheid racism.

Another story from that trip relates to my meeting with an outstandingly courageous opponent of apartheid, the retired Catholic archbishop of Durban, the late Denis Hurley, then in his early eighties. It had been arranged that Clodagh and I would travel with him to the town of Phoenix, outside Durban, which is close to the Phoenix Settlement established by Mahatma Gandhi. We soon discovered that Hurley was transporting a bust of Gandhi on behalf of an inter-Church peace organisation that would be unveiled in our presence by another visitor – the Prime Minister of India.

In conversation the archbishop told me that his father had come from West Cork. What part, I asked, since my father also had come from West Cork. Skibbereen, he replied, from the parish of Caheragh. As we talked we realised that his father and my grandmother had come from the same townland, in all probability from neighbouring farms. From then on we talked much more of West Cork than either South Africa or Northern Ireland. As we drove along the dirt roads leading to Phoenix I glanced at Clodagh in the row of seats behind us. There she was clinging on to Gandhi, with whom she was being bounced to and fro.

It was a very wet day and we were grateful for the four-wheel drive vehicle, which did not get bogged down in the mud. But other vehicles were not so lucky. When we got out to help push one of them I found myself beside a very well-spoken and appreciative Indian gentleman. When we returned to our own vehicle someone said to me did I know that I had just been helping Gandhi's grandson out of the mud. What an unexpected privilege!

After the ceremony I was introduced to some of the other special guests, including some of the representatives of political parties. I was greatly impressed by my conversations with two in particular: members of different and opposing parties who were working together in a constructive political power-sharing arrangement. It was confirmation for me that such an agreement really can work.

Apart from the experience of meeting Archbishop Hurley, I was deeply impressed by stories that I heard about several other courageous pastors and preachers both from within and outside Methodism.

There was George Irvine, a lad from the Shankill who had gone to South Africa following a pre-ministerial year at Cliff College in Derbyshire and went on to become Bishop of the Natal Coastal District of the Methodist Church of South Africa and an active advocate for reconciliation in the new South Africa, subsequently becoming the first bishop to stand down to make way for a woman bishop, who was also Black. It was a delight and a privilege to spend time with George and his wife, Lynette. Again, a reminder of the 'village' we call Northern Ireland – George's brother Frank was our gifted organist and choirmaster in University Road.

And there was Pastor Danny Chetty, a brave young anti-apartheid activist from a Coloured family, based near Durban, who hosted Clodagh and me in his own home. We have been greatly saddened to hear of his untimely death from brain cancer at the age of 63 in 2022.

Danny shared some very personal experiences with us. Such as the Sunday evening when three white men and their families who had become 'enthusiastic' members of his church were inexplicably absent and how during that service the police arrived and arrested him for 'offences' related to what he had been saying from his pulpit. It turned out that the three new parishioners were undercover police who had been keeping a record of his sermons and anti-apartheid activities.

His lovely wife took Clodagh for a walk on the nearby beach and told her how Danny had been arrested for leading anti-apartheid protests on that beach. But with the collapse of apartheid they could now walk, and swim and mix as they pleased, enjoying freedoms long denied that white citizens had always taken for granted.

Another outstanding figure who left his mark on me was the Black South African Methodist minister Bishop Mvume Dandala. An impressive and articulate pastor, he had completed postgraduate studies at Cambridge University. I found his accounts of the security forces' surveillance of clergy, and their arrest and detention for so-called incitement and 'subversive activities', as compelling as they were chilling.

He told of how often he was arrested and taken to a police interrogation station. On one such occasion he was handcuffed and suspended from the ceiling (in what was called a 'turkey' something), suffering torture in an attempt to obtain from him the names of those he knew to be so-called subversives. When he refused and was dumped in a cell, one of his interrogators/torturers arrived to say how moved he was by Mvume's courage and witness to his faith. The person who had earlier tortured him said that he now wanted to become a Christian and asked him would he forgive him. Which Mvume did.

'Now,' said his captor. 'Now that we are brothers in Christ can you give me the names for which we asked?' He continued to decline and retained his dignity. It was an incredible story that I will not forget. Mvume went on to become the presiding bishop of the Methodist Church of Southern Africa, and later still head of the All-Africa Conference of Churches and pastoral confidant to President Mandela – whose marriage to Graça Machel he conducted.

On a pre-arranged visit to the offices of the Truth and Reconciliation Commission in Cape Town I briefly met with Desmond Tutu, who was called away to an emergency but graciously left me with his deputy chairman, Dr Alex Boraine, who back in 1970 had, at 39, become the youngest ever President of the Methodist Church in South Africa before entering the purely political arena. At the conclusion of our conversation I asked, if invited, would he come to Northern Ireland to help us in our search for post-conflict healing. He generously replied in the affirmative. Upon my return home, as chair of NIACRO, together with our chief executive, Dave Wall, we met with Oliver Wilkinson, CEO of Victim Support, and agreed that our two organisations, representing former combatants and victims respectively, were ideally placed to explore a new initiative to address issues around legacy.

Alex Boraine accepted our invitation and, following his visit in 1999, we found funding to establish a new cross-community forum to be known as 'Healing Through Remembering' in 2001. Under the direction of Kate Turner, it is an organisation which has been responsible for a hugely significant, if not fully recognised, contribution to our ongoing conversations on the healing of our hurts. I remember at our first submission to the Eames–Bradley Commission, the Co-Chair Robin Eames acknowledging that in HTR we had already done the groundwork for what was to follow.

Our experience in South Africa confirmed for me that the stories of suffering and discrimination about which we had read and heard were not exaggerated.

As I returned home with memories swirling in my head of Robben Island, Cape Town's District Six and that drive through the mud with Archbishop Hurley – and so much more besides that I don't have space to recall here – I was overwhelmed with a sense of admiration for the courage and integrity of those in leadership – especially fellow pastors – who challenged and confronted the apartheid state and were prepared to go to jail to support necessary change and help secure justice.

During this time I was struck by the need for healing and the willingness of South Africans to embrace a healing process. Their TRC process – while not perfect and not necessarily a 'blueprint' for us or for other arenas of conflict – did provide an example of one way for all parties coming out of conflict. It underlined the need to engage in honesty, truth and acknowledgement and recognise these as essential steps towards healing and reconciliation.

I watched on South African television some of the hearings from the TRC and noted how the media refrained from creating confrontation between those participating in the proceedings. There is as yet no analogous process here and no sign of one, notwithstanding the excellent work of Eames–Bradley and Richard Haass, and that is a scandal. When asked about media restraint in South Africa it was explained that following the 'new beginning' there was a self-regulatory agreement on the part of media in the interim period to refrain from doing or saying anything that would be unhelpful or destabilising. I confess I have not seen such media restraint here. Which is a conversation which we ought to have with Stephen Nolan[xi] as well as others.

This was not to be my last visit to South Africa. Indeed it was the first of eight. Following my sabbatical my next visit to South Africa was during my Presidential Year in July 2001 when I was asked to represent the British and Irish Conferences at the Triennial Conference of the Methodist Church of Southern Africa on the campus of the university at Port Elizabeth. While much of the proceedings were similar to any Methodist conference, it was for me a happy and moving experience to share in such an event in the then still 'new' South Africa with a mosaic of white, Black and Coloured Methodists praying and singing loudly and lustily together. The climax to our conference was to be the ordination service of 28 presbyters who had completed their studies and their period of training. The night before those of us who were overseas representatives were given to understand that there would be tight security around the service, and we were asked to come at an earlier hour. We would understand why when we got there. It was rumoured that the world's most famous political and moral leader par excellence would grace us with his presence.

[xi] A controversial BBC broadcaster in Northern Ireland.

And so it was. Next morning those of us who were to occupy privileged seats were guided through airport-style security checks ahead of the arrival of Nelson Mandala, who had shown his sublime selflessness by voluntarily vacating the state presidency two years previously and making way for a younger man. He was now the world's pre-eminent elder statesman. We stood before him as he and his wife Graça arrived and were introduced as representatives of the world Church.

As the service proceeded Graça was the first to speak, recalling the debt that she and her husband owed to Methodism. It was the Methodist Church which provided for their schooling and it was the Church which had provided the moral foundation upon which they had built their personal lives and values. For her in Mozambique and for Nelson in the rural South African village of Qunu.

Then the president emeritus was invited to address the ordinands. He spoke simply and plainly of their opportunities and responsibilities as leaders within the life of the new South Africa. As I listened to his words I thought this address would be as relevant for ministers and priests of whatever denomination in Ireland, North and South, or for any part of the world emerging from conflict and seeking reconciliation.

While I do not have Mandela's script for that occasion, I can reproduce his challenging words on another occasion from the pulpit of St George's Cathedral in Cape Town:

> In the building of our new nation … we look to the Church, with its message of justice, peace, forgiveness and healing, to play a key role in helping our people … to move from the divisions of the past to a future that is united in a commitment to correct ways and restore a just order.

Put more simply, he is asking us to be the Church we claim to be. How moving was it for me, to be the one chosen to lay my hands on the head of the 28th candidate for ordination: a young Black South African whose name was Patrick. In following years, it was our joy and privilege to re-visit South Africa several times. Twice when we brought more than 40 of our parishioners and their friends on 'Journeys of Understanding'. We continue to observe and grieve for the political instability of that beautiful country.

Hong Kong

Driving through the Kowloon area of Hong Kong I could have been forgiven for thinking momentarily that I was back home when I saw a large sign bearing the words 'Methodist College'. It reminded me of the pervasive legacy of our founder John Wesley and his emphasis on education. That legacy is staggering, with more than 1,000 Methodist-related schools, colleges and universities around the globe.

I was curious to find out how the early transition from British rule was going in Hong Kong and how this was affecting the identity of Christian institutions, schools and churches. Would Churches be free to retain and maintain their distinctive identity and contribution within a very new and different administration? On a Sunday morning we attended the English-speaking Methodist Church with its numerically strong congregation, including a large number of Filipino women who were employed by well-off Hong Kong families as domestic servants. Their lively choir led our singing and we were invited to join them for lunch after the service. This was an obviously happy and inclusive worshipping community but would this survive the transfer of sovereignty to communist China – whatever about Beijing's fancy talk about 'one country, two systems'? At the time, just months after the transfer of power, I did hear concerns, and I was not surprised to hear of the more recent exodus from the former colony following the security clampdown in 2020. The minister of that church, an Englishman, appointed by the Missionary Society of the British Methodist Church, was being recalled and a number of ex-pats in the congregation who worked in the civil service said that they too would be returning to England as their services were no longer required. It obviously was a challenging time for the Christian community.

However, an important lesson from Hong Kong that I took away still pertains today and will remain true always. The life and witness of the Church/es is not determined by what flag flies over Hong Kong or anywhere else for that matter. The Church was and is there to represent and serve within 'the kingdom of God' in whatever earthly kingdom or domain in which it finds itself. It was already an 'indigenous' led church and the withdrawal of Westerners would not affect the ongoing life/witness of the Church.

This truism has of course implications for us in Northern Ireland. What if we found ourselves living under a different flag from the flag of the Union? This is a question of particular interest to the many Protestant churches which display the Union Jack – which I have seen oddly propped up against a Communion Table – and conclude youth parade services and Remembrance Sunday services with the singing of the British national anthem. For the Christian, ultimately there can be only one kingdom, the Kingdom of God under the rule of the 'King of kings', regardless of any merely temporal or temporary earthly dispensation.

CHINA

China, so far away and mysterious with an epic history – especially in recent times – has always been a source of fascination for me. As a boy I used to amuse myself and my friends by showing glass slides of missionaries in China on my father's antique 'magic lantern' and wondered if one day I too might join them. Obviously events in the recent history of that mysterious land put paid to any such possibility. But now was my opportunity to fulfil in part my desire to visit this land so long veiled behind the 'bamboo curtain'.

With encouragement and guidance from the late Rev. Dr Jack Weir, who had been born in China to Irish missionary parents and had himself ministered there, I had corresponded with the leadership of the China Christian Council.

This was the 'umbrella' body permitted to reinstate and 'govern' the Protestant Churches in the post-Cultural Revolution period. The condition set by the communist authorities was that there should be one Protestant Church with no denominations as in the past. The Communists were able to achieve what all the ecumenical councils and movements have failed to do!

At Shanghai Airport we were met and welcomed by a gentleman with a splendid limousine. He was to be our 'guide' in the first few days of our visit. We had no doubt that he was our 'minder' from the government's Department of Religion. On our Sunday in Shanghai we attended the Mu'en Church – formerly a large Western-style city centre Methodist Church, reminiscent of our Donegall Square Methodist Church. It was Advent Sunday and the worship, music and Advent hymns were entirely familiar.

Apart from the language we could have been in our own church, and before our eyes we felt the legacy of the tireless work of generations of British and Irish missionaries. The most striking difference from home was that the church was packed and it seemed about 80 percent of the congregation were young people. Most of them had a Bible, and a pencil and notebook taking notes of the sermon. Beside us sat a young woman interpreter who translated the service. Pastor Ho took as his theme 'Advent Hope' and told us of his own very personal journey of hope.

In 1966, at the beginning of the Cultural Revolution launched by Mao Zedong, all Christian churches were closed. The Communists desecrated the buildings by turning them into detention centres and other uses. All Bibles, hymn books, worship books and records of membership were destroyed. Pastor Ho and his wife were 'deployed' to a labour camp where for twelve long years, day in and day out, his work for the state was to pedal a tricycle with heavy loads. Had he met a member of his congregation they could not even make eye contact lest they put one or other or both of them at risk. Without a Bible or aids to personal devotion and prayer, he and his wife would whisper Bible passages and prayers to each other. This is how they kept their faith alive.

But one day he had all he could take of this enforced life of spiritual and physical deprivation. He sat on a doorstep with head in hands and had surrendered to hopelessness when he became aware of a man sitting beside him who said, 'I know who you are, you were the pastor of that large church in the centre of Shanghai. I am not a "believer" [as Christians are known in China]. But you must not give up *hope*! One day you will be back in your church with your people.' The pastor continued, 'If someone who was not a believer could speak of hope who was I to give up hope?'

So it was that he literally got on his bike and cycled on until the day came when he and his wife returned to their beloved church and congregation. 'And here we are,' he said as he pointed to his wife presiding at the organ over a splendidly robed choir.

We were invited to share lunch with Pastor Ho following the service. In conversation I asked him to tell me about his return to the church following a gap of twelve years.

As he recalled it, on that Sunday there was a congregation of 500 – similar to the numbers before closure. Did he remember what he said? What was his text?

'Yes', he said, 'I preached from Philippians Chapter 3, verse 13, which speaks of "Forgetting what is behind and reaching toward what is ahead."'

When we visited almost 20 years after the church reopened, that congregation of 500 had grown to 5,000, meeting each Sunday in a series of five services.

There is much more to share about that journey. We were taken to visit new churches springing up – physically overflowing with new 'believers'. And to one of several seminaries full of the brightest of young Chinese students for ministry.

We visited the Amity Christian Printing Press, which has published many millions of Bibles for distribution in China and even the rest of the world – as many as they seek permission to print, we were told. This experience of the Amity operation makes it difficult for me to understand the 'Underground Church' and those who continue to 'smuggle' Bibles into China, but this is another conversation for another time.

Reflecting on what impressions and lessons I took away from my visit to China it is interesting to recall that it was the Communist government that insisted the Protestant Churches must unite if they were to be permitted to re-open. Whatever the arguments around religious 'freedom' and 'diversity', it was in the uniting of the Churches that they have grown and together have been able to build a relationship of respect within Chinese society and with the historically hostile government. To their credit, the formerly divided but now united Protestant Church has concentrated on building trust rather than harbouring bitter resentment for the lost years of harsh treatment. They have chosen to look forward rather than to the past, in the spirit of St Paul and Pastor Ho, by: 'Forgetting what is behind and reaching toward to what is ahead.'

For the Protestant churches this has meant the formal acceptance of the 'Three-Self Patriotic Movement', a movement that actually was first thought of by the churches themselves as far back as 1877, embodying three principles: 'self-governing', 'self-supporting' and 'self-propagating'.

This ensures that it is an authentic and indigenous-led Church, totally free from dependence and therefore the 'demands' of influence and governance from outside of China. Given the history of British imperialism in China, this was understandable and defensible.

As far as I could ascertain the 'rules' were much the same for both Catholic and Protestant churches: while not a part of the Three-Self Patriotic Movement, the Catholic Church agreed to the same principles, in particular to be a self-governing indigenous-led church. In my conversation with a Roman Catholic priest the story was much the same as that shared by former Methodist colleagues in the country. Accepting some restrictions did not demand compromise in things essential.

In all of these conversations and learning about the life and witness of the churches in China I sensed parallels in the story of the early Church and resonances of the never-ending challenge of living out a healthy tension between Church and state and earning the respect of government without being identified with the state. There can be no perfect answer to that conundrum but a wise Church will never accept the patronage of the state nor will it patronise the state, while never hesitating to call out the state when that is required by the demands of the Gospel.

Given the amount of religious freedom that we clearly observed, I was a little confused given the stories that I had heard about the non-registered 'underground' church. Could our hosts enlighten us? 'We do not understand this either,' was the response. 'Sometimes we think that there are people who want to be martyrs.'

We were struck by the faith of the people we met and the freedom and confidence they evinced. Not having a place of 'power' or 'privilege' in that society gave them integrity. And we were reminded of what Jesus said about 'salt' and 'light' and 'mustard seeds'.

I asked a young believing barrister what difference could the church ever make in Chinese society, given that at best it only represents 5 percent of the entire population. In reply he asked me did I know the percentage of Chinese people who were members of the Communist Party. I made a clumsy guess at 60 plus percent.

'It is also a mere 5 percent,' he said, 'and then you ask me what difference we can make!'

He went on to say that Christians (believers) were increasingly to be found in positions of influence and responsibility where it matters because they were trusted and respected for their values. That observation added to the hope that I sensed around me in China that Advent.

NEPAL

Like so many others, Clodagh and I have always been haunted by the plight of those in developing countries who suffer the ravages of disease, not least leprosy, an affliction we all recall from the story of Jesus and the ten lepers in the Bible.

So, I was pleased when I came across an appeal from the Leprosy Mission for someone to make 'pastoral visits' to their personnel scattered throughout Nepal. Such an opportunity coincided with my planning for my sabbatical.

We set out on a remarkable journey to remarkable projects and remarkable people across Nepal, the Hindu kingdom nestling in the Himalayas, bordered by India and Tibet, and encircled by the most spectacular scenery on earth. Amongst the most unforgettable views ever was the sunrise over the stunning Annapurna Mountain Range. We were flown and driven to some of the most remote areas where the Leprosy Mission is involved in the care of people suffering from or at risk of being infected by leprosy and other diseases.

To reach one of the most inaccessible mission stations we were driven across spectacular mountain ranges and riverbeds for twelve hours in a four-wheel drive. To reach another we had to take to the skies in a small plane and we landed in a field which had been cleared for our arrival. Surprisingly, one of the smoothest landings ever.

The Leprosy Mission is also responsible for some of the most well-equipped and professionally staffed hospitals and clinics in the country, such as the Anandaban Hospital close to Kathmandu. It was here in 1993 that those most moving images of Princess Diana embracing the patients did so much to challenge and change the stigma of leprosy.

To do justice to this part of our sabbatical story would call for a book on its own. Up to 1955 there was no known Christian community in Nepal, which was not surprising since until then it was illegal to either practice or promote any religion other than Hinduism. We were told the story of how a small number of Nepalese, returning from a spell in India where they had been converted to the Christian faith, began to share their newfound faith with family and neighbours. It is estimated that there are now over half a million practising Christians in Nepal, Roman Catholic and Reformed.

While officially Christians are permitted to gather for worship, there are remote areas where this is not easy. On one Sunday we worshipped with a small village congregation in a discreet upper room. We were told that the previous Sunday there had been a Communist-inspired raid during the service with the men being taken for intensive and aggressive questioning.

While the Church is growing under indigenous leadership, 'foreign' missions and missionaries are not permitted to operate as traditional 'missionaries' in Nepal. They are admitted only as aid workers to be involved in purely 'secular' humanitarian activity such as medical care and dentistry, and engineering projects such as the building of bridges and dams. In the churches these very skilled and professional 'humanitarians' sit very significantly and symbolically in the back seats of the churches, under the leadership and ministry of Nepalese pastors.

So once again, I found an authentic indigenous Church worshipping and serving the community without 'the fear of favour' from government. As in China, the churches were allowed to exist but not permitted to 'evangelise' nor to receive support from abroad – other than the welcome presence of aid workers from two outstanding Christian-inspired organisations from the UK: the Leprosy Mission Nepal, an international NGO of which I am now a proud patron, and the Inter-Church International Nepal Fellowship.

With not a little humility we observed volunteers from those organisations, doctors, nurses, paramedics, engineers and others bring their skills to bear to make a big difference on the ground, coming to serve rather than to dominate, enabling and encouraging the indigenous leadership to grow in confidence, asking for nothing in return and seeking no reward, save that of knowing what it means to fulfil the law of Christ. And, importantly, earning the respect and gratitude of an otherwise unsympathetic government.

One's experience was of a growing Church in spite of laws prohibiting evangelism with people being drawn to the churches and into a living faith by what they saw to be very visible 'signs and wonders' in the form of care being provided without conditions, and especially to the poorest, the shunned lepers and those of the lowest castes.

It made one think with sadness of how mainline churches in the West have so largely abandoned our inner cities and disadvantaged communities. We have much to learn from the 'incarnational' servant role of the Church in Nepal.

Sadly there were those – largely American 'evangelicals' – who were trying in not so subtle and devious ways to circumvent the law to 'infiltrate' and quite literally buy over some of these new and vulnerable churches. For example, in one case the lure of a 'gift' of a battery of computers for which the church had neither need nor knowledge. This kind of practice resulted in competitive division and compromise, a sad reflection of what we are all too familiar with in the West.

However, I was heartened by the work of those volunteers and the growth of the Church. And my heart was warmed to see the Christian community refusing to ally themselves with one side or the other in a politically and culturally divided society.

15

GUNS AND NO GUNS!
UP CLOSE WITH ETA AND FARC

'Peace cannot be achieved through violence, it can only be attained through understanding.'

Ralph Waldo Emerson, essayist

The destruction of the remaining huge stocks of guns and explosives under IRA control at numerous secret sites throughout Ireland in September 2005, witnessed by Fr Alec Reid and myself, was a major international news story.

While it was welcomed from 10 Downing Street to the White House, and from Brussels to the Vatican, interest in it was nowhere more intense than among those striving to secure a peace settlement to Europe's remaining longest-running conflict – that between the Spanish government and the Basque separatist guerilla group ETA, Euskadi Ta Askatasuna, 'Basque Homeland and Liberty' or 'Basque Country and Freedom'.

In time, it also became a development of great interest in Colombia, where the authorities and FARC guerillas had been engaged in deadly combat for more than 50 years.

ETA's violent campaign for independence from Spain began in 1968, roughly at the start of our own Troubles. Few outside of Spain were much aware of the group until it assassinated the Spanish Prime Minister, Admiral Luis Carrero Blanco, Franco's chosen successor, by putting a bomb under his car in December 1973.

ETA's campaign claimed 829 lives and wounded more than 22,000 people before it formally ended in 2018 after a weapons decommissioning process in which I was privileged to be involved, along with an Italian Catholic archbishop, now Cardinal Matteo Zuppi – the Pope's emissary on Ukraine and considered a potential successor to papal office.

The Spanish peace process had some marked similarities to ours. A hardline attitude by a deeply conservative Spanish government not interested in serious engagement with ETA, even after it had declared a ceasefire, had prolonged the conflict. It was also fascinating to hear officials from Eusko Alkartasuna – a moderate Basque social democratic party resembling the SDLP – confide to me their ambivalence about ETA decommissioning because it might mean that ETA's political wing, Batasuna, 'would steal our votes'.

ETA had actually declared a truce in September 1998 which coincided with elections and was thought to have been influenced to some extent by the success of our peace process and the Good Friday Agreement of that year. But the truce did not hold and they resumed their campaign at the end of 1999.

Unbeknown to all but a very few, one of those beavering away in the background to secure peace in Spain was the remarkable Fr Reid. I knew that Alec had made many trips to the Basque Country since 2003 in the cause of peace without seeking or being given details.

After our verification of the secret decommissioning of IRA arms in September 2005 everything changed for Alec and for me. Never again could the naturally private and reserved Alec escape the glare of media attention, and I too needed to be on guard. As my son Richard had presciently observed, following my now very public role in the historic destruction of the IRA's arsenal, life would not be quite the same again. Fr Alec and I received numerous awards and invitations to speak at various conferences at home and abroad. And the ever-inquisitive media still wanted to hear more about what had transpired in those IRA bunkers.

But nowhere was there more interest in all of that than in the Basque Country. So it was that in mid-December 2005 Alec and I received the most potentially significant call of all. It was from the Office of the Lehendakari, or President of the Basque government, in Vitoria-Gasteiz in the Basque Country in northern Spain, to say we were to get the René Cassin Award, as I recalled in Chapter 13.

Bilbao is not the easiest place to fly to from Northern Ireland. But this was to be the first of many such journeys which were made easier by the generous and thoughtful arrangements that awaited us upon our arrival in Bilbao where we were greeted as VIPs and driven to Vitoria-Gasteiz, the Basque capital. What is a beautiful drive at any time of the year was made all the more spectacular by the snow-peaked mountains with the fields and valleys wrapped under a very pure white blanket.

The official residence of the Lehendakari proved to be a magnificent setting for the ceremony to follow. After his generous speech of welcome, in the presence of an invited audience and the media, the Lehendakari, Juan José Ibarretxe Markuartu, made his presentation and invited us to respond. Being in an unfamiliar setting and not knowing who might be present, it was the kind of event for which one could not easily prepare. So much of what I said was very much off-the-cuff.

However, with my newly acquired/Googled knowledge of René Cassin in mind and having served as a member of the Northern Ireland Human Rights Commission, I thought I would play it safe and centre my thoughts on the importance of human rights in the search for the resolution of any conflict. Without having been prompted, or having had adequate time to prepare, it was obvious from the response that I had touched on a very central theme, particularly in my reference to our treatment of prisoners as well as victims of the conflict. What I could not have known was that within the invited audience were ETA activists as well as sympathisers in the Basque separatist movement's struggle.

I have to say that as an introduction to the many visits that were to follow, the welcome we received, along with the attention from the media, was quite overwhelming. And over the years to follow that media interest did not abate – all of which was to emphasise to both of us the significance of any contribution we might have to offer.

Our next day began with a news conference, reminiscent of the day Alec and I joined John de Chastelain and his colleagues in front of the world's media at the Culloden Hotel for our post-decommissioning press conference. Again, with no prepared scripts, Alec and I were questioned at length and in depth about our peace process, the Good Friday Agreement and the decommissioning of the weaponry of the IRA. It was only then that I understood the real reason behind our invitation. The Lehendakari and his party colleagues and like-minded people from other parties, as well as civil society, were anxious to bring the issue of decommissioning onto the public agenda, envisaging a similar approach there to what had succeeded in Northern Ireland.

Following two days of further conversations and interviews with the media, we were given private tours of the restoration project of the cathedral in Vitoria-Gasteiz and of the famous Guggenheim Museum in Bilbao.

As our homeward-bound plane descended from the clouds, so did our VIP status as we shared a belated post-Christmas party with our noisy and much less respectful grandchildren. But this was to be but the beginning of a protracted and very special relationship with some of the most genuine seekers of peace that it has been my privilege to know and work with.

Over the years that followed, until his health no longer permitted, Alec and I made several shared visits and then, sadly, I continued to go solo. I soon realised how much Alec's quiet and persistent presence had been appreciated by those who were aware of him and his contribution to the ongoing search for peace in that beautiful but sad region, with its 40 and more years of civil conflict.

Just a few months later, in March 2006, after ETA announced a 'permanent ceasefire', Alec and I were walking through Bilbao when cars started slowing up, horns hooting, and we heard shouts of 'Eskerrik asko' (Basque for 'gratitude, thanks') or 'gracias.' Others were giving a 'thumbs up' as a sign of appreciation and approval. While many citizens of Spain and some from within the Basque Country itself would not have shared these sentiments, on that day I felt as if I was walking with something of a national hero.

Confirmation that not all were on the same page as Alec came when I sought a meeting with a Señor Carmelo, the chief executive (secretary-general) of the main opposition People's Party (Partido Popular), which had ruled Spain under Prime Minister José María Aznar from 1996 until 2004 but had lost the general election after controversially and erroneously blaming the Madrid Bombings on ETA – bombings which were later proven to be the work of an extreme militant Islamic group.

When I was told that a meeting was problematic as Señor Carmelo saw me as indistinguishable from Fr Alec, I asked an intermediary to assure him that I was 'my own man'. Only then did he agree to meet me. We had a very cordial but frank meeting during which I conveyed to him my willingness to facilitate a conversation between him and a prominent representative of the DUP. I explained that it was a party which shared and understood the reluctance of the People's Party to engage with representatives of a proscribed organisation but was willing to share some recent positive experiences arising out of their engagement with Sinn Féin.

I followed up this meeting with a letter in which I re-emphasised my thoughts and suggestions. While I did not receive a reply and my suggestion was not followed up in the way that I had offered, I was very pleased when an all-party delegation from Spain accepted the invitation of our then Assembly Speaker William Hay to come and visit Stormont. I was particularly pleased to find Señor Carmelo within that delegation. He greeted me most cordially and I had reason to believe that what I had suggested would now be achieved in another way.

Obviously, much of his concern was based on the many parallels in the Basque situation and our past history on the island of Ireland, both in terms of constitutional aspiration and the recourse to violence in the pursuit of a political objective. For me it was revealing to discover how much the Basque separatists looked to representatives of Irish republicanism in their search for an alternative strategy. The significance of that positive role has not been fully understood or acknowledged.

For example, I have in my possession the cutting of an extensive Basque newspaper interview with Martin McGuinness in which he was clearly encouraging ETA, from his own experience, to pursue another and a better way. I was also present at events in the Basque Country at which Gerry Adams and Bertie Ahern shared their experiences of the Irish peace process, following which I had opportunity for a very personal conversation with Bertie on the flight back to Dublin.

Sadly the time came when Alec could no longer make these journeys and I missed his company as I continued on my own. In particular I recall sharing a platform with Roelf Meyer, the South African National Party's chief negotiator during the dismantling of apartheid and the establishment of Black majority rule. And an event in the Basque town of Oñati when I delivered an address entitled 'Rights, Religion and Restoration', combining my very personal and passionate commitment to what for me is the indistinguishable relationship between faith, justice and reconciliation. This was to be followed by a similar address at an international human rights conference on conflict resolution in Bilbao in November 2006. In both of these events I summed up what I sought to say in a paraphrase of the prophet Micah, who exhorted the people of his time to 'Do justice, be generous in your judgements, and refrain from arrogance', emphasising to my hearers that my message to them was based on what had been my appeals to people across the community in Northern Ireland.

On that occasion I argued that conflict resolution requires a consensus on ten core principles and common values which I listed as:

- Truth – confessing what we have done to one another.
- Honest dialogue.
- An empathetic understanding of 'the other'.
- An openness to a truly inclusive concept of society.
- Commitment to exclusively democratic and peaceful means.
- Generosity and reciprocity.
- Being prepared to do the unthinkable.
- Trust – beginning with trust in ourselves, only then can we begin to trust one another.
- Hope. Like the Old Testament prophet Zechariah, we must be prepared to become 'prisoners of Hope'.

A tall order? Yes! But think of the lives that are saved and all the joy that flows – as opposed to grief and suffering – when we embrace the ways of peace.

In each of my visits to the Basque Country, whatever the publicised event, I was given opportunity to speak with representatives of political parties and with individuals, some of whom no doubt were close to and perhaps a part of outlawed organisations. On every visit I was a person of interest to the local and sometimes national media, including TV and newspapers.

I have to say that for me personally it was a disappointment to discover that with one exception, neither the Catholic Church nor anyone from the minority Reformed Churches in the Basque Country was represented at events organised by the pro-independence movement. For me it was, therefore, regrettable that there was no opportunity to engage in even private conversations with representatives of the Churches. From what I could gather, given the history of Spain and his treatment of the Basques, the influence of General Franco to some extent remains alive and well.

The exception to this was when at one event Alec and I did share a platform with an elderly, outspoken and radical bishop who was an unapologetic critic of the status quo. So much so that the government in Madrid had appealed to the Vatican to have him transferred from the Basque Country. Therefore I was encouraged when, much more recently, I was invited to Loyola, the birthplace of St Ignatius, founder of the Jesuits. In his memory stands a spectacular cathedral, adjacent to an impressive Jesuit House which plays an important role in the provision of a place of learning and training for laity as well as for the clergy. I had been invited to meet with a small and inquisitive group of five Jesuit priests who wished to hear about the Northern Ireland peace process. Within that conversation I learned that this was something of a clandestine event – the purpose of which was concealed from their superior.

Clearly, the Church of which their order is a part had no wish to be in conflict with the state, or with sections of society with whom they would find themselves in ideological or theological conflict. To me from Northern Ireland, it all sounded sadly familiar. The Jesuits with whom I spoke confessed to having been excited and challenged by what I shared, particularly of the role of individual clergy and lay members of the churches who were prepared to act outside the formal structures of the churches in the cause of anchoring peace.

In each and all of my visits and conversations there were two recurring issues that were so familiar to me: prisoners and decommissioning. Something else that was familiar was the tortuous nature of the Spanish peace process with numerous turns and twists and false dawns. Seven or so years elapsed between the ETA truce of 1998–1999 and the 'permanent ceasefire' of March 2006 when, as I have recalled, Alec was greeted so enthusiastically when we walked on the streets of Bilbao.

Sadly, in the absence of any positive response from the government in Madrid that ceasefire was formally ended in June 2007 and only reinstated in January 2011. Although ETA did carry out a partial act of decommissioning in February 2014, in which I was not involved, it was dismissed by the Spanish government as a 'theatrical exercise'. So it was that in mid-December 2016 ETA organised another attempt at the decommissioning of their weapons. Having agreed to assist in any way I could and having visited the region many times in the intervening years, I was not altogether surprised when the invitation finally came and I found myself once more on a plane to the Basque Country. But this time it was to Biarritz in the Basque region of southwest France, with which I was less familiar.

This time I found myself in something of a covert role. I was not to bring my mobile phone or any electronic device which could be tracked. Upon arrival I would be given an alternative mobile phone with a different number which would conceal my identity. After landing I was met by the person who was to be my host for my short stay. He brought me to a comfortable rural farmhouse with a well-concealed bedroom in a loft to which I would be returned after the completion of the act of decommissioning. This act of decommissioning, which promised to be the defining moment in signalling ETA's irrevocable rejection of armed struggle, was planned to take place very early the following morning on the premises of a nearby farm.

It was explained to me that very early the next morning, in the presence of a small but representative group of honourable local citizens, together with myself and a priest as independent witnesses, members of ETA would assemble and begin the physical destruction of their weapons which were to be brought to that discreet rural location.

However, during a splendid Basque evening meal for which I was more than ready, my host received an urgent call. What was then to unfold was a drama as bizarre as it was unhelpful. A combined posse of French and Spanish anti-terrorist police had swooped on the nearby farm where the decommissioning was to take place and had arrested that group of respected and trusted citizens who were awaiting the arrival of representatives of ETA and their deadly weapons. Those arrested were now in custody and on their way to Paris for questioning for allegedly aiding and abetting an illegal organisation. This was a bombshell and all the carefully laid plans were in tatters.

I was then left on my own in my upstairs billet for what was to be a long and anxious night. I assured myself that I was not important enough to be a wanted man while fearing that every vehicle which passed might well be the security forces coming to arrest me. I hardly slept a wink!

As it turned out nobody came looking for me, no dreaded vehicle slowing down, no heavy boots crunching on the gravel below, no heavy knocking of the door. Either the police were unaware of my existence or had no idea where I was secreted. But being kept out of sight made for a long next day as my flight home did not depart until midday Sunday. When my kindly 'minder' dropped me at a discreet corner of the airport car park I noticed how well policed the area was with well-armed gendarmes. Were they looking for me? Was I important enough to be a 'wanted man'? All of these questions passed through my head as I walked smartly past them, looking neither to the right nor to the left. So it was with a sense of relief that I finally took my seat and awaited a safe and uninterrupted take-off. Given the bomb attacks in Paris that had killed 130 people a year before, it was not surprising that security throughout France was tight. It was a setback but I was well used to setbacks during our own peace process.

ETA had long crossed the Rubicon and I suspected it would only be a matter of time before another attempt would be made to bring things to a reasonably orderly conclusion. In the grand scheme of things, we didn't have very long to wait before an alternative approach to decommissioning was to be agreed. This time, crucially, there was agreement in advance between the three principal players – ETA (or their representatives), and the Spanish and French governments – with Spain consenting to the French authorities taking the lead. The chosen day was Saturday, 8 April 2017, dubbed 'Disarmament Day' by Basque nationalists.

I flew to Bilbao the day before and was driven almost 100 miles through a most scenic route across the border to the city of Bayonne in the Basque region of France. This time I travelled without any fear of arrest because what was to unfold had been agreed in advance in what Irish peace process veterans would call a 'choreographed operation'.

So it was that on that Saturday morning I was driven to the City Hall in Bayonne where I was to meet for the first time my fellow independent witness, Archbishop Matteo Zuppi. In Northern Ireland terms it was an unlikely partnership, but as pastors we felt privileged and humbled to be asked. Also present were members of the International Verification Commission (IVC), including its chairman, Dr Ram Manikkalingam, who had helped with peace efforts in Sri Lanka and, to my delight, my good friend Chris Maccabe, whom I have known for many years and who since his retirement from the Northern Ireland Office – where he made a significant contribution to our peace process – has dedicated himself to peace building in many parts of the world.

On this occasion, resulting from the delicate negotiations that had been successfully conducted behind the scenes, there was to be no visible public decommissioning of arms. Instead, there would be a very public demonstration by ETA of their renunciation of violence and their decision to give up their deadly arsenal. At the appointed time, files and folders containing inventories of weapons and weaponry, together with maps of secret arms dumps, were entrusted to Archbishop Matteo and myself who, in turn, handed them to Dr Manikkalingam, the chair of the IVC. For me it was another historic, memorable and moving moment. I thought of the day that Father Alec had whispered in my ear, 'there goes the last gun out of Irish politics'. How he would have rejoiced in this moment also!

Following the inevitable interviews with the media, including BBC World News, I was told of a peace rally which was to take place that afternoon in the spacious public square in the centre of Bayonne. It was anticipated that there could be as many as 5,000 people present. 'Would you address it?', my Basque hosts asked. Thinking it is not often that an Irish preacher would be granted a 'congregation' of that size – other than on Radio Ulster or RTÉ – I felt honoured and agreed.

By the time we arrived at the stage the anticipated crowd of 5,000 had grown to 20,000. Suddenly the enormity of the responsibility that rested on my shoulders dawned on me. This sense of responsibility was considerably magnified when two Spanish reporters asked me for a script of my speech. I hadn't one, of course, but I quickly realised that something significant was expected of me. I would not get away with a simple 'hello, good to be here, and thank you'.

So, quite literally I managed to get hold of a page from a reporter's notebook and began to jot down the main points that came into my head. It is perhaps one of the most important speeches I have given in my life so I think it fitting to recount it in full.

'What a beautiful day!' I cried out at the start, continuing:

> I wish I could 'bottle' this glorious sunshine and bring it home to Ireland, where we have too much rain! But more importantly, I wish I could 'bottle' the incredible spirit of this day and of this incredible gathering on this beautiful day of peace!
>
> I want to congratulate everyone who has brought us to this day. Only they will know the full extent of the time and risk and commitment that has brought us to this historic moment.
>
> As I stand here I cannot but think of my old friend, Father Alec Reid – who worked so quietly 'in the shadows' to help bring us to this day. I know that he was and is one of your heroes. I remember how after the 'ceasefire' of 2006 we were walking together in Bilbao. He almost caused traffic chaos as people slowed down, honked their horns and waved. Father Alec responded with his characteristic 'thumbs up'. I like to think that today he is looking down on all of us and putting both thumbs up. So let us put two thumbs up for Fr Alec!

At that moment all 20,000 people in the massive crowd responded by putting two thumbs up for Father Alec, what a moment. 40,000 'thumbs up' for Fr Alec!

I continued:

> But as I stand here I realise that this may not be an easy day for everyone. Coming from Northern Ireland, I am all too familiar with the hurt and pain of victims and survivors. Today there will

be people across this community who will be grieving for loved ones they have lost and life-changing injuries they will have suffered during these tragic fifty years of violence.

And there is a sense that in every such civil conflict we are all victims. To those who may have difficulty with a celebration associated with the putting of arms beyond use may I say, as I did in Northern Ireland when the IRA put their arms beyond use, remember that every weapon that is de-commissioned represents the potential saving of at least one more life.

So today let us be sensitive to the feelings of everyone and let today be the beginning of a process of healing and reconciliation. And today, as there was with us in Northern Ireland, there will be doubters and dissidents. Some activists who may feel let down, even betrayed, by the leadership of ETA. To you may I plead – trust your leaders and give peace a chance.

And to your leaders may I say, do all you can to ensure that no one will be left behind. Today is but a beginning. But what a beginning! It is a day of new opportunity. Opportunity for healing, restoration and reconciliation.

Last night I visited your wonderfully beautiful Cathedral of Saint Mary. Protestants don't usually light candles in their churches – but last night I lit the biggest candle I could find and knelt and prayed for this day. And already those prayers are being answered.

May I plead with my fellow clergy of the Christian faith, please take the message of Jesus seriously and become more fully involved in this ministry of healing and reconciliation.

I am not here to preach politics. We have enough political challenges where I come from! But politicians – I beg you to listen. Not just to me – but much more importantly to all of these people gathered here in Bayonne and many others in many other places.

Hear me – particularly those of you in government in Madrid and in Paris.

I beg you, respond positively to the events of this day.

Acknowledge what has been achieved. It's not a huge 'ask' but bring the prisoners home. Bring them to where they can be in easy reach of their families.[xii] Not only in the interests of human compassion but to comply with the humanitarian principles of the European Convention on Human Rights. And deal compassionately with those who are frail by reason of serious ill-health as well as age.

In its own interests, the nation that exercises compassion will be a happier nation for all of its citizens. Let this day and all that it represents be a model for other places of as yet unresolved conflict. And let us dedicate this day to your children and to your grandchildren.

From wherever we have come, let us do all we can to ensure that another generation will never again inherit an unresolved conflict of the past. Thank you and bless you.

I was humbled by the loud applause that I received. A truly unforgettable moment.

Sharing in the event was Arnaldo Otegi, a leading Basque separatist politician. Arnaldo had served many years in prison for his suspected involvement with ETA. But as is now known, he was a key figure in persuading ETA to move from a campaign of terror to disarmament and an entirely political non-violent alternative. The fact that he was a pall bearer at the funeral of Martin McGuinness was no coincidence. As friends and confidants they had both made significant personal journeys taking their respective movements with them.

But this was not to be my last visit to my Basque friends.

[xii] In recent years ETA prisoners have been moved closer to their homes. On 14 January 2024 the Anadolu Agency quoted EFE, a Spanish news agency, as reporting that 134 ETA members remain in Spanish prisons, 8 in French prisons and c.20 exiled abroad.

One year later, in April 2018, I was invited to return to Bayonne to give the keynote address at an event marking the first anniversary of the decommissioning of ETA's weapons and declared ending of their campaign, in which I shared with Basques the significance of our sensitive post-conflict work with former prisoners back home through the good offices of NIACRO.[29] (I vividly recall the sterling contribution of Dave Wall, Brian Gormally and Kieran McEvoy in this endeavour. Kieran is currently a professor in the Senator George J. Mitchell Institute for Global Peace, Security and Justice at Queen's University Belfast.)

There was a perplexing moment when I was introduced by the interpreter in the Basque language. The crowd looked puzzled and in turn I wasn't sure what was going on. (Only after my speech did I know why.) But I quickly got into my stride to say the things I wanted to say.

I emphasised not only the significance of the momentous event which we were marking but, from our own experience in Northern Ireland, stressed that decommissioning was not an end in itself but the opening up of a new opportunity for the beginning of reconciliation and the letting go of that from our past which held us back from embracing a new beginning.

I stressed also that while we must try to look forward to a new future we must never forget the plight of victims and survivors and the need to respond with compassion and realism to the issue of prisoners, bearing in mind that the Spanish and French governments did not agree to prisoner releases as per the Good Friday Agreement.

My speech was well received but afterwards I asked the interpreter why there was so much puzzlement and so many surprised faces after I was introduced. She immediately apologised, saying that as I am 'a pastor' she had introduced me as 'a herder of sheep, a shepherd' as that is the literal translation of pastor in the Basque language.

I replied immediately: 'Don't apologise, that is exactly what I love to be known as, a shepherd.' So, I took it as a great compliment to be described as a herder of sheep. A true pastor is called to be a good shepherd and that is what I have always tried to be.

The next morning I was invited to join with the mayor of Bayonne and other members of the Basque peace movement to gather in a park in the centre of the city. The occasion was to be the 'unfurling' of a monument to mark the end of ETA's campaign and the new peace which was now enjoyed. The monument took the form of a twenty-foot-tall axe, with the head buried in the ground and the handle becoming a tree from which sprung new life and foliage. It was a remarkable symbol of all that had been accomplished and all that was yet hoped for.

When asked to speak I explained that being Sunday morning and being a preacher I could not resist the temptation to offer a biblical insight into what we were now sharing.

I spoke of the words of Jesus who reminded us that, as in the world of nature, some things had to be buried in the ground to allow for new life and hope to grow (John 12:24).

Along with the symbolism of the burying of the axe, ETA had also issued an unreserved apology for the years of pain and suffering which they had inflicted upon their victims.[xiii]

Inevitably, as in Northern Ireland, there were those who viewed all of this with scepticism. And as in Northern Ireland there are those who find it hard to forgive and, given the history of hurt inflicted upon victims, this has to be understood. But more importantly, those committed to a sustained process of reconciliation in the Basque Country continue in that task.

As I reflect upon that highly symbolic axe, together with the words of ETA's apology, I yearn for a similar visible sign or symbol in our public squares and unqualified acknowledgment from all of us for our part in our conflict. For what we have failed to do and say as well as for what some of us may have done.

[xiii] The ETA apology is elaborated on in the Epilogue.

WITH FARC IN CUBA AND COLOMBIA

Early in 2015 I was invited by then MLA John McCallister to meet with representatives of 'Justice for Colombia', an organisation run by an indefatigable English woman, Mariela Kohon, and funded by European countries willing to contribute to the search for a resolution of the Colombian conflict, which, like our own, had dragged on for more than 50 years, causing untold suffering and loss.

If, like me, you did not know much if anything about Colombia here is a brief introduction to the background to this conflict, which in terms of scale is utterly horrifying. Around 220,000 people have been killed and eight million driven from their homes in a multi-faceted conflict involving the government, drug cartels and left-wing guerillas. The most prominent guerilla movement is FARC ('Revolutionary Armed Forces of Colombia').

In terms of a link between Northern Ireland and the conflict in Colombia it is widely believed that there had been longstanding links between FARC and the IRA, culminating in the 2001 arrest and subsequent imprisonment in Bogota of 'The Colombia Three'.

But a more positive link was that with the then President of Colombia, Nobel Prize winner Juan Manuel Santos, who has recalled that as a young man in London he was impacted by an IRA bomb and since then retained a particular interest in Irish affairs. And that it was our peace process that had inspired him to work towards reconciliation with FARC. On a visit to Stormont in November 2016, as part of a state visit to the UK, he was encouraged to persist with his peace efforts by Arlene Foster and Martin McGuinness.

It was following my introduction to representatives of 'Justice for Colombia' that in October 2015, together with a small cross-party group of politicians including MPs Jeffrey Donaldson, Mark Durkan and Paul Maskey, I found myself on a flight to Cuba. Being my first visit, I was both curious and pleasantly surprised. I was swiftly disabused of my negative preconceptions. It was a beautiful island, with most hospitable people and a luxurious hotel. While we were treated to a tour of Havana in a distinctive American vintage car, we were not there as tourists. Rather, we were invited for serious conversations with the most senior representatives of FARC who were living in exile in Cuba, having been given asylum and support there by the late President Fidel Castro.

The FARC representatives with whom we met were living in very comfortable bungalows in spacious parkland where we were received by Commander-in-Chief Rodrigo Londoño Echeverri, better known as Timochenko, and his colleagues. We were also aware of discreet negotiations in Cuba between the leadership of FARC and representatives of President Santos and the government in Colombia, which were to conclude with a peace deal in 2016. This was the context in which we found ourselves sharing our experiences from Northern Ireland.

Our conversations covered a wide range of issues. I could not but be impressed by the shared input from my cross-party political friends from Northern Ireland who spoke openly and honestly of the positive outcomes from our Good Friday Agreement, as well as the challenges of our yet unresolved difficulties.

In particular, I was asked to meet privately with three of FARC's most senior representatives, who asked me to share as much as was possible of our story of decommissioning: with whom was it finally agreed, the modalities, and the role of independent witnesses. We talked of the significance of decommissioning in the building of trust and confidence, as well as the challenge of convincing those who did not wish to accept the validity of the process itself.

As I shared in this conversation I could not but contrast the role in which I now found myself with that of the much-publicised 'Colombia Three', the suspected IRA members who in 2003 had been arrested in Colombia for their suspected role in the training of FARC rebels in the making of mortars and the procurement of weapons. Now here was I, the Irish preacher, being asked to advise the same organisation as to how they might rid themselves of their lethal weapons.

As we talked I had no reason to believe that they were anything but genuine in their desire to decommission as part of their journey towards a political settlement. But, as with the IRA, FARC's unwillingness to decommission prior to an acceptable political agreement was a major reason for their failure to convince the 'doubters' who were to vote against the agreement the following year. But as I tried to impress upon them, and which I was able to illustrate from our own experience, the decommissioning of weapons is the surest way of ensuring confidence in the building of a sustainable peace.

It was a cause for celebration when in August 2016 it was announced that a significant peace agreement had been reached between President Santos and Timochenko, Commander-in-Chief of FARC, with whom we had met in Cuba. This sought to address the main causes of conflict and the difficult issues which had to be resolved.

During the signing ceremony Timochenko asked the victims of FARC for their forgiveness, renounced violence and committed his organisation to decommissioning their weapons. In return, FARC were given the green light to re-form as a political party and the government undertook to embark on a massive development programme to address glaring economic inequalities in rural areas. FARC fighters who confessed to crimes would not go to prison but take part in 'reparation' activities such as clearing land mines, repairing damaged infrastructure and helping victims.

As with the Good Friday Agreement, the 'Colombian Agreement' was put to the people in a public referendum. Sadly, it was narrowly defeated. However, rather than accepting defeat, President Santos brought together opposing sides to re-negotiate the more contentious elements within the agreement. He said: 'Colombia needs unity, we have to leave behind our quarrels, the hatred and the polarisation which causes us so much damage.' Wise words, reflecting true leadership.

So it was that in November 2016 a revised deal was ratified by both Houses of Congress. A revision which inevitably involved compromise and something we are familiar with, 'constructive ambiguity'.

As a result, I was very pleased that in June 2017, in a three-way arrangement with the government and the United Nations, FARC finally entered upon a serious process of decommissioning.

Interesting to me was their agreement that the decommissioned weapons will at some future date be melted down and re-created into monuments to the past, to be located in three strategic sites in Colombia. The first of which can be seen in the capital, Bogota.

As in conversations regarding my experience of the Basque Country, I have been asked did I not feel fearful of the people we met. I have to say we were treated and listened to with the utmost respect. We met some very interesting people, such as the extremely intelligent and attractive young woman from Europe who had come to teach in a Colombian school but who, upon coming to understand something of the history of the conflict, volunteered her services to FARC.

'Maria', as I shall call her, introduced us to a group of exiled women in Cuba from a more mature age group, most of whom had been involved for many of the years of this conflict. They shared personal stories which were a mixture of patriotic idealism and victimhood which had convinced them that an armed struggle was the only recourse left to them in their search for justice.

When asked did we not find these women scary I have said that, had I closed my ears to the conversation and been asked to guess with whom I was meeting I could be forgiven for thinking I was in a local branch of the Mothers' Union or the Women's Institute, without the marmalade!

In February 2017, a few months after Congress had ratified the Peace Agreement, I was again invited to join another representative group from Northern Ireland for conversations with elected representatives of the Colombian government, as well as others who had been working for peace with FARC and related organisations.

In Bogota I was joined by other familiar faces from home, including Chris Maccabe, Monica McWilliams, formerly of the Women's Coalition, Eva Grosman of the Centre for Democracy, and Michael Culbert of the republican ex-prisoners' organisation Coiste na nIarchimí. Jeffrey Donaldson was also invited but unavailable on this occasion.

The purpose of this visit was to encourage support for the revised Peace Agreement which, although now ratified, was still opposed in many quarters. As in Northern Ireland, Colombian society remained divided, with serious reservations about issues such as justice for victims, the treatment of prisoners and guaranteed seats in parliament for representatives of FARC.

Also familiar from home was a very clear division of opinion within and between churches and religious organisations. In Colombia, within the Protestant community the strongest opposition was from the fundamentalist Charismatic and the ultra-conservative/Pentecostal community. But within Colombia this opposition united fundamentalist Protestants and the ultra-conservative wing of the Roman Catholic Church – for us an extremely interesting alliance.

It was explained to me by the organisers of our visit that they would like me to address these concerns and the opposition to the Peace Agreement from within the conservative religious communities. In turn, I suggested that since 90 percent of the population in Colombia are Roman Catholics I was hardly the person to address their fears and prejudices. So it was that I was asked to invite a Roman Catholic priest to accompany me. I had no hesitation in suggesting Father Michael Kelleher, a former provincial of the Irish Redemptorists who had travelled with myself and Father Alec on several of our journeys.

While all of our meetings were important, including the opportunity to address an all-party gathering of elected representatives in the parliament, the most memorable part of this visit was a journey which took us into the mountains to visit a FARC camp.

This journey began with a flight to Cali, almost 200 miles from Bogota, followed by a four-hour drive along rough mountainous roads through amazing forests with the only other traffic being the occasional motorcycle or overcrowded bus with passengers clinging to the sides as well as on the roof. Halfway to our destination, we stopped at a basic hut from which we purchased chicken soup and a cup of the finest Colombian coffee. It was a remote mountain version of a roadside service station.

The scenery was spectacular, not least for the acres of 'coca' plant below us. This is the plant whose leaves are used in the manufacture of cocaine, not to be confused with the 'cocoa' in our familiar chocolate drink. The power of drug barons and the disastrous impact of the illegal drug trade is another story, which helps to explain something of the ongoing problems of Colombia.

When we finally arrived at the FARC camp we were greeted by the same attractive Maria who we had met in Cuba, obviously a highly influential figure in the movement and within the peace negotiations. Since the signing of the Agreement camps such as this were no longer deemed illegal, but security measures were very much in place, with another attractive young woman standing guard with an ominous AK-47 on her shoulder. Now where had I seen one of these before?

Since the Agreement and the 'de-criminalising' of the camps, many of the insurgents were being resettled in preparation for a move into a properly planned modern 'transition camp'. However, we were also given to understand that there was frustration at the time this was taking and that further delays could undermine confidence in the government's declared commitment to do all it could to facilitate a new beginning. These conversations resonated with us as we talked about the disillusionment of societies coming out of conflict who failed to see much improvement in their personal circumstances on the ground.

In this we were thinking not just of fellow citizens back home but of similar situations that we had experienced in townships in South Africa. There is a fundamental lesson to be learned here about managing expectations around the speed of change in all societies coming out of conflict.

But coming from our splendid hotel a few hours away in Bogota, it was a revelation to visit a former forest terrorist camp and to realise that comfort matters little to those who are so totally committed to a cause. As in a Boy Scout or Girl Guide camp, the primitive make-do cooking and sanitary facilities were imaginative as well as totally basic. But what for Scouts or Guides would be an exciting overnight diversion from the comforts of home was for these rebels a permanent alternative to what we would consider to be our human right to a decent standard of living.

As well as meeting with much older combatants who had shared responsibility for the organisation of FARC, we met young people who had been drawn away from their homes and families to be a part of this conflict, such as three young teenage girls living in a very basic hut constructed out of branches and waterproof material. I thought of my own daughters and grandchildren. Showing them my camera, I asked if I might take their picture, to which they excitedly said 'Si'. Two of them reached back to their makeshift bed and produced colourful heart-shaped cushions with images of Walt Disney characters. The third girl disappeared, only to return with a large and cuddly Snoopy. Yet these children were drawn into one of the most violent and ruthless campaigns of terror the world has seen. This to me was the really scary memory. How in all of our societies the consummate idealism of youth can be exploited in ways that are potentially so destructive of their futures.

We had in-depth conversations with Maria and others in leadership, such as Pablo, a much older man who had spent his entire adult life in the organisation but who was now fully committed to the peace process, of which he was an influential participant. Now, within the provisions of the Peace Agreement, he is a member of the Colombian Congress – another story with which we also were familiar from home.

In the evening the entire camp came together for a social gathering. Amongst those we met was a young couple with a beautiful baby girl. During the fully active years of FARC cohabiting and childbearing was not permitted, therefore this little one, the first since 'peace had come', was very special to everyone.

Much of the evening was taken up in word games, for which the camp divided into competitive groups. A favourite game focused on synonyms. Interestingly, but not surprisingly, when asked for a synonym for the word 'injusticia' ('injustice') one group suggested 'gobierno' ('government').

I suspected that, having no formal programme of education, these word games were designed to help fill that gap in the learning of those who had been denied proper schooling while receiving less subtle political education.

Camp discipline was strict and when Fr Michael and I retired to our camp beds, it was some time before I slept (partly due to the snores of my Redemptorist companion and partly due to my overactive mind trying to assimilate all that we had heard and experienced on another extraordinary day).

However, the next day, being Sunday, it had been arranged that Fr Michael and I would be visiting a Baptist church in the city of Cali on our return journey to Bogota. This involved another four-hour drive, so we had a very early departure from the camp. After embraces and entirely genuine words of appreciation we bade our farewells and in the very early morning light the scenery was no less spectacular.

The church in Cali was a plain building but the welcome was warm and genuine. There was hearty singing of Gospel hymns accompanied by guitars and drums with a period of informal worship before we were introduced.

In thanking the pastor for his welcome, Fr Michael assured everyone should they ever come to Ireland we would reciprocate their welcome. 'If you come to visit us,' he continued, 'we will give you a céad míle fáilte. A hundred thousand welcomes.' As he spoke these words, I noticed the congregation looking at each other with surprise and concerned expressions. Only afterwards did someone explain the reason. The translator got it rather wrong when instead of the promise of a 'hundred thousand welcomes' she had assured these good folk of a 'hundred thousand *weapons*'! As a priest and a parson who had come to speak of peace and the decommissioning of weapons it was indeed a very mixed message!

In the Q&A which followed our presentation we were asked if, in relation to the Peace Agreement, was it not necessary for FARC to repent before they could be accepted and permitted to participate in government and public life. Remembering the debates that preceded our GFA referendum, it was a question with which I was familiar. In my response I referred to the demand of some Christians for 'sackcloth and ashes' and sought to differentiate between this Old Testament dictum and the teaching of Jesus in the New. I reminded them of His parable of the wayward son whose father did not demand that he 'grovel' before him before he could be accepted.

Once again our lovely translator, who on her own admission was totally unfamiliar with biblical language and imagery, was puzzled, and paused to ask me to help her explain the concept of 'sackcloth and ashes'. Realising the limitations of language, I got down on the floor to demonstrate an act of contrition, which she obviously understood and translated. The only problem was that in the process I did something to my back which resulted in difficulty in getting to my feet again! Later in the day, when we returned to Bogota, we were to have a further conversation on the place of faith in a process of reconciliation with a Redemptorist bishop who was an old friend of Fr Michael's.

All of this, together with time we spent with an impressive proactive, inter-faith peace-seeking group from various Christian traditions, including progressive Mennonites, made us even more aware of the obvious parallels to our own story in Northern Ireland. And of the need for fully informed discussion and debate and understanding, particularly with those whose difficulties are related to their sincerely held religious beliefs, however different they may be from our own understanding of the Gospel.

While there is no way to quantify the impact of the conversations we shared during our time in both Cuba and Colombia, it remains my hope that at least some of what we shared in those conversations will have made a difference in the thinking of some. Unexpectedly, in June 2024 I was asked to speak at a seminar in Dublin City University where I met a delegation from Colombia, one of whom embraced me warmly and recalled that he was one of the FARC representatives with whom I had met in Havana. He thanked me for the insights over decommissioning which I had shared with them, which they had found very helpful. Sadly, in spite of much progress and an overall change for the better in Colombia, much of what was hoped for has yet to be achieved. There are still brutal killings and failings on all sides in the delivery of what was promised. There are FARC dissidents who have never accepted the 2016 Agreement – yet another parallel with here. But the vision and the commitment on the part of so many sincere seekers of peace remains undimmed and undaunted. And Colombia is a much better place for it.

16

QUESTIONS FOR OUR CHURCHES

'In essentials unity, in non-essentials liberty, in all things charity.'
Seventeenth-century tract

It was the nineteenth-century poet Robert Browning who wrote a poem entitled 'A Lovers' Quarrel', the message of which is to remind us that we can quarrel with someone we love but remain in love. Over the years these words will have resonated with many people, including the twentieth-century American poet Robert Frost at whose request these words were inscribed on his tombstone: 'I had a lover's quarrel with the world.'

In his dissertation on the life of the American humourist Mark Twain, one of his biographers wrote of Twain's lover's quarrel with the Church: 'His assault on hypocrisy and mendacity reveals Twain to be a reformer who desires a pragmatic theology and more authentic religious practice'.[30]

In each of these and other such references we read of men of integrity and passion who had reason to question, even quarrel, with the world and with the Church without falling out of love with either. Like others, I can identify with that sentiment. For in my love for the

Church, in its broadest sense, I too have serious concerns and questions to ask of it.

When speaking of my love for the Church I speak of it as the family into which I was born, in which I was nurtured, which from my birth has provided for me and my family every physical need and sustenance but, and most importantly, has granted me the privilege of serving the Church. So whatever rebuke, criticism and challenge I may offer should be read in the spirit of 'a lover's quarrel'.

While I am as aware as any – perhaps more than most – of the shameful failings of Churches in history as well as in our more recent past, I leave it to others to indulge in the all-too-easy dismissive criticism of the Church or Churches which, if not spoken 'in love', will have nothing positive to offer.

When speaking of Church and Churches I have in mind any and all, whatever be their name or sign, who declare themselves to be part of the visible body of Christ and who would seek to be obedient to His mind and will in our world of today. All such are as numerous as they are diverse. But I would hope that in the spirit of what I say that they too will feel included.

Having said that, I am obviously more familiar with what is referred to as the 'four main Churches' in Ireland which, in order of numerical strength, are the Roman Catholic Church, the Church of Ireland, the Presbyterian Church in Ireland and the Methodist Church in Ireland. Since their presence and their governance covers the whole of the island of Ireland these are seen to be the more recognisable face of church life for the greater number of people.

While these four denominations have a special relationship in what is known as 'The Church Leaders' Meeting', they also enjoy an active and visible relationship with other Reformed and Orthodox Christians within the Irish Council of Churches, which was founded in 1922, and with the Roman Catholic Church as members of the Irish Inter-Church Meeting, which came into being in 1973.

It is through these bodies that the voices of these Churches and their leaders are most often heard and oft quoted as representative of the position of 'the Churches' on political and other issues — a formidable challenge as well as responsibility.

While it is easy to catalogue the failings of Churches in both past and recent history, in the interests of balance much more needs to be said about the positive role of Churches across the years and across the island of Ireland. For example, the immense and historical contribution of Churches to the first-class education of our children; the sustained and dedicated service to thousands of young people in youth clubs and uniformed organisations; the care and inclusion of elderly folk in the community and in residential care; and the often thankless challenge that goes with reaching out to the homeless and the most vulnerable in our society.

And not forgetting the unseen and unsung pastoral ministry of clergy, priests and pastors, lay and ordained, who day in and day out share the joys and sorrows of those committed to their care. These are stories which are too personal to share. Such as their ministry to so many grieving families who have been shattered by the unfettered violence of our recent and troubled past. Many such stories are recorded in Gladys Ganiel's and Jamie Yohanis' book, *Considering Grace: Presbyterians and the Troubles* (2019, Merrion Press).

And not to be forgotten are the often-unrecorded stories of people from the Churches who in the most difficult and darkest of times refused to be drawn into the toxic world of 'them and us'. There are many examples, such as Women Together, PACE, the many local all-inclusive councils of churches and individuals such as Ray Davey and those who with him were the founders of the Corrymeela Community. All of which, together with risk-taking clergy and lay folk involved in initiatives such as the aborted Feakle talks and many less visible but focused conversations, remind us that essentially Church is people, whatever about the institutions.

But having affirmed all of that, we dare not deny our failings in the past. Failings which include our 'sins of omission' as well as our more conscious contribution to separation and spiritual 'superiority', reinforcing what at times has been bitter division in an already politically divided society. While by no means alone in our responsibility for this legacy of division across our community, we dare not ask others to acknowledge what we are ourselves are not prepared to admit.

Some of the failings to which I refer were what might be thought of as 'systemic'. One example which comes to mind was the 'rule' which either forbade or discouraged the attendance at services in churches of another tradition. Even at the funerals of friends and neighbours, or the assumed betrayal of one's own faith by attending a 'mixed' marriage of one's own son or daughter in the church of another tradition.

An ironic and extraordinary example of this is the account of the funeral of Douglas Hyde, first President of Ireland. The service took place in the Protestant St Patrick's Cathedral with the Catholic government ministers sitting outside in their official cars.

Regrettably, there are other stories which emphasise the point. Such as that of the 'mixed' marriage couple and their family embroiled in the saga of the boycott of Protestant businesses in Fethard-on-Sea when the parents chose to 'disobey' the unjust *Ne Temere* decree.

While the examples I quote are thankfully from the past, no less hurtful and divisive are much more recent stories of exclusion, such as the selective but deliberate exclusion of Roman Catholic women from participation in local services for the Women's World Day of Prayer. Or in some areas the failure to invite Roman Catholic clergy to participate in neighbourhood services to mark the annual Week of Prayer for Christian Unity.

Regrettably, for Churches of both traditions there has been the largely unchallenged assumption that confessional and political identities should be one and the same. The result is that, whatever their personal preferences, Protestant ministers were expected to be unionist in their sympathies while Catholic priests were assumed to be nationalist in theirs. Inevitably, for many this resulted in a conflict between a theological understanding of the Kingdom of God and their loyalty to the kingdoms and constitutions of this world. Thankfully, the sectarian notion of a 'Protestant Parliament for a Protestant people' no longer applies, nor does 'the special position' of the Roman Catholic

Church in the Constitution of the Republic of Ireland. But while no longer acceptable, the legacy lingers on. So it was that the systemic sectarianism which fuelled fear and suspicion within and across our community largely went unchallenged, giving 'justification' for the emergence of militant forces on both sides of our divide.

Thankfully, particularly in rural areas, the well-rooted spirit of decency and good neighbourliness helped to combat the seasonal discordant rhetoric from pulpit and platform at events to mark anniversaries of best forgotten battles and events.

But, having said all of that, what now is the challenge for our Churches and for all people of faith to redress this painful legacy of our past and bring healing to our land? What does it mean to do justly, to love mercy and to walk more humbly as children of the one God whom we all refer to as 'Our Father'?

The 'timelessness' of scripture is particularly relevant when it speaks to us of what is required of those who would aspire to be faithful to the teaching and example of Christ. As St Paul so clearly reminds us in his second letter to the church in Corinth, having reconciled us to Himself, God has entrusted to us His ministry of reconciliation, not as an optional extra, but as the very core of the mission entrusted to us by Christ Himself (2 Corinthians 5:18–19).

How then are we to fulfil this sacred mission in our time and in our place? I suggest that, given the will to do so, there are many relatively obvious opportunities. For some this will be a new experience, and for others a building on what has been done before, but maybe with need for 'refreshing'.

Given the Churches' role in youth services and education, this should provide opportunity for imaginative as well as pleasurable inter-church and cross-community events to ensure that a next generation will not imbibe the prejudices of the past. What other corporate, voluntary or statutory partnership could boast of an outlet at almost every street corner with significant human resources as well as financial assets to call upon? And what in the past might for some have been considered a risk too far should be now thought of as an obvious opportunity for a witness to the reconciling power of faith in practice. Such as very deliberate and public signs of 'togetherness' when neighbouring churches and clergy reach out to one another in more than symbolic gestures.

The first step in any journey towards reconciliation is in an understanding of 'the other'. How much do we really understand one another? Over the years, Clodagh and I have organised and led 'Journeys of Understanding' to places as far apart as South Africa and China. But very surprisingly, the most memorable and in some ways the most important was one which I led for members of my east Belfast congregation to a west Belfast parish. As fellow 'pilgrims' in what for many may well be a first step in our search for reconciliation, let us seek opportunities to walk with one another in our own enlightened journeys of understanding.

And let us not be deterred by memories and stories of the past. Such as the furious reaction of one congregation when their minister and a local priest, the Rev. David Armstrong and Fr Kevin Mullan, crossed the street to exchange Christmas greetings to their neighbouring churches. That reaction did not come out of nowhere. It was from an instinctive and inherited false assumption that there were differences which must not be compromised, without any reference to the teaching and example of the Jesus whose timeless story is at the heart of the message and meaning of Christmas.

All of this is not to pretend that there are not differences in doctrine and practice between our Churches within and across denominational boundaries, to which each tradition is entitled. But as many of us have discovered, it is in the sharing of that which is central to us all that we have come to understand and respect the richness of each other's traditions, without being any less committed to our own.

Having said that, let us be honest about some of the barriers in either faith or practice that do compromise us when we talk about our ministry of reconciliation. And here I tread softly. As one who cherishes the practice of Holy Communion, or the Lord's Supper as many of us know it, I feel personal pain when I am unable to joyfully celebrate at the sacramental table of my Roman Catholic friends, be it at a wedding or a funeral.

One minister of the Church of Ireland has described Holy Communion as 'Holy Hospitality'. I know it is not intended, but to be invited to come to that table with folded arms for a blessing but not permitted to receive is as if I were to welcome you to my home, ask you to fold your arms during the blessing and quietly observe while my family shared their meal.

Well remembered will be the occasion when President Mary McAleese received the Eucharist in the Protestant Christ Church Cathedral in Dublin, in spite of the fact that Catholics are forbidden by Canon Law from taking Communion in this way. While there was predictable criticism, it was welcomed by most as a very visible sign of reconciliation.

I have to confess that on more than one occasion I too have shared in what for some might be seen as an act of 'ecclesiastical disobedience', such as on a night following my brother Peter's very sudden death. As the Methodist minister in Omagh, Peter had formed a very special relationship with his neighbour, the late Fr Kevin Mullan (mentioned above). Kevin telephoned me to say that he was dedicating his evening Mass to Peter's memory and hoped that I and members of our family might attend, inviting me also to read the Gospel.

We were deeply moved when in offering the host Kevin looked directly at our family and said, 'In the sharing of our brokenness, let us share this broken bread.' And with tears of joy we did. For as well as embracing one another in our grief this was a visible sign of our oneness in Christ and the breaking down of the single most visible barrier between us. To me it was like the renting of the veil in the temple.

I pray for the day when we will no longer be constrained by rules and regulations and allow ourselves to be led by the Spirit. What a sign of unity this would be. And in the same spirit, is it not time for a revision of the sentiments contained in some of the long-outdated seventeenth-century Protestant articles and confessions of faith with archaic and intemperate references to the Pope. While I fully accept that these are considered to be subordinate standards of faith and no longer reflect the official position of governing bodies, a revision as suggested would be a sign and confirmation of a desire for 'oneness', as well as a healing of historic hurt. In the same spirit as the Second Vatican Council declaration that recognised Protestants as 'separated brethren' (rather than being 'heretics'), which if drafted today would make clear that this includes 'sisters'!

In acknowledging how far we have come, let us not grow either weary or complacent in the fostering of understanding, respect and tolerance which are prerequisites for true reconciliation. And while rightly expecting a 'top-down' lead from those responsible for the governance of our Churches, let those of us 'on the ground' commit ourselves more wholeheartedly to an authentic and focused ministry of reconciliation in our yet divided homeland and in the very broken world beyond our shores. As Ray Davey, founder of Corrymeela, never tired of reminding us, 'If we cannot speak of reconciliation, we have nothing to say.'

In today's world it is no longer a rarity for young people from Catholic and Protestant families to fall in love and decide to marry. Happily, at 'official' level there is now a much more enlightened and pastoral approach with guidance to celebrants as well as for the couple themselves, with much credit to the work of NIMMA, the Northern Ireland Mixed Marriage Association. Thankfully, in spite of that title, we are now encouraged to speak of 'inter-church' marriages.

In general, it is a far cry from the day when many such couples would be ostracised by their families and their community, including their Churches. But as was expressed to me by a loving couple seeking counsel for their marriage, there can still be the perception that we are 'from two different religions'. Sadly, the compromise for many (if not most) couples is for one or the other or both to opt out of a meaningful relationship with either or any tradition of faith, rather than a considered and shared decision for themselves and their children to choose a 'spiritual home' in which they can share love and faith as a family.

This should be an objective and shared decision which as pastors and parents we should encourage and respect. The hope must be that they will find that 'spiritual home' in which their relationship with God and with themselves will flourish, thus demonstrating a hugely visible and joyful sign of reconciliation where it matters most, within the family.

While appealing to the Churches to be true to their high calling to be reconcilers in a fragmented society, I am very conscious of the history as well as the potential for fragmentation within Churches themselves. At times this is due to selfish and petty preferences, as in any human institution. But in the present day, within debates on what are considered to be major issues to do with 'faith and order' there is the potential for critical division obscuring who and what we are called to be, which renders the Church impotent and regarded as irrelevant when it comes to the exercise of a wider ministry of reconciliation.

In particular, I am mindful of the ongoing and divisive debates on 'human sexuality'. My fear is that in these debates, as we have seen elsewhere, we have the potential to tear ourselves apart and surrender any credibility we may still have to offer a ministry of reconciliation to others in their brokenness, be that in personal or communal life. While fully cognisant of the arguments supporting various and conflicting views, can we not differ in such a way as to respect the views of others and, above all, remain open and caring for those about whom we speak.

These paragraphs are only examples and pointers. Obviously, there is much more to be shared and debated. But in the spirit of those who are open to the guidance of the Spirit, as Jesus himself promised in his parting words to his first followers, 'When the Spirit of truth comes, he will guide you into all truth' (John 16:13).

Anticipating their questioning, there will be those who will want to ask of this Wesleyan preacher what all this talk of reconciliation has to do with the sharing of the Gospel. Coming from an evangelical tradition, I too am anxious to share the Good News which is precious to me. This is why I am so fixed on what Jesus said to His followers in one of his final conversations: 'I pray for your oneness, so that the world may believe.'

In my final word to the Churches and all people of faith across our island home, it would be remiss of me not to refer to 'the elephant' in many of our rooms, including our sanctuaries and vestries. I refer to the difficult conversation on the future shape of the island of Ireland, to which I have alluded in my prologue. A conversation that takes place in many corners and car parks, but for fear of dissension is largely avoided within the Church itself.

Within a divided community, dominated on the one hand by historic resentment and on the other by fear of the future, for most people this cannot be other than 'an uncomfortable conversation'. For me this in itself is the very reason for our Churches to be involved. Not in any partisan sense, but in a pastoral role. And for those of us who represent 'all Ireland' Churches there must and will be a special responsibility.

From a personal point of view, like so many others I do not have a 'fixed' view on 'how' and 'what' as regards the future of this our island home. And at this stage I am reluctant to either predict or pontificate. But of the need for an honest, dispassionate, realistic and respectful conversation I have neither hesitation nor doubt. We must not and we dare not allow our future to be decided by either default or distain. Whatever about the outcome, let Brexit be our warning and not our template.

While politicians and their parties have a right as well as a responsibility to have a major part in this conversation, it must not be left to them alone. Nor must there be any place for the threat of violence. Whatever be the future political shape of this island let it be decided and governed by the principle of consent, as guaranteed in the Good Friday Agreement.

So while we do not compete in the stadium of partisan politics we must remain unapologetic in our insistence that, whatever the future, let it be based on the fundamental values and principles of mutual respect, rights, equanimity and equality. Be that an Ireland in two parts as is, or one or even four. And in doing so let us be clear, our mutual and ultimate loyalty must be to the values of what we speak of as the Kingdom of God, so clearly defined in our scriptures. And contrary to what some would have us believe, this 'Kingdom of God' is not to be confused with either a united Ireland or a United Kingdom or any other political realm.

Similarly, let us be wary of a 'chosen people' theology, with its divisive influence on politics here as in other parts of the world.

This was brought home to me in a totally unexpected way while preparing to give a lecture at the University of St Thomas in Texas, within which I would warn against the practice of lifting biblical references and stories out of context to justify our practices and personal prejudices.

As I was thinking of a relevant example to illustrate my point, my eye caught the wording on the milk carton on our breakfast table declaring that it was a product of the 'PROMISED LAND DAIRY'. Under the logo were words from the biblical book of Deuteronomy which read: 'This is the land that God gave us.' Holding up the carton in front of the class, we talked of how a misconstrued 'chosen people' theology can divide communities around the world. In places as far apart as South Africa, the US Bible Belt, Israel–Palestine, and Ireland.

All options for our future must be on the table. And let those with fixed ideas in one direction or the other be open to listen as well as to speak. And in whatever way and by whatever means may the reasoned and reasonable voices of people of faith be included in the conversation.

So, when the time is right, with others who will have their own agenda, I would ask our Church leaders, and others of goodwill who are willing to join them, to facilitate such a conversation within and across our Churches, without either fear or prejudice. And let us learn from the mistakes of the past for which we have paid dearly, some much more than others in very personal and grievous ways.

As a start to this conversation, we might do well to re-visit the alternative Covenant of 1912 drafted by the Presbyterian Rev. J.B.

Armour of Ballymoney, in which he sought to emphasise how much we had to offer one another, as Catholics and Protestants, unionists and nationalists, the Planter and the Gael in whatever was to be the future shape of the island of Ireland.

In January 2023 I was invited to preach in St Anne's Cathedral at a service to celebrate the centenary of the Irish Council of Churches and the fiftieth anniversary of the Inter-Church meeting, which brings all of the Churches together. In emphasising our fundamental calling to a ministry of reconciliation, I chose to speak of 'Humility and Hope'. In speaking of *humility* I spoke of admitting our failures of the past and of the need to remind ourselves that we do not have a monopoly on the things which make for peace. But in speaking of *hope* I said:

> As the Easter people it is to us that God has entrusted this Gospel of HOPE. But this hope of which we speak is not to be confused with a benign optimism which chooses to ignore the realities of the world in which we must live our daily lives. The HOPE of which we speak is rooted in reality.
>
> It was St Augustine who said: 'Hope has two beautiful daughters; their names are Anger and Courage. Anger at the way things are, and Courage to see that they do not remain as they are.' So Hope looks at the world as it is and responds with a determination to change it.

Epilogue

'Those who forget the past are condemned to repeat it.'
George Santayana, philosopher

As I strive to find the right words to conclude this memoir I have been watching television images of the state visit of King Charles III to Germany, and of his enthusiastic welcome at the Brandenburg Gate. How things have changed. Having been born prior to – and having lived through – the Second World War, it was for me an astonishing scene, although the late Queen had visited both West Germany and a united Germany many times.

The significance of the King's visit could not be understood by my children let alone by my grandchildren and great-grandchildren. For it signalled an ever-deepening friendship between two nations that had engaged in an all-consuming conflict that engulfed the world resulting in death on an unimaginable scale, up to an estimated 55 million civilians and 25 million military. And all in my lifetime.

What a contrast to the uplifting images of King Charles and the German President. I then switched on my local lunchtime radio news to hear the sadly predictable voices of out-worn and self-defeating local politics, ignoring new realities and new opportunities for all the people of our blighted but beloved Northern Ireland and the whole of our island home. Sadly, such voices and sentiments are not to be heard on one side only of our still sadly divided community. In recent years much time and effort has been devoted to 'Dealing with the Past', with a plethora of consultative groups, conferences, inquiries and tribunals. Sadly, while it has not been for the want of trying, none of them has taken us very far and it could be argued that some have been counterproductive.

Whatever the future may hold for Northern Ireland, remaining in the UK with one leg in the EU, or becoming part of a united Ireland with full European membership, or being somewhere in between, we continue to be haunted by the ghosts of our unresolved past. After all that we have endured together during the past half century, we can never truly heal until we have adequately contended with the painful legacy of the past in as fair a way as is humanly possible. As many of us on behalf of victims and survivors have protested, recent legislation passed by the Tories following Boris Johnson's glib call to 'draw a line under the Troubles' will not do that.

It is unacceptable that entirely subjective and partisan attitudes should have been allowed to dismiss balanced and nuanced proposals such as those offered by Eames/Bradley, Richard Haas, and the Stormont House Agreement, preventing us from fully embracing the spirit of the Good Friday Agreement. I welcome the pledge of the newly elected British Labour government to 'repeal and replace' the Legacy Act.

When speaking of 'the past' we need to be reminded of the bitter and at times bloody past which takes us back well beyond the more recent period which we euphemistically refer to as 'the Troubles'. To fully understand the present and our recent past, we need to re-visit our history and the legacy of such consequential developments as the Tudor Conquest, the Penal Laws, the Flight of the Earls, the Plantation of Ulster, the Irish Rebellion of 1641, the Cromwellian conquest, the United Irishmen, the Great Famine, the Home Rule Crisis and the Ulster Covenant, the Irish War of Independence and the Irish Civil War.

An objective reading of our shared history will reveal that in the main Ireland was 'sinned against' rather than being the architect of its own misfortunes, being something of a chess piece within the context of a wider Europe divided by religion, as exemplified by the Battle of the Boyne, where the Williamites and Jacobites were joined respectively by the Dutch and the French.

As unionists and nationalists, Catholics and Protestants, we need to re-visit these stories to help us understand what it is that we have carried from our separate and shared histories which we have allowed to shape us in our largely inherited fears and prejudices. But to do so in the spirit of a journey of understanding, rather than the re-opening of old wounds or the re-kindling of resentment. And most certainly not to seek to legitimise the terrifying violence of the recent past. Rather, as on any journey, we cannot fully appreciate where we now are without an understanding of where we have been.

This requires humility, openheartedness and magnanimity of the kind so spectacularly displayed by the late Queen Elizabeth II at Dublin Castle when she declared: 'To all those who have suffered as a consequence of our troubled past I extend my sincere thoughts and deep sympathy. With the benefit of historical hindsight we can all see things which we would wish had been done differently or not at all.' It was a brief but sincere statement which has had a huge impact upon Anglo-Irish relationships at every level. Not least upon many of those who were actively involved in the turmoil of recent years.

Watching the Queen utter those words on TV, I recalled the occasion in November 2006 when I had the privilege of being seated on her left at an intimate two-hour long private luncheon party that she co-hosted with Prince Philip at Buckingham Palace, attended by just seven other guests. Her keen interest in and commitment to reconciliation in Northern Ireland and between both parts of Ireland and between the Republic and Britain was evident to me.

The Queen asked me if I thought the time might be right for her to make what would be an historic visit to the Republic – the first of a reigning British monarch since independence and the first to what became known later as the Irish Free State since her grandfather King George V in 1911. I shared my personal view that I did indeed believe that the time was right and that she would be warmly welcomed by the vast majority of the citizens of Ireland.

I told her of the time I met her son, Prince Charles, at the Glencree Centre for Peace and Reconciliation in County Wicklow. And how welcome he was made by the people who lined the route as well as by those of us who had the privilege of meeting him more personally. She seemed pleased and reassured by what I said and I felt that I was confirming what her advisers had been told, even though it would be another four-and-a-half years before the timing for such a visit would be considered right by the Irish government following the devolution of policing and justice powers to Stormont in February 2010.

It was a memorable conversation. As if choreographed, and right on cue, two corgis appeared from under the table, which obviously was a signal that our lunch was over. But not before they received their reward from the royal handbag. It was all so relaxed that it did not dawn on me that it could have been an 'off to the Tower' moment when I commented on how her doggies were allowed privileges denied to mine. 'You will notice that they did not beg', replied Her Majesty. Wisely I refrained from a mischievous response, such as 'one wouldn't, would one?'

I was pleased that her memorable visit in 2011 was as I had predicted: a visit which did so much to heal the historic hurt between our two countries. And one that would not have taken place as it did and achieved so much in terms of reconciliation without the initiative and diplomacy of the Queen's host, President Mary McAleese.

It was in 2009 that my good friend Fr Martin Magill invited me to give the annual 'St Oliver Plunkett Lecture' within the programme of Féile an Phobail, the West Belfast Festival. As I explained on the night, I knew little or nothing about St Oliver, the archbishop of Armagh and the last man to suffer martyrdom for the Catholic faith in England. But I appreciated the challenge to think more seriously about how do we deal with our past in a way which can help in the healing of our hurts. So I entitled my presentation 'Hearts and Minds'.

Following a positive response to what I had to say that night I have re-presented it and shared it with many audiences over the years since. These audiences have ranged from entirely academic and 'secular' gatherings such as Rotary, Probus and University of the Third Age, to open and thoughtful inter-church and community groups. And I offer it now as the core of the 'Epilogue' to this memoir because I believe that the values, virtues and principles embodied in it hold the key to addressing the legacy of our shared and painful past without which we cannot be truly reconciled to one another.

Recently we have been celebrating the 25th anniversary of the Good Friday Agreement, for which I remain an unequivocal supporter and advocate. But as I emphasised on that night in west Belfast, laws and agreements per se, however skilfully framed and well intentioned, are not in themselves a panacea to conflict and hatred.

In his excellent book *The Audacity of Hope*, Barack Obama reminds us that legislation without values cannot transform society. It was Martin Luther King who said, 'The Law may prevent my brother from lynching me, but it cannot make him love me.' For others, peace-making is an 'intellectual' exercise, based on pragmatism. At Glencree I listened to F.W. de Klerk, former President of the apartheid government in South Africa, as he described his personal journey. He spoke of his resistance to the idea of releasing Nelson Mandela and all that this would involve. But he knew that as a result of an international boycott his country was on the verge of economic ruin and was faced with increasing isolation from the rest of the world, as well as the prospect of a bloody civil war. While it was the last thing he wanted to do, he had to accept that there was no alternative to do what must be done. 'But then', he said, 'I distinctly remember the day when I knew what we had done was morally right.' While pragmatism may for some be the starting point, our search for genuine peace, the healing of our past and our hope for the future must move well beyond that.

In the Basque Country I shared a platform with Roelf Meyer, former Minister of Security in the South African apartheid government who had been a reluctant negotiator with Cyril Ramaphosa, the

State's current President. Very eloquently, he outlined the ten essential steps towards a peace deal in South Africa. When he spoke of step number nine as 'a change of mind', I wondered what could follow. As a preacher I should have known. Number ten was 'a change of heart'. Hence my theme of 'Hearts and Minds' for the St Oliver Plunkett lecture.

In response to an oft-asked question as to what we as churches or people of faith have to offer in our longing for healing, reconciliation and a lasting peace, I begin by emphasising that none of us, from whatever sector we may come, has a monopoly on 'the things which make for peace' (Romans 14:19). To suggest that would be insufferable arrogance. Thankfully God does not confine himself to Church synods, conclaves, assemblies or conferences. But all of us, from whatever sacred or secular sector of society we may come, will have something distinctive to bring to the table.

For those whose perception of our conflict is based entirely in the context of an historic 'religious war', it is understandable that there will be those who will argue that 'religion' has nothing positive to offer in our search for reconciliation. Perhaps it is with intentional irony that some would argue, 'For God's sake keep religion out of it.'

As one whose whole life has revolved around the Church, I make no attempt to defend the negative and at times destructive role of churches in our troubled history, particularly in the nurturing of sectarianism in subtle and not so subtle ways. But for those of us for whom faith is very personal and has not been compromised by the confusion of culture, ethnicity and politics, we would maintain that the faith we profess and share has a profound contribution to offer, particularly when it comes to 'dealing with the past' and providing a path to personal and collective healing. In our understanding of the gospels we are left in no doubt that the transformation of hearts and minds was central to the teaching of Jesus – transformation so radical that He described it as a 'new birth'! In a tragically broken and divided world what more persuasive offering have we to bring?

Perhaps this is best understood in the sharing of three words from our distinctive faith vocabulary. Those words are:

- Confession
- Grace
- Forgiveness

As a Protestant minister invited by a Catholic priest to deliver a keynote address in a Catholic church I knew that these concepts of *confession*, *grace* and *forgiveness* would resonate with my hearers of both traditions. And this is why I so passionately believe that these key words from our shared vocabulary should be seen as our distinctive offering towards true reconciliation in the changing of hearts and minds and the healing of our hurts.

However, living as we do in a secular and at times cynical world, it will be noted that for some who may see our vocabulary as a bit too 'churchy' I have suggested synonymous words and phrases, without compromising the profoundly spiritual and biblical concepts which are at the heart of these words.

Confession/Acknowledgement

In both of our traditions, we fully recognise the value of confession at a personal level, be it in within the confidence of the confessional or in the solitude of one's own bedroom. And we are no less mindful of the importance of collective confession as we gather for public worship when together we confess to one another, as well as to God, that we have sinned in what we have failed to do as well as in what we may have done.

But should 'confession' appear to be too 'churchy' a word for some, let's talk about 'being honest with ourselves and with each other', about 'acknowledgement' or 'accepting responsibility', individually and collectively, for what has taken place over the past nigh 60 years. Lest I be misunderstood, in emphasising the need for the acceptance of responsibility I am in no way suggesting that innocent victims of violence are in any way responsible for what has been inflicted upon them. Nothing could be further from my mind.

There is a compelling story from the records of the South African Truth and Reconciliation Commission. Just before the cut-off hour for those who wished to apply for amnesty, a group of young adults arrived at the door of the Commission's office in Cape Town. They had come, they said, to apply for amnesty. Amnesty for having remained silent and for having done nothing about a situation which they knew to be so very wrong.

What a difference a statement such as this would make in Northern Ireland! In stark contrast to the 'blaming', the 'scapegoating', the 'whataboutery' and the denial at which we are all so well practiced, on every side. It is not for any of us to dictate what others should say or do. But I would hope that those of us from within the Churches would be the first with both hands up. For none of us has any right to ask of another what we ourselves are not prepared to say and do.

Amongst examples of very public and unambiguous acknowledgement was the statement of then Prime Minister David Cameron to the relatives of those who had died on what is known as Bloody Sunday when he stated that the killings on that day were 'unjustified and unjustifiable'.

Searching online for the term 'public apology', I found seventy-three further examples of 'confession' from both state and religious institutions. That scene of David Cameron in the House of Commons on that giant screen in 'Derry's Guildhall Square was almost identical to a very similar scene and screen with an unequivocal public apology from then Australian Premier Kevin Rudd, to the indigenous people of Australia for how they had been mistreated over many decades.

From Canada there were similar stories of public regret and acceptance of responsibility for the abhorrent mistreatment of totally innocent indigenous Inuit people. And one also recalls then Taoiseach Bertie Ahern's public apology on behalf of the state and the Irish people to the victims of institutional child abuse.

Epilogue

In their response to the Truth and Reconciliation Commission, the leadership of the Dutch Reformed Church in South Africa stated: 'We should have seen but we did not, we should have spoken but we remained silent, we should have acted but we were afraid …'.

And further back in time, in relation to the atrocities for which their country was responsible during the Second World War, the United Church of Christ in Japan confessed and sought forgiveness for their failure:

> As our nation committed errors, we as a church, sinned with her. Now with deep regret in our hearts we confess this sin, seeking the forgiveness of our Lord, from churches and our brothers and sisters of the world.

More recently from the Basque Country, in announcing an end to their 'armed struggle' and following their commitment to the decommissioning of their weapons, in which I personally was involved, in a full and unambiguous apology accepting that it bore direct responsibility for years of bloodshed and misery, the leadership of ETA declared:

> We know that we caused a lot of pain during that long period of armed struggle, including damage that can never be put right. We wish to show our respect for those who were killed or wounded by ETA and those who were affected by the conflict. We are truly sorry.

For an unreserved apology we can revisit that offered by the late Gusty Spence on behalf of the loyalist paramilitary organisations on the declaration of their ceasefire. For his own part, Gusty Spence, as a UVF activist, had served eighteen years in prison for the murder of a young Catholic in west Belfast. His voice broke as he read:

In all sincerity, in all sincerity, we offer to the loved ones of all innocent victims over the past twenty-five years abject and true remorse. No words of ours will compensate for the intolerable suffering they have undergone during the conflict.

I am of course very conscious of those who understandably will argue that since they took no part in the events of which we speak, they should feel no need to acknowledge or accept responsibility for any of these atrocities. But in saying this, I am reminded of a young man from Germany with whom I had a conversation when he visited Corrymeela. He was on a 'pilgrimage' from his native Berlin to Jerusalem, walking through all of the European countries which had been deeply affected by the nightmare that was the Second World War. His mission was to personally apologise to all he met for what 'his people' had inflicted upon 'their people' during those years. He who had not even been born at that time. I cannot help but wonder what would be the impact if each of us were to cross the street to a neighbour from a different tradition to ours, or to cross from our church to another, to acknowledge what those from our community may have inflicted upon them.

Imagine if you will, the impact of a carefully crafted opportunity in the Chamber in Stormont in which politicians might cross the floor to sincerely acknowledge and apologise for the hurt that members of their respective communities have at various times inflicted on 'the other side', either through deed or omission.

In Australia, every 26 May is observed as 'National Sorry Day', when all Australians are asked to reflect on their painful past as they commit themselves to a very different future. In Northern Ireland on 21 June each year (the 'longest day'), the organisation known as Healing Through Remembering promotes a 'Day of Reflection'. It is an important opportunity for all of us to reflect and remember the victims and survivors of our conflict. I suggest that now is the time for this to be declared as a statutory 'Day of Acknowledgement', providing an opportunity for all of us, individually and collectively, to acknowledge to ourselves and to one another our part in our troubled history. To acknowledge those things we should not have done and the things we have failed to do.

So, call it what you will, in any situation of brokenness, being honest and true to ourselves and to one another does inevitably bring us into a new relationship with our neighbours as well as with our God.

Grace/Generosity

In church and theological thinking confession is but a first step in the journey towards the healing of fractured relationships. But in the offering and in the receiving of genuine regret and acknowledgement there is a need for what is best described as 'Grace' before that acknowledgement will make a discernible difference. As a deeply 'spiritual' experience, 'grace' is difficult to explain or define. Perhaps it is one of those ethereal words that you can only recognise when you see it – or feel it.

For many people the most difficult part of the Good Friday Agreement was the provision concerning the early release of prisoners and the ensuing images of them walking free. It was especially difficult for many victims and survivors and their families. At that time I was chair of NIACRO and we sought to be helpful by facilitating informed discussion on this hugely contentious issue. In some ways it was not surprising but yet disappointing that amongst those who found this most difficult were many people from the Churches. So it was that I invited representatives from the Churches to a conversation with a South African lawyer called Brian Currin, who talked about his involvement in the South African Commission for Truth and Reconciliation.

After he spoke of the release of prisoners the first question was, 'very interesting Mr Currin, but what about justice?'

I vividly remember his response. 'This is not about justice. You cannot go to a widow or an orphan and say we are doing this in the interests of justice. This is about giving all parties to the conflict an opportunity to share in a new beginning, whether you believe they deserve it or not.'

To which I replied: 'Brian, I don't know whether you are a "religious" person or not. But most of us around this table are pastors and preachers. Our word for what you have just described is "Grace!"'

'If that is your word,' he replied, 'keep preaching it for you are going to need a great deal of it!' And how right he was. However you and I may choose to describe it, we are all going to need a great deal of this 'amazing' thing we call 'grace' if we are to be serious about our search for healing.

Again, for those who may feel this word is too 'churchy' I have suggested 'generosity': an unconditional generosity with no strings attached. The generosity of spirit that will neither withhold nor refuse a handshake. The generosity of spirit which makes it possible for us to sit with anyone, including our historic enemies. Even those at whose hands we may have suffered.

The generosity of the spirit of 'wounded healers' such as Gordon and Joan Wilson, the parents of Marie, who died at her father's side in the Remembrance Day bomb in Enniskillen. Of Alan McBride, who lost his wife in the horrific bomb in her father's Shankill Road fish shop. Of Maura Kiely, whose son Gerard was murdered as he left his church. Of Michael McGoldrick, a grieving father who at his murdered son's graveside pleaded with all involved in violent word or deed to bury their pride as he buried his son and was later to speak of 'the power and the *grace* to forgive from the heart which was such a freedom and release.' And it was grace which inspired him and his wife to found a life-changing charity in memory of their son, which has transformed the lives of countless orphans in Romania.

All of these stories and countless more help us to understand how transforming this 'amazing grace' can be. For those of us who would seek to practice a conscious faith, however imperfect we may be, 'grace' is the word which describes the undeserved, unconditional acceptance of a God who is best understood in the story of the Prodigal Son and asks no less of us in our troubled relationships with one another.

Forgiveness

Here I tread softly – for this is the most difficult and sensitive word of all.

On several occasions following my having spoken of forgiveness, one or more persons have spoken to me of their deeply personal loss and of their struggle with forgiveness. The last thing we must ever do is to suggest that anyone who finds it difficult to forgive is in any way less worthy than others who apparently can. For none of us knows how we might respond in the situation of another. And 'forgiveness' can mean different things to different people in different situations.

Having offered alternative and less 'churchy' words for 'confession' and 'grace', I have invited others to suggest another word for 'forgiveness'. To date, neither I nor any I have asked have offered an alternative.

I remember the first visit of the Dalai Lama to Belfast. As an invited audience, we were packed into the Ulster Hall to hear a message of peace from this remarkable man. Then came the questions. 'Your Holiness, what can you say about forgiveness?', asked a member of the audience. We waited with eager anticipation for his response. 'Forgiveness', he repeated many times, looking somewhat perplexed. In his characteristic way he looked in turn to the ceiling and then to the floor for inspiration and said, 'Forgiveness … forgiveness … forgiveness. Who knows what forgiveness is?' And that was it.

After a moment of surprised silence, his audience broke out in rapturous applause. An ovation for saying nothing, I thought, and wished that I had that gift! And then I wondered, was his answer a 'cop out' or might it have been a much more profound answer than at first it seemed? On reflection I suggest it was the latter. But whichever, his answer reminds us that forgiveness is as difficult to define as it is to practice. For who does know what forgiveness is?

I wanted to shout out that from our understanding of the gospel story of Jesus He knew what forgiveness is. He who from the Cross could look upon his accusers and tormentors and pray, 'Father, forgive; for they know not what they do'. These words both inspire and haunt us. As do the words of the Lord's Prayer when we pray: '... forgive us our trespasses, as we forgive those who trespass against us'.

Like others, I have read many books and essays on the subject of forgiveness. But upon reflection and pastoral conversations with many people, victims and survivors, I have concluded that the only people who can help me to understand forgiveness are those who have themselves forgiven or who have been forgiven. Everything else is mere speculation or academic theory.

Following his release from 27 years of imprisonment, Nelson Mandela wrote: 'As I walked out the door that would lead to my freedom, I knew that if I didn't leave my bitterness and hatred behind, I would still be in prison.'

Closer to home, on the night of my presentation at the West Belfast Festival, I was deeply moved by two responses during the question time which followed. A Catholic lady reminded me of the terrifying night she and her husband had been driven from their home and were welcomed and cared for in our church at Agnes Street. She spoke of the bitter resentment that she had carried in her heart for almost 40 years. 'But', she said, 'tonight I am going to let it go.'

And in a quiet corner Alan McBride, who lost his wife and father-in-law in an IRA bomb on the Shankill Road, shared with me his need 'to make his peace' with Gerry Adams, who was at the back of the church that night. I advised Alan that this was too public a setting with too many cameras around for a personal conversation and suggested that if Gerry was up for it they could meet in my home. They both accepted my invitation and not long afterwards it was my privilege to sit with them as they reached out to one another in an honest but reconciling conversation.

A gospel story that continues to fascinate me is the story of the paralysed man at the pool of Bethesda (John 5:1–15), a place where the water was believed to have healing powers. Here was a man who had lain at this pool for 38 years in the hope of being cured. Upon spotting him in this extraordinary situation Jesus asked him if he really did want to be healed. After 38 years was this not a stupid if not an offensive question?

That story begs a question for us, in our own time and place. After whatever number of years we measure our troubled past, and our individual and collective suffering, do we really want to be healed? As people who seek to live by faith, however imperfectly and however we define it, let us walk more humbly with all who have lingered much too long waiting for healing as we share our distinctive insights and experiences of confession, grace and forgiveness. And like the man at the pool and those around him, let us be prepared to be amazed at what may yet be possible.

ENDNOTES

1. britannica.com/place/Alsace-Lorraine
2. J. Crowley, W.J. Smyth, and M. Murphy (eds) (2012) *Atlas of the Great Irish Famine, 1845–52*, Cork University Press, 372.
3. B. Lalor (ed.) (2003) *The Encyclopaedia of Ireland*, Gill & Macmillan, 776.
4. 'Methodist Meets Republican', *Irish Times*, 15 June 1959.
5. W.H. Lax (1928) *Lax of Poplar*, Epworth Press. (William Henry Lax: 1868–1937).
6. Wilfrid Thomason Grenfell (1919), *Grenfell of Labrador: A Labrador Doctor*, Hodder and Stoughton.
7. Frank Ormsby, ed. (1991) *The Collected Poems of John Hewitt*, Blackstaff Press.
8. *Ibid*.
9. CAIN archive, Ulster University, 'Fact sheet for the conflict in and about Northern Ireland', 21 June 2007.
10. Richard Deutsch and Vivien Magowan (1973), *Northern Ireland 1968–73, Chronology of Events Vol. 1*, Blackstaff Press, 119.
11. *East Antrim Times*, 26 January 1973.
12. *News Letter*, 29 December 2020.
13. *Belfast Telegraph*, 27 April 2009.
14. PRONI CENT/1/25/70A.
15. Dennis Cooke, (2005) *Peacemaker: The Life and Work of Eric Gallagher*, Methodist Publishing House, 169–170.
16. *Ibid* 167.
17. A religious affairs and ethics programme, producer Martin O'Brien, 1996–2011
18. Martin McKeever (2017) *One Man, One God – The Peace Ministry of Fr Alec Reid*, CSsR, 12.
19. Brian Rowan (2005) *Paisley and the Provos*, Brehon Press, 89.
20. Full text in Appendix II.
21. Full text in Appendix I.
22. Patrick Marrinan (1973) *Paisley: Man of Wrath*, Anvil; Ed Moloney & Andy Pollak (1986) *Paisley*, Poolbeg Press; Steve Bruce (1989) *God Save Ulster – The*

Religion and Politics of Paisleyism, Oxford University Press; Dennis Cooke (1996) *Persecuting Zeal: A Portrait of Ian Paisley*, Brandon; Steve Bruce (2007) *Paisley: Religion and Politics in Northern Ireland*, Oxford University Press; Ed Moloney (2008) *Paisley: From Demagogue to Democrat*, Poolbeg Press; William Brown (2022) *Ian Paisley as I Knew Him*, BTP Books.

[23] Full text in Martin McKeever CSsR (2017) *One Man, One God: The Peace Ministry of Fr Alec Reid CSsR*. Redemptorist Communications, 139–146.

[24] *Ibid* 84.

[25] *Ibid* 34.

[26] *Ibid* 28–29.

[27] See Appendix IV.

[28] This can be accessed on the following link: https://www.youtube.com/watch?v=O-2Q9AeLkiDo; The main event can be accessed on this link: https://www.youtube.com/watch?

[29] Full text in Appendix IV.

[30] Timothy G. Esh (2018) 'Mark Twain's Lover's Quarrel with God; or, Satirizing All God's Children: Mark Twain's Uses of Religious Satire', D.Phil. dissertation, Drew University.

Appendix I

Joint Statement by the Independent Eyewitnesses, Reverend Harold Good and Father Alec Reid, on the Decommissioning of IRA Weapons (26 September 2005)

'Fr Alec Reid and I are making this statement on the basis of our role as independent eyewitnesses of the process of IRA decommissioning, which has been carried out by the Independent International Commission on Decommissioning.

We found ourselves in this role when a person who is intimately involved in the work for peace came to each of us, individually and separately, to ask if we would be willing to witness the process of IRA decommissioning. We both agreed to do so.

It is our understanding that a series of consultations then took place between those who would be responsible, either directly or indirectly, for the implementation of that process.

Sometime later, we were informed that we had been accepted for the role of independent eyewitnesses.

This role was to be clear and focused. It would involve watching the whole process of decommissioning, minute by minute, from beginning to end. This would enable us to testify to the reality of the decommissioning itself and to verify the truth of the report of the Independent International Commission on Decommissioning.

Here, we would like to say that we were not appointed by the IRA to do this work.

We would wish to emphasise that our role as eyewitnesses is a completely independent one. Throughout this process, we have taken our own counsel and made our own decisions about everything we have done and will say.

We now wish to verify the truth of the statement on IRA decommissioning which has been given by General John de Chastelain in the name and with the authority of the Independent International Commission on Decommissioning.

We are certain about the exactitude of this report because we spent many days watching the meticulous and painstaking way in which General de Chastelain, Brigadier General Tauno Nieminen and Ambassador Andrew Sens went about the task of decommissioning the huge amounts of explosives, arms and ammunition that they have just described in their statement. The experience of seeing this with our own eyes, on a minute-to-minute basis, provided us with evidence so clear and of its nature so incontrovertible that, at the end of the process, it demonstrated to us, and would have demonstrated to anyone who might have been with us, that beyond any shadow of doubt, the arms of the IRA have now been decommissioned.

In light of this, and in order to create universal confidence, we wish to assure everyone, but especially those in Northern Ireland who may yet have misgivings, that the decommissioning of the arms of the IRA is now an accomplished fact.

We also wish to assure the British and Irish governments that, in so far as they relate to the decommissioning of the arms of the IRA, the objectives of their Decommissioning Acts have now been achieved.

We hope that this development will become a benchmark for the peaceful resolution of political conflicts everywhere and that, for the people of Northern Ireland, it will herald the dawn of a new era of peace.'

This statement was read by Rev. Harold Good to media from all over the world at a news conference in the Culloden Hotel, Cultra, Co. Down on Monday, 26 September 2005.

APPENDIX II

REPORT OF THE INDEPENDENT INTERNATIONAL COMMISSION ON DECOMMISSIONING

INDEPENDENT INTERNATIONAL COMMISSION ON DECOMMISSIONING

Brigadier Tauno Nieminen   General John de Chastelain   Andrew D. Sens

Address in Dublin

Dublin Castle
Block M, Ship Street
DUBLIN 2

Tel No: (01) 4780111
Fax No: (01) 4780600

Address in Belfast

Rosepark House
Upper Newtownards Road
BELFAST BT4 3NX

Tel No: (028) 90 488600
Fax No: (028) 90 488601

REPORT OF THE INDEPENDENT INTERNATIONAL COMMISSSION ON DECOMMISSIONING

To:

The Rt. Hon. Peter Hain, MP
Secretary of State for Northern Ireland
BELFAST

To:

Mr. Michael McDowell, TD
Minister for Justice, Equality and Law Reform
DUBLIN

1. Over the past number of weeks we have engaged with the IRA representative in the execution of our mandate to decommission paramilitary arms.

2. We can now report that we have observed and verified events to put beyond use very large quantities of arms which the representative has informed us includes all the arms in the IRA's possession. We have made an inventory of this materièl.

3. In 2004 the Commission was provided with estimates of the number and quantity of arms held by the IRA. These estimates were produced by the security forces in both jurisdictions and were in agreement. Our inventory is consistent with these estimates and we believe that the arms decommissioned represent the totality of the IRA's arsenal.

4. The manner in which the arms were decommissioned is in accordance with the remit given us by the two governments as reflected in their Decommissioning Acts of 1997.

5. A Protestant and a Catholic clergyman also witnessed all these recent events: the Reverend Harold Good, former President of the Methodist Church in Ireland, and Father Alec Reid, a Redemptorist priest.

6. The new single inventory of decommissioned IRA arms incorporates the three we made during the preceding IRA events. This lists all the IRA arms we have verified as having been put beyond use. We will retain possession of this inventory until our mandate is complete.

7. We can report, however, that the arms involved in the recent events include a full range of ammunition, rifles, machine guns, mortars, missiles, handguns, explosives, explosive substances and other arms, including all the categories described in the estimates provided by the security forces.

8. In summary, we have determined that the IRA has met its commitment to put all its arms beyond use in a manner called for by the legislation.

9. It remains for us to address the arms of the loyalist paramilitary groups, as well as other paramilitary organizations, when these are prepared to cooperate with us in doing so.

Tauno Nieminen   John de Chastelain   Andrew Sens

26 September 2005

Appendix III

Address at a Graduation Ceremony in Queen's University Belfast, 3 July 2008

Vice-Chancellor, Professor English, ladies and gentlemen and graduands, it is my privilege to second the sincere words of appreciation proposed by my good friend, Father Alec. In recent years he and I have shared some interesting journeys, but this one is rather different. Not least because, today, we know where we are!

On the day that this honour was made public, I received a text message which read, 'Granddad, which is better, an hon. doc. or an "A" in the 11+ for which you have to work?'

Even on a proud day such as this, families will find a way to keep us humble!

Many years ago, in the early days of what we euphemistically call 'the Troubles',

I was in the middle of a riot – skilfully orchestrated by a rather intimidating individual.

As he slashed the fourth tyre of an overturned and burning police vehicle, I asked him what did he think he was *at* – or words to that effect. He paused, looked up and said, 'Reverend, all we want is a wee bit of law and order!'

Students of the law us will quickly recognise that there was more than a slight incongruity between his aspiration and his actions.

As good citizens we would all want to be assured that we live in a society governed by more than just a 'wee bit' of law and order. Since the beginning of human habitation, the fair and impartial administration of law has been a pre-requisite for the governance of a secure and just society.

In recent years, an unprecedented series of reviews and revisions of the law have contributed to growing confidence in the administration of justice in this part of our island home.

This morning, those of you who have graduated in law are of a generation that will see legislation which guarantees equality and human rights for all as the norm. And rightly so.

Having said that, we know that it takes more than law to build a happy and healthy society. This is why it is significant that, this morning, the two disciplines represented in this ceremony are Law *and* Theology or, as referred to in ancient scripture, 'The Law and the Prophets.'

In the first century there was a man called Paul who, as a 'Pharisee of the Pharisees,' was well versed in the laws of his day. Yet, in one of his many letters, he speaks of 'that which the law cannot do,' rightly reminding us of a limitation in the scope and application of law.

In his challenging book *The Audacity of Hope*, presidential candidate Barack Obama speaks of our need for cultural transformation as well as legislation. He reminds us that policy without values will not create the kind of society we desire.

> 'We must hang on to our values,
> even if at times they seem tarnished and worn;
> even if, as a nation and in our own lives,

we have betrayed them more often than we care to remember. What else is there to guide us,'

he asks.

It was the civil rights crusader Martin Luther King who said,

'The law can keep my neighbour from lynching me,
…. but it cannot make him love me!'

Last year, in the Basque Country, Father Alec and I shared a platform with Roelf Meyer, one time Minister for Security in the discredited apartheid government of South Africa. He spoke of 'ten steps in the South African peace process', in which he himself played a crucial role. When he stated that step number nine was 'a change of mind', we wondered what could top that for number ten!

As preachers we should have known. Number ten was 'a change of heart'. Without that change of heart, however sound our laws may be, we will not rebuild trust nor restore relationships – without which *our* peace process will not be complete.

Lawyers and theologians have distinct but related responsibilities in the creation of a just and peaceful society. Society rightly expects those who study and administer the law to do justly at all times and in all things. And of those who study the ancient scriptures from which we draw our common values we ask that, like the prophets of old, you will be fearless and unequivocal in the preaching and practice of a theology which leads us to action – not abstraction: a theology which will be as relevant to the legislator and the 'slasher of tyres' as it is to the person in the pew.

Sadly, as we reflect on the past, neither of our two disciplines have been without fault in the fulfilling of our mutual responsibilities. But you are the new generation, and it is to you that we look for the creation of the new society which we crave for ourselves and covet for our children – and their children.

We ask you therefore, as lawyers and theologians, to **respect** one another; **listen** to one another and **learn** from one another. As guardians of just laws and custodians of our timeless values it will be you, successors to the 'Law and the Prophets' of old, who will have a particular responsibility for the shaping of our future.

So, today, we entrust that future to you. With confidence and with great expectation.

APPENDIX IV

'FROM PRISON TO PEACE' ADDRESS IN BAYONNE, BASQUE COUNTRY, SOUTHWEST FRANCE, 7 APRIL 2018, TO MARK THE FIRST ANNIVERSARY OF THE DISARMAMENT OF ETA

I wish to thank you for the invitation to share this day with you. As always, for us older folk time passes all too quickly. It is hard to realise that it is almost twelve months to the day since we gathered here in Bayonne to witness the completion of the decommissioning of the weaponry of ETA. What a significant day that was. And what a significant day is this as we remember that event.

Coming from Northern Ireland and having been a witness to the decommissioning of the arms of the IRA, I can fully share your feelings this weekend. And I am honoured by your invitation to be here and to address this important gathering.

As I said on this day last year – when we gathered in the square in Bayonne for that remarkable and moving demonstration for peace – while decommissioning represents a hugely significant and symbolic commitment to peace, in itself it is but a beginning, not an end. As we discovered in Northern Ireland, by removing the visible and tangible threat to peace, decommissioning provides the opportunity to begin the search for a lasting peace.

This is why I emphasise that disarmament, is a beginning, not an end.

As that wonderful Hebrew word 'Shalom' reminds us, the peace we seek is about much more than the absence of violence ... or of weaponry.

This morning I have been asked to specifically refer to the situation regarding prisoners, and lessons we have learned from our story in Northern Ireland with particular reference to the role of former combatants in a post-conflict situation.

It is important for me to emphasise that I have not come to tell you or others who may be a part of your story what you must or must not do. That would be both impertinent and inappropriate. But what I can do – and will hope to do – is to share something of our story and the lessons we have learned from where I come. Some of these lessons we have had to learn the hard way.

To give you some understanding of the scale of our problem in relation to the treatment of prisoners, it is estimated that there were upwards of 40,000 people who were interned and/or imprisoned at some time during our 30 years of conflict. Within a relatively small population where there had never been a large prison population, this statistic speaks for itself. The vast majority of our prisoners would never have seen the inside of a prison had it not been for our years of political turmoil and conflict.

Appendix IV

For many years the British government refused to recognise the term '*political*' prisoners. It was only after many years of dismissal and protest, including 'hunger strike' deaths, that the term 'politically motivated' was accepted, with reluctance. But this was an important step forward as it allowed for the inclusion of politically motivated prisoners in the search for a resolution to our long-running and bloody conflict.

In saying this, it is important for me to emphasise that this in no way legitimises or endorses the activities of either republican or loyalist paramilitaries. Their respective campaigns of terror brought unspeakable grief upon our relatively small community. This cannot be forgotten, particularly by the victims and survivors most personally affected.

Having said that, I want to focus on the status and the role of former combatants in the post-conflict period following ceasefires and decommissioning and within our peace process. In talking about the role of former political prisoners in this period it is important to emphasise the difference between 'PEACE-MAKING' and 'PEACE-BUILDING'. Initially their contribution was to the '*making*' of peace.

It was in 1995 – at which time I was chairman of an organisation known as the Northern Ireland Association for the Care and Resettlement of Offenders – that we began to think more seriously about the role of politically motivated prisoners. Prior to this all prisoners were seen as criminals and warmongers who could have nothing to contribute to the things which make for peace.

However, within that context, we set aside two senior members of our staff to take time to travel to other places of conflict to see what lessons we might learn. Upon their return they published a comparative study of what they had learned from their visits to South Africa, Israel and Palestine, Italy, and Spain – together with a fresh understanding of the historic treatment of political prisoners in Ireland by British and Irish governments.

In summary they reported:

Our first and overriding conclusion is that the early release of politically-motivated prisoners was critical to any peace process which follows a violent political conflict. Whatever the particular positions taken up by negotiating parties at any given time we would argue that, until the question of prisoners is agreed then nothing that will create a final solution will be agreed.

In short, the reality was that it was the prisoners who held the key to the *making* of peace. For it was within the prisons that prisoners from both sides of our conflict were receiving political education, many of them for the first time. And it was within the prisons that the leaders of republicanism and loyalism were giving much thought to the ending of conflict – a conflict which they knew had not achieved what they had hoped for and a conflict which they did not wish to pass on to their children and grandchildren.

Around the same time, all-party conversations were taking place between most of the political parties, under the facilitation of Senator George Mitchell from the USA. Those at the table included those who were the political representatives of the organisations to which the prisoners belonged.

While it might have appeared that the outcome of these talks was entirely in the gift of those around the table, it was not so. For without the agreement of prisoners nothing could be finally agreed. This reality was confirmed on the day that the British Secretary of State had to go into the prison to persuade the loyalist prisoners to accept the terms of what would become known as the Good Friday or Belfast Agreement.

So in this week during which we will be marking the twentieth anniversary of our Good Friday Peace Agreement – and you are marking the first anniversary of the decommissioning of the weaponry of ETA – we reflect upon a clear message from the history of Ireland, that without the engagement and inclusion of ALL prisoners groups there would have been no Agreement.

So it was that within the Agreement there was a clear position relating to the treatment of political prisoners. I quote:

Both governments will put in place mechanisms to provide for an accelerated programme for the release of prisoners, including transferred prisoners, convicted of scheduled offences in Northern Ireland or, in the case of those sentenced outside Northern Ireland, similar offences. Any such arrangements will protect the rights of individual prisoners under national and international law.

But it also makes very clear:

Prisoners affiliated to organisations which have not established or are not maintaining a complete and unequivocal ceasefire will not benefit from the arrangements.

Obviously, following so many years of cruel and bloody conflict inflicted upon our community by many of those who were now to be released, this was an incredibly difficult part of the agreement for people to understand, let alone accept.

But in support for this part of the Agreement it was President Bill Clinton who stated:

Those who renounce violence and take risks for peace are entitled to be full participants in the democratic process. Those who do show courage to break with the past are entitled to their stake in the future.

Nevertheless, there were those who continued to have understandable concerns and reservations. I know that there will be many victims here who will fully understand how difficult this was for so many of the victims in Northern Ireland. It was because of this that I invited the South African lawyer Brian Currin to address a gathering of people from the Churches. I know that Brian Currin is well known to many of you. After he had spoken to us of the work of the South African

Truth and Reconciliation Commission the first question asked of Brian was 'All very well Mr Currin, but what about justice?'

I remember his reply.

> This not about justice. You cannot go to a widow or orphan and say that we are doing this in the interests of justice. This is not about justice. This is about giving all parties to the conflict an opportunity to share in a new beginning, whether you feel they deserve it or not.

As a preacher I found myself saying, 'Mr Currin, I don't know whether you are a man of faith or not, but our word for what you have just said is "GRACE".'

So it was that the Good Friday Agreement was endorsed by 82 percent of the people of the island of Ireland. It should be noted that amongst those who voted 'Yes' were many victims and survivors and those who had lost loved ones. It was their hope that this Agreement would bring violence to an end and spare others what they had suffered.

It was through a carefully managed process, that within two years 428 prisoners benefited from early release. And to date, only a very, very small percentage of them have had their licence revoked – in most cases for offences unrelated to the political process.

In time, this was to be followed by the decommissioning of the weapons of the IRA. Which opened the way towards the formation of a power-sharing Assembly and Executive.

But as I have suggested, there is a difference between PEACE-MAKING and PEACE-BUILDING.

PEACE-MAKING being the beginning of a new journey.

PEACE-BUILDING being the continuation of that journey.

Having played a significant role in the making of a peace which allowed for their early release, it was the responsibility of ex-prisoners to play their part in the building of a sustainable peace. Inevitably there have been some individuals who have had agendas of their own. And there were doubts about the sincerity and the ability of ex-prisoners. But in spite of this, the organisations which represent the majority of ex-prisoners have accepted their responsibilities and have continued to make a significant contribution towards the building of a more peaceful, just and reconciled community.

In the years since the Good Friday Agreement a number of credible organisations have evolved with the purpose of supporting and re-integrating ex-prisoners. Most of them are recognised and respected and are supported with funding from British and Irish governments, European Community Peace Funds and grants from corporate and voluntary funders. This illustrates the confidence that is now invested in the role of ex-prisoners.

And this they have earned in a number of ways. Through credible community development projects within and between divided communities. With an emphasis on:

- Employment and training
- Children and young people
- Community safety and cohesion
- Anti-racism and anti-sectarian initiatives
- Study tours to places such as Auschwitz
  - » to better understand the consequences of racial and religious intolerance

And by former enemies seen to be working together in positive ways such as:

- Joint guided tours of our city and a shared interpretation of our recent history
- A shared educational project known as 'From Prison to Peace'

Through which they help young people to understand the cost of violence and realise that there is a better way for all of us. And through joint projects involving children and young people from opposing communities.

Even if it were within my power to do so, I would not wish to be seen as 'canonising' ex-prisoners, nor would they wish me to do so. They, as well as we, are well aware of the hurt they have inflicted upon our community. But having worked very closely with both republican and loyalist ex-prisoners, over a long period of time, I can say that from my experience I have no reason whatever to doubt the sincerity of their intentions as well as the worth of their efforts.

PEACE-BUILDING can be driven at various levels, 'bottom-up' or 'top-down'. Ideally, we need a combination of both.

This is why I must also emphasise the role of several high-profile ex-prisoners who have shared responsibility for government at the highest level, including a First Minister, a deputy First Minister, ministers of government departments and their special advisers.

It was a former prison warder, now a security guard in our parliament, who told me that he now opens the door and says 'Good morning Sir' to people he used to lock up in their cells every evening. When I asked how he felt about this he replied, 'It was the right thing to do.'

May I say again what I said at the beginning of this presentation.

It is not for me to tell the government in Vitoria-Gasteiz or in Madrid what they must do. To do so would be improper and impertinent. I can only tell you our story and speak of our experience and the lessons we have learned.

However, it would be my hope that in the sharing of our story there may well be lessons which we have learned which have relevance for the situation in this beautiful land, in this post-conflict period of time.

Yes, I do know from where I come how difficult much of what I have said must be for many of your victims and survivors – as it has been for so many of ours.

But may I appeal once more to those in whose gift it is – as I did in Bayonne on this day last year – as a first but incredibly important step towards healing and reconciliation, hear the pleas of concerned citizens as well as families and bring prisoners closer to their homes.

Especially those who have served long sentences and those who may be frail in health.

In doing so you will not only be helping to build peace but by responding with compassion you will be helping to restore confidence between government and people. It is a well-known fact of life and history that a compassionate society is a much more contented and peaceful society.

It is with respect, but from personal experience of a situation similar to your own, that I have to ask:

How can there be reconciliation among the people of this country as long as hundreds of your fellow citizens, the families of more than 280 prisoners who are being held in prisons so far from home, are given no reason to hope for a realistic and compassionate resolution of this issue?

I firmly believe that it is in the interests of everyone, not just the prisoners and their families, that those in whose gift it is to make decisions must do so NOW. Remembering that massive and moving rally for peace in Bayonne. I have no doubt that this is the deep desire of the people.

Out of our experience in Northern Ireland I can assure you, with confidence, difficult as some decisions so obviously may be, your reward will be seen in the creation of a more just, inclusive and peaceful society, for this generation and the next.

Thank you and bless you.

Index

A

Adams, Gerry 135, 140, 171, 190, 262, 308
   letter from Harold Good to 214–16
   Methodist Church meeting with 113–14
   Paisley–Adams meeting 217, 218
Agápē Centre, Belfast 112
Agnes Street, Belfast 60
Agnes Street Methodist Church, Shankill Road 61, 62–3, 160
Agnes Street Youth and Community Centre 77–8
Ahern, Bertie 205, 233, 262, 302
Alderdice, John 218
Allen, Dorothy Mildred (Doris) (mother) 10, 12, 13, 14
Allen, Elizabeth (Lizzie) 10, 11–12
Allen, Ephraim (great-grandfather) 10–11, 12
Allen, Hugh, Rev. 43
Allen, Isaac (grandfather) 12, 13, 29, 40, 148
Allen, Muriel 13
Alliance Party 24
Allister, Jim 209
America *see* United States of America (US)
America, SS 48
Amity Christian Printing Press 251–2
Ancram, Michael 166
Anderson, Martina 211
Anglo-Irish Agreement (1985) 123–4, 186–7
Annan, Kofi 167
apartheid 240
apprenticeships, in family retail firms 7–8
Arbuckle, Victor 68, 161
Ardill, Austin 84
The Argory, Moy, County Armagh 12
Arlow, William, Canon 123
Arminianism 117
Arminius, Jacobus 117
Armour, J.B., Rev. 293–4
Armstrong, David, Rev. 288
Attridge, Harold 232
The Audacity of Hope (Obama) 299, 318
Augustine, St 294
Austin family 15
Australia
   'National Sorry Day' 304
   public apology to indigenous people of 302
awards
   Gandhi Foundation's International Peace Award 231
   René Cassin Human Rights Award 229, 259
   World Methodist Peace Award 125, 129, 138, 184
Aznar, José María 261

Index

B

B-Specials 67, 68, 160
Bakewell, Kathleen 92
Ballinamallard Methodist Church 37
Ballycastle, County Antrim 91–2, 178
Ballynahinch, County Down 102–7
Ballynahinch Free Presbyterian Church 104
Balmoral Furniture Company, Shankill Road 81
Bangkok, Thailand 91, 240
  World Council of Churches (WCC) conference 88, 238
Bannside, Lord *see* Paisley, Ian, Rev.
Bardon, Jonathan 127
Barre, William J. 111
Barritt, Denis 101
Basque Country 168, 229–30, 239, 258, 259–72, 299, 303, 319
Bates, Robert 84
'Battle of the Bogside,' 'Derry 66
Battle of the Boyne 41n, 297
Baxter, Ralph, Rev. 123
BBC Radio Ulster 139
Belfast, Dalai Lama visit to 307
Belfast Agreement *see* Good Friday Agreement
Belfast (film) 73
Belfast South Circuit 111
Belfast Voluntary Welfare Society, Bryson House 101
Bell, Mrs 68
Bellevue Zoo 21
Bessbrook, County Armagh 37–8
Bibles, in China 251–2
Birkenhead, HMS 12–13
Blair, Sir Tony 139, 172, 203, 205, 231, 233
Blair, Wesley, Rev. Dr 192
Blitz Square, High Street, Belfast 156
Bloody Friday 182
Bloody Sunday 83
Boesak, Allan, Rev. Dr 59
Bombay Street, Belfast 67
Bond-Shelton, Ralph MacGeough, Captain 12–13
Booth, William 119
Boraine, Alex 245
bovine tuberculosis (TB) 15–21, 29
Brady, Seán, Archbishop 171–2, 203
Branagh, Kenneth 73
Brett, Bernard 95
British-Irish Association 171
Brokenshire, James 197
Brookeborough Primary School 34–5
Browning, Robert 283
Bruce, Hugh 82
Bush, George W. 173, 184
Butler, Arthur, Dr 123
Byrne, Gay 114

C

Callaghan, James 69
Callaghan, Sydney, Rev. 62, 63, 109, 123
Calvinism 117
Cameron, David 83, 302
Campbell, Francis 203
Canny, Michael, Fr 197
Carmelo, Señor 261–2
Caroline, HMS 107
Carrero Blanco, Luis 258
Carroll, Lesley, Rev. 187
Carson, Eric 66, 67
Cassin, René 229
Castro, Fidel 274
Catholic Church 11, 284
  in China 252
Catholics
  grievances of 38–9
  relations between the RUC and 67
Census
  1901 5
  1911 5
Charles III, King 295, 298
Chetty, Danny 243–4

child abuse 19, 302
children, involved in rioting in Belfast 78–9
China 143–4, 240, 249–53
   Catholic Church in 252
   Protestant Churches in 250, 252
China Christian Council 249–50
Christ Church Cathedral 144
Christian socialism 118
Christian Theological Seminary (CTS), Indianapolis, Indiana 52
'The Church Leaders' Meeting' 284
Church of Ireland 119, 284, 289
Churches
   failings of 285–6
   fragmentation within 291
   positive role of 285
Civil Authorities (Special Powers) Act (1922) 39n
civil rights marches 61
civil rights struggles, in mid-1960s America 51
Clements, David, Rev. 201
Clinton, Bill 197, 325
Clonard-Fitzroy Fellowship 226–7
Clonard Monastery, Belfast 139–40, 223
Cloughjordan, County Tipperary 60
Clyde Valley, SS 164
Coad, Clodagh (wife) (Good) 46, 48, 52–3, 138–9, 218
Coad, Richard 47
Cole, John 96
Colombia 176, 239, 257
   conflict in 273
   FARC in 273–82
   Peace Agreement 276–7, 279
'Colombia Three' 274
'Colombian Agreement' 275
Community Forum 195
confession 301
   /acknowledgement 301–5
Confirmation 32–3
conflict resolution 224, 229, 262–3

Considering Grace: Presbyterian and the Troubles (Ganiel and Yohanis) 285
Cooper, David, Rev. 190, 200
Correll, Jabez 9
Corrigan, Mairead (Maguire) 88, 89, 240
Corrymeela Community 91–100, 186, 285
   'An Croí' 94
   'Policing and Community' weekend event 97–8
   volunteer programme 93
   workshops 94–6
Craig, Bill 84
Cranbrook Park, Belfast 80
Crawford, Fred, Colonel 13, 138, 148
Crumlin Road, Belfast, parades and protests in 194–6
Crumlin Road prison 102, 164
Cuba, FARC in 273–82
Culbert, Michael 276
Cultural Revolution, China 250
Cummings, Mrs (teacher) 21
curfew 39
Currin, Brian 180–1, 305–6, 325–6

D

Dalai Lama, visit to Belfast 307
Dandala, Mvume, Bishop 244
Darling Street Church, Enniskillen 34
Davey, James Ernest, Rev. Professor 157–8
Davey, Ray, Rev. 91, 92, 290
'Day of Acknowledgement' 304
de Chastelain, General John 134, 146–7, 149, 150, 151, 154, 313
de Klerk, F.W. 299
Decommissioning Acts (1997) 149
decommissioning of arms 100
   by ETA 100, 230, 239, 264–8
   by the IRA 100, 131–54
Democratic Unionist Party (DUP) 132, 134, 137, 195
Derry City Mission 25
Deuteronomy, book of 293

'Women Together' 87, 126
Women's World Day of Prayer, exclusion of Roman Catholic women from participation in 286
Wood, Derek 222
World Council of Churches (WCC) 72, 88
World Methodist Council 125
World Methodist Peace Award 125, 129, 138, 184
world, the, as a parish 238–56
Worrall, Stanley 122
worship, acts of 109

Y

Yale University 231, 232
Yohanis, Jamie 285
'Youth for Christ' 156

Z

Zuppi, Matteo, Cardinal 230, 258, 267

Index

T

Taggart, Norman, Rev. 117
Talkback (BBC) 226
Thatcher, Margaret 123
Thompson, Maggie 63
Thompson, Sam 42
'Three-Self Patriotic Movement' 252
Tindley, Charles Albert 66
Trade Union movement 118
Triennial Conference of the Methodist Church of Southern Africa 246
Trimble, David 132, 137, 168, 203
'The Troubles' 61, 68, 80–3, 96, 121, 296
    victims of 68, 75, 161
Truth and Reconciliation Commission 303
truth and reconciliation (TRC) process 245–6
tuberculosis 15–21, 29
Turner, Kate 245
Tutu, Archbishop Desmond 88–9, 240, 244–5
Twain, Mark 283
Twelfth, the (12 July) 41

U

UDA (Ulster Defence Association) 83, 84
Ulster Unionist Party (UUP) 66, 137, 202
Ulster Vanguard 84
United States of America (US)
    civil rights struggles in the mid-1960s 51
    Good family in 2
    Indiana (1966–1968) 52–60
    Ohio (1964–1966) 47–52
    trips with Fr Reid to 230-1-2
University of St Thomas, Texas 293
University Road church 111–12, 165, 200, 201
UVF (Ulster Volunteer Force) 84, 121, 148

V

Velsheda Park, Belfast 80
Victim Support 245
Victoria Methodist Church, Bristol 83
Volf, Miroslav 175, 231
Voting Rights Act 51

W

Wall, Dave 133, 245, 271
Walpole, Chris, Rev. 165, 190
Walshe, Carol 241
Warren, Ohio 48
Waterford 45–7
'We Shall Overcome' (US civil rights anthem) 66
Week of Prayer for Christian Unity 286
Weir, Jack, Rev. Dr 122, 249
Wellington Hall, Belfast 31
Wesley Chapel, Cork 43–4
Wesley, Charles 6n, 115, 118, 119
    Advent hymns 173
Wesley College, Dublin 119
Wesley, John 6n, 115–16, 236, 238
    legacy of 248
    Letter to a Roman Catholic 120
    as a radical social reformer 118
Whelan, Pax, Commandant 8–9
Wilkinson, Oliver 245
William III of Orange, King 41n
William J. Flynn Center for Irish Studies, University of St Thomas, Houston 230
Williams, Betty 89
Wilshaw, Mervyn, Rev. 83
Wilson, Des, Fr 67, 70–1
Wilson, Gordon 29, 126–7, 128–9, 306
Wilson, Harold 118, 122
Wilson, Joan 126, 128, 306
Wilson, Marie 126–7, 306
Wilson, Sammy 207, 209
Winter, Dan 12, 40, 137
Winter, Hannah 12

Reid, John 132, 135, 172, 203
religion, and reconciliation 300
René Cassin Human Rights Award 229, 259
Reynolds, Albert 135
Reynolds, Gerry, Fr 187, 226
Richardson family 37
Richhill Friends' (Quaker) Meeting 10–11
Robinson, Eliza 10–11
Robinson, Peter 197, 209, 213–14, 217
Roddy, Jim 194, 196
Roman Catholic Church 284
Rose, F.P. 22–3
Ross, Andy 65
Rowan, Brian 135n
Royal Belfast Hospital for Sick Children 17
Royal Irish Constabulary (RIC) 3, 4
Royal Naval Reserve 107
Royal Ulster Constabulary (RUC) 96–7
    Community Relations Branch 97
    Historical Society 3, 4
Royal Victoria Hospital 82
RTÉ, *The Meaning of Life* 114
Rudd, Kevin 302

S

St Andrews Agreement 205, 231
St Anne's Cathedral 294
St Francis of Assisi, Prayer of 145, 152
St Gerard's Redemptorist Retreat Centre 141
Saint Michael's Church of Ireland 162
'St Oliver Plunkett Lecture' 298, 300
Salvation Army 119
Santos, Juan Manuel 273, 275
Saville Report 83
Second Vatican Council 290
sectarianism 51, 54, 67, 80, 287
Sens, Andrew D. 134, 147, 313
'the Shankill Butchers' 84
Shankill Road 68

Simms, George Otto 66
Simpson, David 168
Simpson, Robert 77
Sinn Féin 132, 169, 171, 188, 200
    Ard Chomhairle (National Executive Committee) 206, 208, 210–11, 213, 214, 216
    Ard Fheis (conference) 206–7, 210, 216
    support of the PSNI 205–6
Skainos Centre, Belfast 21
Skibbereen, County Cork 2, 3
Skibbereen Eagle 4
slavery 118
Smyth, Fr 103
Smyth, Peter 113
social holiness 118
Society of Friends (Quakers) 10–11, 37
The Song of the Cradle (Allen) 11
South Africa 240–8
    Dutch Reformed Church 240–1, 303
    peace process in 319
South African Truth and Reconciliation Commission 302
Spain
    ETA's campaign for independence from 258
    Jesuits in 264
    peace process 258
Special Powers Act 39, 121
Spence, Gusty 303–4
Stafford, Wilfred, Rev. 69–70
Staten Island Hospital 50
'Stationing Committee' 88
Stephenson, Thomas, Rev. 119
Stone, Michael 222
'Stormontgate' 132
Stout, Bob 124
Strandtown school, east Belfast 36
Stranmillis Teacher Training College 35, 36
Sunday Sequence (BBC Radio Ulster) 139
Suonio, Aaro 153

Index

response to Methodist 'Open Letter' 114
retirement from the office of First Minister and Moderator of the Free Presbyterian Church 155
Paisley, Rhonda 169
'Paisleyism' 156
Parliament Buildings 172
Pastoral Psychology 19
Patten, Chris (Lord Patten of Barnes) 110–11
Patten Report 111, 205
Patterson, Ian 70
Patterson, Mary (Minnie) 4, 5, 6, 7, 8
Patterson, Saidie 126
Paul, St 57
    letter to the Ephesians 148, 198
    Second Letter to the Corinthians 81, 287
Pax Christi (Peace of Christ) 187, 200
peace-building 326, 328
peace-making 326
    Fr Alec Reid's golden rule of 234
'The Peace People' 89
peace rally, in Bayonne 267–70
Peter's Hill, rioting at 75–6
petrol bombs 79
Philbin, William 70
Philip, Prince, Duke of Edinburgh 129–30
PIRA (Provisional IRA) 67, 122, 123, 183
Police Service of Northern Ireland (PSNI) 205
Pop Goes Northern Ireland (BBC series) 69
Poplar, London 30–1
Porter, David 187
Powell, Bruce 91
Prayer of St Francis of Assisi 145, 152
Presbyterian Church in Ireland 284
Presbyterian General Assembly 72
prison chaplaincy, in Crumlin Road prison 164
prisoners
    political 323, 324–5
    treatment of 322–4
Protestant articles, revision of sentiments in 17th-century 289–90
Protestant churches 249
    in China 250, 252
    inter-church relationships between 103
Provisional IRA 67, 122, 123, 183
public apologies 302–3
puritans 130

Q

Quakers (Society of Friends) 10–11, 37
Queen Elizabeth, RMS 60
Queen's University Belfast 231
    Harold Good's address at a graduation ceremony in 317–20
Quigley, Sir George 166, 187

R

racism 51, 54
Ramaphosa, Cyril 299
Rathgael (boys' borstal) 64
Rea, Desmond, Professor Sir 22, 123, 124
Rea, Jim, Rev. 192
reconciliation 288, 300
Redemptorists 236
Reid, Alec, Fr 139, 140–1, 142, 148, 153, 168, 190, 198, 219–37
    death of 234
    on Devolution Day (8 May 2007) 172
    involvement in the Spanish peace process 258–61, 268
    joint statement with Reverend Harold Good on the decommissioning of IRA weapons 166, 312–14
    at LaGuardia Airport, New York City 224–5
    lecture at St Clement's Retreat House, Belfast 220–1
    tribute to Tony Blair 233

Morris, Gladys 20, 29
Morrison, Danny 127
Morton, Harry, Rev. 122
Mowlam, Mo 114
Mu'en Church, Shanghai 250
Mullan, Kevin, Fr 288, 289
Munn, Helen 82
Munn, Tracey 82
Murphy, Conor 218
Murphy, Pádraig, Canon 71, 76
Musgrave Park Hospital, Belfast 18

N

The National Children's Home (Action for Children) 119
Ne Temere decree 11, 286
Neal, Richie 230
Neill, John 124
Nepal 240, 253–6
    Leprosy Mission in 254, 255
New Ireland Forum 125
New York 133
Newell, Ken, Rev. 138, 139, 146, 187, 226, 227, 228
Newry, protest against curfew in 39
Newton, John 177
Nicholl, Colin 81, 82
Nieminen, Tauno 134, 147, 313
NIMMA (Northern Ireland Mixed Marriage Association) 96, 290
Nolan, Stephen 246
Northern Bank Robbery 142
Northern Consensus Group 124, 187
Northern Ireland
    'Day of Reflection' 304
    orthopaedic nurses in 19–20
Northern Ireland – Untying the Knot (pamphlet) 125
        Northern Ireland Association for the Care and Resettlement of Offenders (NIACRO) 133, 181, 271, 305

Northern Ireland civil rights movement 39n
Northern Ireland Civil Service 189
Northern Ireland Policing Board 22
Nuffield, Lord 20

O

Obama, Barack 299, 318
The Observer 96
O'Hare, Margaret 182
Ohio, US 47–52
O'Leary, Olivia 220
Oliver, St 298
O'Meara, Margaret 229
One Man, One God: The Peace Ministry of Fr Alec Reid CSsR (McKeever) 221
O'Neill, Terence 66, 84, 121
'Open Letter,' to Northern Ireland political party leaders, Rev. Ian Paisley's response to 114, 165
Orange Order 12, 40–1, 137
Otegi, Arnaldo 270
Over the Bridge (Thompson) 42

P

PACE [Protestant and Catholic Encounter] 76
Paisley, Eileen 169, 175–6
Paisley, Ian, Junior 168, 169, 199
Paisley, Ian, Rev. 61, 66, 121, 132, 134–5, 139, 154, 155–77, 206, 225
    burning of Prof. Davey's writings 158–9
    meeting with Gerry Adams 217, 218
    meetings with Harold Good 174
    meetings with Martin McGuinness 170
    memorial service for 176
    response to decommissioning of arms by the IRA 166–7

M

McAleese, Mary 221, 289, 298
McAllister, Billy 92
MacArthur, Arthur, Rev. 123
McAteer, Aidan 132, 136, 204, 206, 207, 212, 218
Macaulay, Ambrose, Monsignor 112
MacBrádaigh, Caoimhín 222
McBride, Alan 306, 308
Maccabe, Chris 267, 276
McCall family 38
McCallister, John 273
McCambridge, Gerry 92
McCreary, Alf 92
McElhinney, Ivan, Rev. 211
McEvoy, Kieran 271
McGaughey, David, Rev. 135
McGibbon, Michael 195
McGoldrick, Michael 306
McGuinness, Bernie 172, 196
McGuinness, Martin 132, 136, 138, 140, 141, 178–99, 211, 218, 273
   Basque newspaper interview with 262
   books and biographies written about 180
   Christmas greeting to Harold Good 185
   on Devolution Day (8 May 2007) 172
   funeral of 197, 270
   Ian Paisley Junior's tribute to 199
   letter from Harold Good to 214–16
   meetings with Harold Good 178
   meetings with Ian Paisley 170
   meetings with Jeffrey Donaldson 203
   resignation as deputy First Minister 196
McGuinness, Peggy 172
Machel, Graça (Mandela) 244, 247
McKeever, Martin 221
McKittrick, David 90
McLachlan, Peter 101–2
McLaughlin, Mitchel 128–9, 188
McLernon, Desi 92
McMaster, John 107
McQuade, Johnny 63–4
McQuiston, Billy 82–3
McWilliams, Monica 276
Magee, Winifred 18
Magill, Martin, Fr 298
Mahoney, James 3
Major, John 190–1
Mammoth Cave Park, Kentucky 54–6
Mandela, Graça (née Machel) 244, 247
Mandela, Nelson 239, 244, 247, 299, 308
Manikkalingam, Ram 267
Mao Zedong 250
Martyrs Memorial Church 159, 160
Maskey, Alex 188
Maskey, Paul 273
The Meaning of Life (RTÉ) 114
Mennonite Christians 1
Methodism 115–20
   'The Four Alls' of 117
Methodist Church in Ireland 7, 25, 119, 284
Methodist city missions 118
Methodist College, Belfast (Methody) 22, 23, 36, 119
Methodist Conference, in 1966 in Dublin 121
Methodist 'cottage meetings' 6
Methodist Council on Social Responsibility 124, 186, 187
Methodist Hospital, Indianapolis 53
Methodist ministry, entrance exams 33
Methodist Recorder 83
Methodist World Development Service 110
Meyer, Roelf 262, 299, 319
Meyer, Ted 50
Mitchell, George 324
'mixed' marriages 95–6, 290–1
Moltmann, Jürgen 89
Montgomery, Jack 78
Moore, William 84

International Verification Commission 267
internment without trial 80
IPLO (Irish People's Liberation Organisation) 107
IRA (Irish Republican Army) 9, 38–9, 67, 82, 97
  ceasefires 113, 191, 231
  decommissioning of arms by 100, 131–54, 205, 257, 312–14
  links between FARC and 273
Ireland
  future of 292
  Methodist schools and colleges in 119
Irish Civil War 8–9, 47
Irish Council of Churches 284, 294
Irish Inter-Church Meeting 284, 294
The Irish News 166
Irish Special Branch 186
Irvine, Frank 243
Irvine, George 243
Irvine, Lynette 243
Irvine, Winston 195

J

Jaffe, Alex 72
James II, King 41n
Jarlath McKenna, Sister 103, 105
Jesuits, in Spain 264
Jewish community 72
Jewish Synagogue, Somerton Road 162
John Paul II, Pope 104
Johnson, Boris 296
Johnson, Donald C. 134
Johnson, Lyndon B. 49, 51
Johnson, Paul E. 52, 59
Johnston, Timothy 207, 208, 211, 212
'Journeys of Understanding' 143, 248, 288
July 12 (the Twelfth) 41
justice 305, 326
'Justice for Colombia' 273

K

Kasper, Walter, Cardinal 120
Kelleher, Michael, Fr 176, 232, 277, 280
Kennedy, Danny 167
Kennedy, Robert F. 59
Kenny, Enda 197
Kerr, David, Rev. 201
Keys, Henry, Rev. 189, 190
Kiely, Gerard 306
Kiely, Maura 306
Kilmacabea parish, Co. Cork 3
King, Harold 82
King, Martin Luther, Jr, Rev. 51, 58–9, 299, 319
Kingsmills, County Armagh 39
Kingston, Tom, Rev. 3–4, 5
Kirkpatrick, Charlie 34, 35
Knock, east Belfast 107–8, 110, 184
Knock Methodist Church, Belfast 32
Knox, Ian 166
Kohon, Mariela 273

L

Labour movement 118
LaGuardia Airport, New York City 232
Lambe family 27
Lambe, Paddy 27
Lamont, Jim, Rev. 103
Lax of Poplar 30, 33
Laytown, County Meath 43
Legacy Act 296
Leonard, Bob 106
Leprosy Mission, in Nepal 254, 255
Levin, Rick 232
Liguori, Alphonsus 236
  Road church 165, 200
London Docklands bombing 190
Lord's Prayer 308
'A Lovers' Quarrel' (poem by Browning) 283
Lowe, Fred 183
Lynn, Dave 50

Index

trial sermon at Ballimamallard Methodist Church 37
in Waterford 45–7
Good, Peter (brother) 2, 7, 14, 33, 289
Good, Peter (grandfather) 2, 3–5, 29
Good, Peter (great-grandfather) 2
Good, Peter (uncle) 2
Good, Richard (son) 218, 228
Good, Robert James, Rev. (Bob) (father) 4, 9–10, 14, 28, 148
Good, Robin (brother) 14, 34
Good, Sharon Ruth (daughter) 54, 59
Good, Thomas Albert 4
Goodville, Lancaster County, US 2
Gormally, Brian 271
grace 117, 301
/generosity 305–6
graffiti, sectarian 106
Graham, Edgar 204
Graymount Hospital 17
Great Famine 3
Greenisland, County Antrim 17, 86, 87
Greenisland Hospital 18–19
Gregg, Thomas Cecil J., Constable 28
Grenfell, Wilfrid Thomason 31, 33
Grosman, Eva 276
Grosvenor Hall 31
Guess Who's Coming to Dinner? (film) 58
Gurteen College, County Tipperary 119

H

Haass, Richard 246
Habitat for Humanity 138
Hadden, Winifred, Dr 16
Hamilton, George 197
Hamilton, Sir Nigel 124
'Hammer Playground' (Lower Shankill) 64–5
Hanna, Jean 73–4
Hanna, Thomas 73–4
Hart, Sir Anthony 75
Hartley, Tom 188
Hassard, Marina 182–3
Hassard, William 183
Hawe, Herbert 161
Hay, William 218, 261
Hayes, Maurice 76
'Healing Through Remembering' forum 245, 304
Heath, Edward 122
Henning, Reggie 21
Hermon, Jack 98, 99
Hermon, Lady Sylvia 167
Hewitt, David 125
Hewitt, John 62
Hewitt, Robert 62
Higgins, Michael D. 197
Ho, Pastor 250–1
Holiday Fellowship Centre 91, 92
Holy Cross Church, Crumlin Road 162, 163
Hong Kong 240, 248–9
hope 294
Howes, David 222
Human Rights Commission 182
Hume, John 135, 141, 190, 223
humility 294
Hunt Report 68, 160
Hurley, Denis 242
Hyde, Douglas 286

I

Ibarretxe Markuartu, Juan José (Lehendakari (President) of the Basque government) 229, 259, 260
Ignatius, St 264
Independent International Commission on Decommissioning (IICD) 134, 144, 153, 154, 312, 315–16
Indiana, US 52–60
institutional abuse 75, 302
Inter-Church International Nepal Fellowship 255
'inter-church' marriages 290

Frazer, Willie 227, 228
Free Presbyterian Church of Ulster 104, 157, 160
Free Presbyterian Church, Ravenhill Road 159
Friends School, Lisburn 11
Frost, Robert 283
Fuller, Millard 138
'fundamentalism' 116

G

Gallagher, David, Dr 190, 192
Gallagher, Eric, Rev. 29, 69, 90, 100, 122, 123, 129, 192
Gallagher, Lori 230
Gandhi Foundation's International Peace Award 231
Gandhi, Mahatma 242
Ganiel, Gladys 285
Gaston, Mike 127
generosity, of spirit 306
George V, King 297
Germany, state visit of King Charles III to 295
Gibney, Jim 188
Gildernew, Michelle 183
Gillies, Donald, Rev. 69, 71, 72
Glass, Anna 92
Glencree Centre for Peace and Reconciliation, County Wicklow 298
God, closeness to 40
'Going to church' (poem by Hewitt) 62
Goldwater, Barry 49
Good Brothers 8–9
Good, Carolyn Anne (daughter) 52, 53
Good, Clodagh (wife) (née Coad) 46, 48, 52–3, 138–9, 218
Good, Dorothy Mildred (Doris) (née Allen) (mother) 10, 12, 13, 14
Good family, origins of 1–3
Good Friday Agreement 22, 124, 125, 132, 133, 296, 299, 305, 324, 326

Good, Harold
  address at a graduation ceremony in Queen's University, Belfast (3 July 2008) 317–20
  address in Basque Country to mark the first anniversary of the disarmament of ETA 321–9
  as assistant teacher at Brookeborough Primary School 34–6
  at Bessbrook 37–42
  bovine tuberculosis (TB), battle with 15–21
  childhood 15–29
  Confirmation 32–3
  as director of the Corrymeela Community 92–3
  in Dublin Central Mission 42–3
  at Edgehill Theological College 43
  friendship with Martin McGuinness 179, 181
  in Indiana (1966–1968) 52–60
  joint statement with Father Alec Reid on the decommissioning of IRA weapons 312–14
  MBE and OBE honours received by 77
  meetings with Martin McGuinness 192–3
  meetings with Rev. Ian Paisley 169, 174, 175
  at Methodist College, Belfast 22–3
  in Ohio (1964–1966) 47–52
  ordination 43–4
  perspective on Irish history 24
  preparation for entrance exams for the Methodist ministry 33
  as President of the Methodist Church in Ireland 203
  at primary school 21–2
  reference from F.P. Rose 23
  reflection at funeral mass of Fr Alec Reid 234–7
  speech at peace rally in Bayonne 267–70

Devolution Day (8 May 2007) 171
Dewer, Canon 41
Diana, Princess 254
Dickie, George 161
Dickson, Brice 183
direct rule, from Westminster 132
Dodds, Nigel 195, 209, 217
Donaghmore townland 38
Donaghy, Terence 124
Donaldson, Denis 133
Donaldson, Sir Jeffrey 136, 171, 184, 203–4, 209, 211, 213, 218, 273, 276
   conversations with Martin McGuinness 181, 206
   endeavours to remove obstacles to Paisley–Adams meeting 217
   private conversations with Harold Good 137, 202
Donegan, Gary, Fr 195
Donnelly, Tom 182, 183
Drimoleague, County Cork 3
Dublin Central Mission 42–3
Dugdale, Mary 109
Dugdale, Norman 108–9
Dundonald Church, Ballybeen estate 185
Dunlop, Alastair 203
Dunlop, John 76
Durkan, Mark 203, 273
Dutch Reformed Church, South Africa 240–1, 303

E

Eames–Bradley Commission 245
Eames, Christine 183
Eames, Robin, Archbishop 22, 138, 190, 203, 245
East Antrim Times 90
Echeverri, Londoño (Timochenko) 274, 275
ecumenical carol service 105–6
ecumenism 120
Edentubber, County Louth 38

Edgehill Theological College 43
education, provided by Methodists 119
Egan, Fr 67
Eli Lilley Foundation 56
Elizabeth II, Queen 127, 129, 295, 297–8
Enniskillen 28, 33–4
   bomb on Remembrance Sunday (8 November 1987) 126
Ervine, David 113, 114, 213
ETA 257, 303
   address in Basque Country to mark the first anniversary of the disarmament of 321–9
   campaign for independence from Spain 258
   decommissioning of arms by 100, 230, 239, 264–8
   public apology by 303
Eusko Alkartasuna (Basque social democratic party) 258
'evangelical' 116
exclusion 90
Exclusion and Embrace (Volf) 175

F

FARC 176, 239, 257, 273–82
Farrington Gardens, Belfast 80
Feakle, County Clare, talks between Protestant clergy and the IRA 29, 90, 123, 186, 192
Féile an Phobail, West Belfast Festival 298
Fell, Sir David 189
Fermanagh County Education Committee, Enniskillen 34
Fethard-on-Sea, boycott of Protestant businesses in 286
First Methodist Church, Warren, Ohio 50
Fisher, Geoffrey, Archbishop of Canterbury 159
Flanagan, Sir Jamie 97
forgiveness 301, 307–9
Foster, Arlene 196, 197, 273